Paul, the Community, and Progressive Sanctification

Paul, the Community, and Progressive Sanctification

Studies in Biblical Literature

Hemchand Gossai
General Editor

Vol. 90

PETER LANG
New York • Washington, D.C./Baltimore • Bern
Frankfurt am Main • Berlin • Brussels • Vienna • Oxford

James M. Howard

Paul, the Community, and Progressive Sanctification

An Exploration into Community-Based Transformation within Pauline Theology

PETER LANG
New York • Washington, D.C./Baltimore • Bern
Frankfurt am Main • Berlin • Brussels • Vienna • Oxford

Library of Congress Cataloging-in-Publication Data

Howard, James M.
Paul, the community, and progressive sanctification: an exploration into
community-based transformation within Pauline theology / James M. Howard.
p. cm. — (Studies in biblical literature; v. 90)
Includes bibliographical references and index.
1. Bible. N.T. Epistles of Paul. 2. Sanctification. 3. Community—
Religious aspects—Christianity. I. Title.
BS2650.52.H69   234'.8—dc22   2006022879
ISBN-13: 978-0-8204-7928-6
ISBN-10: 0-8204-7928-4
ISSN 1089-0645

Bibliographic information published by **Die Deutsche Bibliothek**.
Die Deutsche Bibliothek lists this publication in the "Deutsche
Nationalbibliografie"; detailed bibliographic data is available
on the Internet at http://dnb.ddb.de/.

The paper in this book meets the guidelines for permanence and durability
of the Committee on Production Guidelines for Book Longevity
of the Council of Library Resources.

© 2007 Peter Lang Publishing, Inc., New York
29 Broadway, 18th floor, New York, NY 10006
www.peterlang.com

To Jaquelyn Louise Harton Howard and Carl Mabry Howard[†]:
My understanding of your love for me grows with time.
Thank you!

TABLE OF CONTENTS

Editor's Preface ix

Acknowledgments...xi

List of Abbreviations...xiii

1   Introduction 1

2   Approaches to Progressive Sanctification...................................11

3   Definitional Considerations 41

4   The God Who Initiates 61

5   Solidarity of the Redeemed Community 83

6   Solidarity and Progressive Sanctification in Paul 105

7   Community in the Pauline Epistles... 141

8   Conclusion 183

Bibliography... 189

Author Index 207

Scripture Index 211

EDITOR'S PREFACE

More than ever the horizons in biblical literature are being expanded beyond that which is immediately imagined; important new methodological, theological, and hermeneutical directions are being explored, often resulting in significant contributions to the world of biblical scholarship. It is an exciting time for the academy as engagement in biblical studies continues to be heightened.

This series seeks to make available to scholars and institutions scholarship of a high order, and which will make a significant contribution to the ongoing biblical discourse. The series includes established and innovative directions, covering general and particular areas in biblical study. For every volume considered for the series, we explore the question as to whether the study will push the horizons of biblical scholarship. The answer must be *yes* for inclusion.

In this volume Jim Howard, building on the theological notion of progressive sanctification argues for an intrinsic and essential relationship between the role of the individual and that of the larger community of believers. In addition to the exploration of biblical texts and themes as a principal focus in this regard, the author argues that much of the emphasis placed on the role of the individual is not biblically generated but has come about through the western emphasis on individualism. The argument in this volume on the centrality of community is thorough and cogent, and will be embraced and used extensively particularly by evangelical scholars.

The horizon has been expanded.

Hemchand Gossai
Series Editor

ACKNOWLEDGMENTS

Publishing a book with an emphasis on community and its role in progressive sanctification necessarily requires that community be involved. With this in mind, this book is the presentation, with revisions and updates, of a Ph.D. dissertation accepted by the Faculty of the Department of New Testament Studies at Dallas Theological Seminary in 2004. I am grateful for the encouragement and valuable criticisms of Drs David K. Lowery, John D. Grassmick, and Stephen R. Spencer (Wheaton College), all of whom were members of my dissertation committee. Without their rigor, this book would be less than it is.

The renewed and growing focus on community in New Testament studies has involved scholars and authors at a variety of levels. I cannot claim to have utilized all of the studies which have appeared, but I have attempted to identify the works which seem to be the most significant and utilize them to further the discussion. My acceptance or criticism of their arguments in no way diminishes my appreciation for their contribution and, of course, none of these people should be held responsible for the use which I make of their ideas and arguments.

Having said this, these two groups are not the sum total of the community that generated these ideas. I am also grateful for the members of the Mannheim and Darmstadt Hospitality Houses and other members of Cadence International whose early discussions laid the groundwork for this study. This study would not have been initiated without Drs Mark Young and Dorian Coover-Cox, and Chuck Cox, who initially challenged me to write in this area and have journeyed with me through the project. I would be remiss if I did not mention my appreciation for the many friends at Pathfinders Community Church who patiently endured as I "tried on" these ideas. And of course, Dave Schlup, my good friend and peer in a variety of contexts, whose consistent encouragement and technical expertise made this project delightful.

Finally, I am most grateful for Nancy and my children, John, Cassie, Molly, and Andrew, all of whom I love deeply and who consistently encouraged me through the process. They shared in the cost, with little benefit to themselves personally, except for my growing appreciation for their significance and role in my life.

LIST OF ABBREVIATIONS

ASNU	Acta seminarii neotestamentici upsaliensis
AnBib	Analecta biblica
AThR	*Anglican Theological Review*
AB	Anchor Bible
AsTJ	*Asbury Theological Journal*
BDAG	Bauer, W., F. W. Danker, W. F. Arndt, and F. W. Gingrich. *Greek-English Lexicon of the New Testament and Other Early Christian Literature.* 3d ed. Chicago, 2000
TBT	*The Bible Today*
BT	*The Bible Translator*
Bib	*Biblica*
BSac	*Bibliotheca sacra*
BNTC	Black's New Testament Commentaries
BDF	Blass, F., A. Debrunner, and R. W. Funk. *A Greek Grammar of the New Testament and Other Early Christian Literature.* Chicago, 1961
BBB	Bonner biblische Beiträge
BBR	*Bulletin for Biblical Research*
BASP	*Bulletin of the American Society of Papyrologists*
CTJ	*Calvin Theological Journal*
ChrCent	*Christian Century*
CNT	Commentaire du Nouveau Testament
DBI	*Dictionary of Biblical Imagery.* Edited by L. Ryken, J. C. Wilhoit, and T. Longman III. Downers Grove, 1998
DJG	*Dictionary of Jesus and the Gospels.* Edited by J. B. Green and S. McKnight. Downers Grove, 1992

DNTB	*Dictionary of New Testament Background.* Edited by C. A. Evans and S. E. Porter. Downers Grove, 2000
DPL	*Dictionary of Paul and His Letters.* Edited by G. F. Hawthorne and R. P. Martin. Downers Grove, 1993
Epiph	*Epiphany*
ETR	*Etudes théologiques et religieuses*
EvQ	*Evangelical Quarterly*
ExpTim	*Expository Times*
GNS	Good News Studies
GOTR	*Greek Orthodox Theological Review*
GBS	Guides to Biblical Scholarship
ICC	International Critical Commentary
Int	*Interpretation*
JSNT	*Journal for the Study of the New Testament*
JSNTSup	*Journal for the Study of the New Testament: Supplement Series*
JBL	*Journal of Biblical Literature*
JES	*Journal of Ecumenical Studies*
JRE	*Journal of Religious Ethics*
JETS	*Journal of the Evangelical Theological Society*
LEC	Library of Early Christianity
LXX	*Septuagint*
NA^{27}	*Novum Testamentum Graece*, Nestle-Aland, 27th ed.
NDBT	*New Dictionary of Biblical Theology: Exploring the Unity & Diversity of Scripture.* Edited by A. T. Desmond et al. Downers Grove, 2000
Neot	*Neotestamentica*
NET	New English Translation
NICNT	New International Commentary on the New Testament
NIDNTT	*New International Dictionary of New Testament Theology.* Edited by C. Brown. 4 vols. Grand Rapids, 1975–1985
NIDOTTE	*New International Dictionary of Old Testament Theology and Exegesis.* Edited by W. VanGemeren. 5 vols. Grand Rapids, 1997
NIGTC	New International Greek Testament Commentary
NSBT	New Studies in Biblical Theology

NovT	*Novum Testamentum*
NovTSup	Supplements to Novum Testamentum
NTS	*New Testament Studies*
OiC	*One in Christ*
ProEccl	*Pro Ecclesia*
RefR	*Reformed Review*
RelEd	*Religious Education*
SNTSMS	Society for New Testament Studies Monograph Series
SBL	Society of Biblical Literature
SBT	Studies in Biblical Theology
SN	Study Note, NET Bible
SwJT	*Southwestern Journal of Theology*
TBT	*The Bible Today*
TDNT	*Theological Dictionary of the New Testament.* Edited by G. Kittel and G. Friedrich. Translated by G. W. Bromiley. 10 vols. Grand Rapids, 1964–1976
TNIV	Today's New International Version
TS	*Theological Studies*
TWOT	*Theological Wordbook of the Old Testament.* Edited by R. L. Harris, G. L. Archer Jr. 2 vols. Chicago, 1980
ThTo	*Theology Today*
TJ	*Trinity Journal*
TynBul	*Tyndale Bulletin*
TNTC	Tyndale New Testament Commentaries
VT	*Vetus Testamentum*
WW	*Word and World*
WBC	Word Biblical Commentary

CHAPTER 1

Introduction

A review of the books and articles on the subject of sanctification reveals both a long history and a list of topics that in some way contribute to our collective understanding of it. They include the biblical definition, distinctions between the "old man" and "new man," the concept of "the flesh" and its control, the distribution and use of spiritual gifts, the freedom that believers have in Christ, differences between position and practice, the phenomena of transformation, growth and renewal, the fruit, baptism, filling, and control of the Holy Spirit, evidences of sanctification, individual versus corporate sanctification, and more.

With this complexity in view, this study explores and analyzes the Pauline Epistles exegetically and theologically in order to reexamine the role of the believing community in the process of the individual believer's transformation. The primary thesis is that the redeemed community, at all levels of relationship, is an essential element in the process of growing in Christ.

The Need for the Study

Historically, the role of the redeemed community in sanctification has been discussed separately from treatments of the topic. Perhaps this is because the various theological positions are oriented more toward the role that God, especially the Holy Spirit, plays in the believer's growth. At the same time, because life as a believer often involves intense struggle, the believer deeply desires (and rightfully so) God's refreshing involvement with them, and they hope for relief from the struggles.

The various theological positions evaluated in chapter 2, in some sense, all reflect a profound optimism and the deepest hopes of believers on how to survive and win in this "present evil age." It is clear from biblical teaching, secular and ministerial experience, and the development of theology within church history that people innately seek to find value extrinsic to their own being. For the believer, this process necessarily orients one toward God and the hope found with him, rather than the empty and deceptive pleasures found in the world around us.

Meanwhile, the role of the believing community in this process has consistently been overlooked in traditional exegetical and theological studies related to sanctification. A review of the standard systematic theologies confirms this. Where sanctification and the community are addressed together, the community is viewed either as the *environment* in which growth occurs, or from the more traditional perspective of Paul's *ethics*, that is, as something in which the believer should participate. Both the environmental and the ethical perspective implies that the community, while important, is not essential in the process of growing in maturity. While many believers may agree that the community is important, it is questionable whether they would agree that it is a means of progressive sanctification. The quip that all that is needed for Christian growth is "me and the trinity" does not stand up to the teaching of the New Testament.

This study intends to show that the redeemed community plays an essential role in the process of progressive sanctification in Pauline theology. Along with the indwelling Holy Spirit and the Word of God, it is a necessary ingredient for growth in Christ. In other words, the community is required for the believer to grow in Christ-likeness.

In addition, exegetical and theological studies, especially in the Western world, have long emphasized the individual aspect of biblical truth. This has resulted in a highly individualized systematic theology in the Western church in which believers are taught to engage God's truth in all aspects of life primarily from an individual orientation. Thankfully, New Testament scholarship is gaining momentum in every area to overturn this trend and look at the community aspect as well.

Therefore, this study also intends to demonstrate that there is a consistent pattern of movement from the individual to the redeemed community in the Epistles of Paul. In other words, while many of the biblical teachings start with the individual, they find their consummation in community. In fact, it is impossible to understand accurately much of the teaching of the New Testament, especially involving the growth of the believer, without taking this into account. The community texts begin with the individual and the individual texts usually find their resolution in community. This is a consistent pattern that permeates most of the texts about Christian growth. Failure to understand this results in a distorted view of how the believer grows in Christ.

Moreover, when believers do not fully understand their sanctified position in Christ and the role of the community in the process of growth, they are left to journey alone at the deepest level of relationship. This seems to be the habit in much of Western Christianity. Christians operate at one level in community, but they operate at a deeper and different level in the struggles related to growth and exposure of sin as the Holy Spirit engages believers in his transforming work.

At its core, this study asks, "Is it possible to grow to maturity in Christ without the believing community?" The answer, found in the following pages, is no, not any more than it is possible to grow to maturity without the Word of God. To validate this answer, there are several issues that will be addressed. First, are there features intrinsic to the concept of sanctification in general that require community involvement for accomplishment? Second, does the example of a God who relates to his creation provide theological insight into the process of sanctification? Third, is there development in the biblical understanding of community under the New Covenant that impinges on transformation and Christian growth? Finally, do the community texts in the Pauline corpus reveal any necessary community or relational features on which the progressive sanctification of the believer depends?

Method

The following study answers these questions using a combined theological and exegetical approach. However, before these questions are answered, historical considerations related to the issue of progressive sanctification are reviewed and summarized in chapter 2 to identify patterns of thinking and how they impinge on the issue. Then chapter 3 evaluates definitional considerations including the related concepts and terminology found in both the Old Testament and the New Testament. Chapter 4 analyzes the primary example of an initiatory God and how he is related to progressive sanctification. Chapter 5 evaluates the need and benefit of solidarity among the redeemed and the corresponding union with God, especially as it develops under the New Covenant. Chapter 6 further evaluates solidarity as it develops in the Pauline corpus to determine how he relates it to progressive sanctification. Chapter 7 analyzes the community texts within the Pauline corpus in light of these theological considerations to determine what role Paul specified for the community in the growth and transformation of the believer. Finally, chapter 8 summarizes the study and the significant findings and suggests implications for both the individual and the community for future study.

Assumptions

It is necessary to make several assumptions, given the limitations of the study.

First, the triune God is ultimately responsible for the sanctification, transformation and growth of the believer. Broadly speaking, there is general agreement that God is the ultimate source and sanctifier of the believer, as the following survey reveals.[1]

Karl Barth speaks of

> the Holy One who encounters the man who is so very different from Himself, and who does so in that unapproachable majesty, and therefore effectively, but who demonstrates and reveals Himself as the Holy One in the•fact that He sanctifies the unholy by His action with and towards them.[2]

Louis Berkhof states, "[Sanctification] is a supernatural work of God. Some have the mistaken notion that sanctification consists merely in the drawing out of the new life, implanted in the soul by regeneration, in a persuasive way by presenting motives to the will. But this is not true."[3] Emil Brunner states, "It is the Holy Spirit who sanctifies. He alone can effect sanctification. The whole Christian existence as such is the work of the Holy Spirit and, as such, is sanctification."[4] Millard Erickson, in his discussion dealing with the continuation of salvation—what he terms sanctification—emphasizes that it is a work of God. "It is something done by God, not something we do ourselves."[5] Stanley Grenz states, "In the strict theological sense sanctification is the Holy Spirit accomplishing God's purpose in us as Christian life proceeds."[6] Finally, Charles Hodge says, "This reference of sanctification to God proves it to be a supernatural work. It is because men cannot cleanse or heal themselves."[7]

The general consensus that God is the ultimate source of sanctification in no way minimizes the role of the believer. Beyond this point of consensus, the various traditions move in different directions as they attempt to understand and explain the events that make up the sanctification, transformation, and growth of the believer. Many of the theologians cited above go on to articulate some role that the believer plays in this growth process. They use a variety of concepts and terms to explain this phenomenon such as people in partnership with God, people having a task to accomplish as given by God, people in obedience before God, people submitting to God's gracious work of maturing, and so forth. This survey supports the assumption that God is the sanctifier, and the current study then concentrates on the role of people in the growth process.

Second, the truth contained in the scriptures is necessary for sanctification and growth. Here, the disparity in theology becomes more apparent. For example, Barth is reluctant to associate sanctification and growth with the more evangelical concept of truth contained in God's Word. His view is deeply rooted in the mystical relationship of the believer with God, as expressed in the work of Christ in our lives. Concerning John 17:17 he states, "But He Himself is the fulfillment of this request as the Son of the Father." Further, "Sanctification takes place as history because and as this man [Christ] who is directly sanctified by God is its acting Subject in the royal authority thereby given Him by God, God Himself being the One who acts through Him." After an extensive evaluation of Christ's accomplishments, he concludes, "Everything that follows flows from this source and is nourished by this root."[8] In contrast, Berkhof states clearly that, "the principal means used by the Holy Spirit [in this process] is the word of God." While, in and of itself, the Word is not effective for sanctification, he goes on to explain that it "presents all the objective conditions for holy exercises and acts" and "serves to excite spiritual activity by presenting motives and inducements."[9] Similarly, Erickson clarifies that the Word of God is the means to Christian growth.[10] Pentecostal theologians develop the idea that it is the "truthfulness" of the Lord which is the vehicle for growth.[11] In an apparent attempt to avoid "Phariseeism," they focus on the experience with the Spirit who "opens" the Word of God to the believer.[12] This is consistent with their focused approach on the role of the Spirit and his supernatural manifestation of gifts in the life of the believer.

What is clear is that truth is important in the process of growing to maturity. What is not clear is how and in what way. As noted above, Berkhof places some emphasis on the objective nature of the Word as it relates to sanctification and growth. It is intriguing that in each discussion the "jumping off point" is the specific commands and statements in the scriptures. Even Barth, who consistently moves toward a relational emphasis with Christ, grounds his discussion in specific verses and precepts.

The position argued here is that the Word of God, taken in its entirety, provides an objective conceptual and theological framework for assessing the process and progress of growth in the life of the believer. As is well known in hermeneutical studies, the principles involved in distinguishing between eternal and absolute truths versus cultural and relative truths are complex and debated. With this in mind, this study focuses on the truth contained in God's Word as the objective and central means for framing the discussion while concurrently allowing for great flexibility in cultural adjustment regarding behavior.

Third, faith is necessary for sanctification and growth. Berkhof states, "Faith is the mediate or instrumental cause of sanctification as well as justification. It does not merit sanctification any more than it does justification, but it unites us to Christ and keeps us in touch with Him." He goes on to say that the path to holiness is a "constant exercise of faith."[13] This sentiment is echoed by all of the major traditions.

The exercise and practice of faith is developed extensively in the Epistle to the Hebrews. After devoting significant attention to the superiority of the priesthood of Christ (Heb 4:14–10:18), the author then turns the argument to the superiority of the life found in Christ (Heb 10:19–13:19). It is in this later section that the concept of faith is treated extensively. Faith is the basis for the exhortation to draw near to God with confidence (Heb 10:19–22). And, although the technical word for faith does not occur, the concept is very clear and a necessary ingredient for maintaining consistency when the author says, "And let us hold unwaveringly to the hope that we confess, for the one who made the promise is trustworthy" (Heb 10:23).[14] This establishes the background for the famous chapter 11 which deals with examples of faithful believers down through the ages. This chapter serves as an encouragement to the recipients that they too can stand in faith and remain true to the Lord.

Fourth, Paul authored the New Testament letters traditionally attributed to him. While it is not the purpose of this study to establish the authorship of the Pauline corpus, and recognizing that this is an area of significant debate in New Testament studies, it is necessary to make an assumption regarding that authorship. In addition, assuming Pauline authorship brings with it certain other assumptions. Inherent in the assumption is also the idea of coherence within the theology developed and expounded by Paul. This is not to say that there is no progression. On the contrary, New Testament scholarship has long demonstrated evidence of progression in Pauline theology. However, progression does not necessitate disparity or discontinuity in his theology. Rather, it reflects an unfolding nature of how God is at work in creation.[15] Therefore, the assumption is made that Paul authored the letters traditionally attributed to him and that his theology, while evidencing progression, is coherent in its development regarding the role of community in the process of growth.

This is not a study in the behavioral sciences specifically as it relates to sociology or psychology. Much work has been done in each of these areas in recent times regarding sanctification and Christian growth and is worth reading.[16] Since this is about the role of the community of believers, it is first a study about the process of growing in Christian maturity and the role that the community plays in that process, rather than the goal of sanctification.

Argument

To accomplish this goal, it is first necessary to survey the current approaches to sanctification; specifically the process that believers go through post-regeneration (traditionally referred to as progressive sanctification). This is accomplished in chapter 2.

In chapters 3–5, after development of brief definitional considerations (chapter 3), theological considerations are addressed that have historically been omitted from the discussion of Christian growth. They are theologically oriented and reflect a transcultural nature. In other words, they are not limited by cultural practices, but are theologically central to understanding what God is doing in the life of the individual believer to grow them to maturity. In addition, they exhibit continuity between the Old Testament and the New Testament. In other words, what was begun in the Old Testament has found further clarification and expansion in the New Testament with the coming of the New Covenant and the finished work of Christ on the cross.

The first theological consideration is a study of the God who initiates (chapter 4). From the beginning of time, as recorded in scripture, God always moves toward individuals for the purpose of redemption and relationship. In this respect, he is an "initiatory" God. His movement toward humanity in general and to individuals in particular presents a consistent pattern of how to "move" dynamically and actively in relationships. This is a significant theological example related to the role of community that is ultimately the basis for Paul's exhortation to imitate God.

The second theological consideration involves the solidarity of the redeemed community (chapter 5). This concept permeates the biblical story, starting with Israel and ending with the eschatological community of God in the eternal state. This solidarity is both a gift and a responsibility that is to be used to generate unity within the church as well as to invite the unregenerate into relationship.[17] This concept is central to Paul's community texts. It finds its expression in the form of unity, which is then applied to the lowest level of solidarity: relationship. Where the individual, rather than a group, is addressed, it is in the context of the necessity of being integrally involved in mutually edifying, life-changing relationships that guard the unity of the Spirit and promote Christian growth.

In Chapters 6–7, the community texts within the Pauline epistles are evaluated exegetically to demonstrate that in Pauline theology, the solidarity of redeemed is essentially related to progressive sanctification (chapter 6), and the community plays an essential role in the maturing of the individual believer, ultimately leading to an eschatological community of mature saints (chapter 7). Here, the theological considerations developed in chapters 3–5 will also be taken into account and applied to the Pauline community texts to support the primary thesis and demonstrate continuity throughout God's historical plan of total and complete redemption. Also, it will be demonstrated that for Paul there is a necessary movement from individuals to the community. While many of his exhortations originate at the individual level, they are incomplete unless they find their consummation in the believing community.

Finally, in chapter 8 a summary and conclusion of the findings will be presented.

NOTES

1   For the current study, only traditions within the broad range of Protestantism were considered. This in no way is intended to imply that Roman Catholic, Orthodox, or even non-Christian theologies, make little or no significant contribution to the discussion. Rather, it is a reflection of the assumptions controlling the study. In addition, the traditions considered are only to provide a framework for comparison and contrast, rather than an analysis into specific beliefs. More analysis is performed later in the section entitled "Approaches to Progressive Sanctification."

2   Karl Barth, *Church Dogmatics*, ed. G. W. Bromiley and T. F. Torrance, trans. G. W. Bromiley, vol. 4 (Edinburgh: T&T Clark, 1958), 500.

3   Louis Berkhof, *Systematic Theology* (Grand Rapids: Eerdmans, 1941), 532.

4   Emil Brunner, *The Christian Doctrine of the Church, Faith and the Consummation*, trans. David Cairns, vol. 3 (Philadelphia: Westminster, 1962), 290–91.

5   Millard J. Erickson, *Christian Theology*, 2d ed. (Grand Rapids: Baker, 1998), 982.

6   Stanley J. Grenz, *Theology for the Community of God* (Grand Rapids: Eerdmans, 1994), 440.

7   Charles Hodge, *Systematic Theology*, vol. 3 (London: Scribner and Company, 1872; reprint, Grand Rapids: Eerdmans, 1940), 216.

8   Barth, *Church Dogmatics*, 4:515.

9   Berkhof, *Systematic Theology*, 535.

10 Erickson, *Theology*, 1021–25. It is interesting to compare this discussion on the importance of the Word with his discussion concerning the nature of sanctification where very little is said about the Word and its role (pp. 980–83).

11 Russell E. Joyner, "The One True God," in *Systematic Theology: A Pentecostal Perspective*, ed. Stanley M. Horton (Springfield, MO: Logion Press, 1994), 127.

12 Timothy P. Jenney, "The Holy Spirit and Sanctification," in *Systematic Theology: A Pentecostal Perspective*, ed. Stanley M. Horton (Springfield, MO: Logion Press, 1994), 419.

13 Berkhof, *Systematic Theology*, 537.

14 Unless otherwise indicated, biblical quotations are taken from the NET Bible.

15 William J. Webb, *Slaves, Women & Homosexuals: Exploring the Hermeneutics of Cultural Analysis* (Downers Grove, IL: InterVarsity, 2001). Webb has demonstrated progression in both the giving of scripture and God's involvement within culture. His "redemptive hermeneutic" is predicated on the fact that God is moving redemptively in culture over time, as evidenced by the historical progression revealed in scripture.

16 For example, note James R. Beck, "Sociopathy and Sanctification," *Journal of Psychology and Christianity* 14 (spring 1995): 66–73; S. D. Gaede, *Belonging: Our Need for Community in Church and Family* (Grand Rapids: Zondervan, 1985); Alistair I. McFadyen, *The Call to Personhood: A Christian Theology of the Individual in Social Relationships* (Cambridge: Cambridge University Press, 1990); Robert J. McShea, *Morality and Human Nature: A New Route to Ethical Theory* (Philadelphia: Temple University Press, 1990); James A. Oakland, "Self-Actualization and Sanctification," *Journal of Psychology and Theology* 2 (summer 1974): 202–9; Thomas Overholt, *Cultural Anthropology and the Old Testament*, GBS: Old Testament, ed. Gene M. Tucker (Min-

neapolis, MN: Fortress, 1996); David Pecheur, "Cognitive Theory/Therapy and Sanctification: A Study in Integration," *Journal of Psychology and Theology* 6 (fall 1978): 239–53; William F. Rogers, "Creation, Redemption, Sanctification, and Mental Health," *Pastoral Psychology* 12 (November 1961): 10–14; F. LeRon Shults, *Reforming Theological Anthropology: After the Philosophical Turn to Relationality* (Grand Rapids: Eerdmans, 2003); and Gerd Theissen, *Psychological Aspects of Pauline Theology* (Philadelphia: Fortress, 1986).

In addition, no analysis is given to the believer in isolation. If community is an essential element in Christian growth, this raises the obvious question about the person who has no access to community. Will that person grow in maturity? While this may constitute a special case, it has traditionally been omitted from the studies of progressive sanctification. The issues in this special case are the same issues facing the believer who has no scriptures available to them. In this later case, while there may be examples of individual believers growing while in some form of isolation, it would be theologically absurd to state axiomatically that the Word is not necessary for growth to Christian maturity. The same argument applies to the believer who is without community.

17   Solidarity should be expressed in the world in incarnational ministry, modeled after the life of Christ. For much of recent North American church history, the evangelistic approach has been first belief, then relationship between the Christian and the non-Christian. Perhaps the more biblical approach is first relationship, then belief. In other words, the more effective strategy is belief that results from genuine love for the world.

CHAPTER 2

Approaches to Progressive Sanctification

The following survey of the various approaches to the study of progressive sanctification reveals how vigorous the debate has been in recent years. Each approach is evaluated in order to understand the core elements in the approach as well as any specific issues that impact the current study. While there are other approaches to progressive sanctification not evaluated, these were chosen as a representative sample to reveal a consistent tendency to deny or overlook the community as a means of sanctification. Following the survey each approach is summarized and evaluated for relatedness to the role of the community in progressive sanctification.

Wesleyan Views

To understand Wesleyan views on sanctification, several concepts need exploration.[1] First is original sin. The Wesleyan tradition affirms the total corruption of Adam and Eve, in keeping with the beliefs of Augustine and the Reformers.[2] This loss of the image of God includes (1) the *natural image*, which gives people understanding, free will, and various affections, (2) the *political image*, or authority over the earth, and (3) the *moral image*, which includes righteousness, true holiness, and the ability to truly love God.[3] Whereas humans retain traces of the natural image and political image, the loss of the moral image was complete and total, thus effecting the need for salvation.

The restoration of the natural image and the political image will only be accomplished at the consummation of all things. However, at the core of Wesleyan understanding of salvation is the belief that through the power of the Holy Spirit, one is enabled to carry out completely the two great commandments of loving God and loving others. This is, perhaps, one point at which Wesleyan writers differ from other Reformation thinkers. In Wesleyan theology, the two commandments lead to the inescapable conclusion that the loss of relationship at the fall of humanity, including the ability to love God, can be fully restored in the sanctification process. Indeed, at the heart of Wesleyan theology is the belief that God's ultimate requirement for humanity is for the perfection, or total holiness, of humanity and that it is achievable in the present life.[4] It is significant in Wesleyan tradition that in the awakening process of salvation of the individual, God's grace leads the fallen sinner from saving grace to grace for sanctification and ultimately to grace that provides the ability to love. This end result is exclusively the result of the atoning work of Christ.[5]

The second important concept for understanding sanctification in Wesleyan thought concerns the relationship between law and love. Invariably, the Reformation generated certain tensions between law in the Old Testament, and gospel, or grace, in the New Testament. In the Wesleyan tradition this tension is mitigated in that the moral intent of the law is captured in the teachings of Jesus in the Sermon on the Mount and the rest of the New Testament. Whereas Reformation theology moved more in the direction of freedom from the moral obligations of the law as a result of the believer's reconciliation, Wesleyan theology developed along the lines of Christ working in believers enabling them to carry out the law's moral obligations. The carrying out of moral obligations, therefore, is integrally related to the process and end of sanctification (p. 25).[6]

The third concept important to Wesleyan views of sanctification involves the work of the Holy Spirit. Since true freedom results in the ability and responsibility to love, the role of the Holy Spirit is significant in that he imparts this ability to the believer. This impartation is an essential and necessary element, since humanity is incapable of achieving the perfection required by God on its own merit.[7] Here, Wesleyan theology sees a direct connection between the essence of God, as characterized by holy love, and a central desire within God to share that image with his children.[8] Impartation of the ability to love is accomplished through the life of Jesus who indwells his children by the presence and power of the Spirit.

This Wesleyan concept of holiness is as dynamic in nature as it is descriptive. The heart of the New Covenant is that God, through the promised Holy Spirit, will completely restore his love in his children and with this love, the ability to fully love God. The centrality of this theme in both the Old and New Testaments is reflected in Wesleyan theology in that, through the power of the indwelling Spirit, the children of God are enabled to live in righteousness and true holiness throughout their entire Christian lives. Inherent in the command is the capability and promise of its fulfillment. This is the essence of the indwelling Spirit and accounts for the prominence given to the Spirit's role in Wesleyan theology. This is what is known as the doctrine of entire sanctification, or Christian perfection, and represents the complete restoration of the *moral image*, which was lost at the fall.[9]

Further, the doctrine of entire sanctification of the believer is rooted in the belief that a person is systematically cleansed, resulting in eradication of sin because, in order for the believer to truly love, sin must be removed by the Spirit. The experience of Christian perfection is the beginning of the holy life, rather than its culmination. Practically speaking, it was identified as a moment in time, an experience that came to be known in various Wesleyan theological traditions as the second blessing.[10] Contemporary Wesleyan theology has developed such that the believer's sanctification is expressed in terms of dynamic relationship, rather than a point-in-time experience. This has resulted in a practical shift from focus on an experience where sin is eradicated to an experience that redemptively cleanses from sin so that the believer is freed to love. One Wesleyan writer defines it as, "the act of God by which the human heart is cleansed from all sin and filled with love by the Holy Spirit who is given, through faith, to the fully consecrated believer."[11]

But is God primarily interested in sanctifying the believer so that they are free to love others, or is there another deeper purpose in mind? Wesleyan theology places a heavy emphasis on obedience and loving others. Granted, in the Wesleyan view the ability to love is the result of entire sanctification, but it seems the goal becomes the means. If the true goal of sanctification is the obligation to love others, this becomes the primary, if not the only, means for what God wants to accomplish in the life of the believer beyond the point of entire sanctification.

This tends to result in downplaying the concept of Christian growth. Wesleyan theology fails to address adequately the fundamental issue of God's holiness versus humanity's sinfulness. If obedience and the ability to love are highlighted as the primary result of sanctification, then the community becomes the object of the sanctification process through the action of loving, rather than the recipient or means of sanctification. Does God give the believer the ability to love in order to fulfill the moral obligation of the law, or does God desire the believer to grow in maturity and therefore use their ability to love to that end?

In addition, is a believer enabled to love only when entire sanctification has been perfected or completed or are there varying degrees of love? How much love satisfies the moral obligation to love? Either the sanctified life starts at regeneration and the believer grows in their ability to love, or it begins at a point beyond regeneration and the capacity to love fully is extrinsically provided, rather than developed. This latter concept is at the heart of the Wesleyan theology of progressive sanctification. The issue is that the Bible consistently presents the believer's ability to love as a developing ability along with spiritual maturity. For example, 1 Tim 1:5 seems to indicate that love is the ultimate goal, rather than the immediate goal. In addition, a process is also in view since love is the goal of Paul's instruction.[12]

Finally, Wesleyan theology tends to overlook the purpose of the community in the process of Christian growth. Where the community is addressed, it is viewed more as the object of love or obedience, rather than an essential part of the process. The Wesleyan teachings on sanctification seem to be more focused on the individual's relationship with God and not on understanding how the community is involved.

Reformed Views

Reformed views of sanctification are rooted in the concept of holiness, specifically as it relates to the process of renewal. It is a process that involves dynamic change, both within the nature of believers and their ability to please God. Sanctification is more than an emphasis on certain behavioral characteristics; it is centrally located in a change in direction rather than a change in substance.[13] In addition, it is balanced between the work of Christ and the Spirit in the life of the believer conjoined with obedience in such a way as to avoid what G. C. Berkouwer refers to as "moralistic improvement."[14] It involves a movement from all that is sinful (a negative) toward a total dedication to God (a positive) rather than an increase in the righteousness of the believer. To understand this process, it is necessary to explore several concepts.

The first involves union with Christ.[15] Believers are sanctified by being united with Christ in his death and resurrection. This is accomplished through the indwelling Holy Spirit and involves a separation from sin through association with Christ in his death.[16] This association effects separation from sin and is rooted in redemptive events in the past, even though the union with Christ becomes a present reality at conversion.[17]

The resultant movement toward righteousness is also related to association with Christ in his resurrection. This association should generate a new awareness that results in a new way of life. Union with Christ is found in both the believer's dying with Christ to sin and being made alive to God in his resurrection.[18] This is the heart of understanding all aspects of sanctification in Reformed theology. In other words, Christ not only *effected* sanctification, he *is* the believer's sanctification. Thus sanctification can be accomplished only through union with Christ.[19]

The second concept central to Reformed views of sanctification involves the Word of God. The Bible is one of the chief means by which believers are sanctified (p. 64). The Reformed writers are careful, however, to assert that the believer has been freed from the requirements of the law (p. 85). In contrast to Wesleyan theology discussed earlier, Reformation theology moved in the direction of freedom from the moral obligations of the law as a result of the believer's reconciliation. The carrying out of moral obligations has more to do with the believer expressing gratitude for all that Christ has done and Reformed theology categorically rejects any form of religious perfection in the present life of the believer.[20] Obeying the Word of God is an expression of believers' love, and living in obedience expresses their image-bearing capacity. So by means of obedience the Word becomes one of the most significant means by which God sanctifies the believer.[21]

The third concept important to Reformed theology involves faith. While the Reformers stressed that the believer is justified by faith alone, they also emphasized that sanctification is likewise by faith. Faith becomes instrumental in sanctification in a number of ways. It allows the believer to grasp the concept of union with Christ. It also allows the believer to live in full awareness that sin is no longer master. Intellectual assent, while the starting point, is insufficient to cause the believer to live an abundant life free from the mastery of sin. Faith moves the believer through this process and allows the Christian to believe that the Holy Spirit indwells the believer and enables them to overcome sin and live for God. It is in the exercise of faith that the believer experiences the reality of Christ's accomplishments. In other words, faith becomes the "how" of experiencing union with Christ, and this faith is only as real as it translates into obedience.[22] Faith is not a "fact producing other facts," but a genuine dependence on God and his accomplishments.[23]

The fourth concept involves renewal and transformation. Though people were created in the image of God, sin so completely perverted that image that holiness was lost. In the process of sanctification, that image is being renewed. In drawing a distinction between definitive and progressive sanctification, Reformed theology holds that the believer is both genuinely and totally a new creation and simultaneously becoming like Christ. This transformation into the image and likeness of Christ is brought about by a partnership with the indwelling Holy Spirit.[24] This partnership predominantly takes the form of "grasping" the truth about one's new position in Christ. Once believers have integrated this truth into their thinking, they are then enabled and responsible to put to death sinful practices and grow in newness of life.[25] At this point the progressive aspect of sanctification comes to the forefront as Reformed theology rightly emphasizes the importance of renewing the mind (Rom 12:2) and growing in Christ (Eph 4:15), while reminding the believer that sanctification in its totality is the work of God.

A final concept important to Reformed theology involves the goal of sanctification. Reformed theology sees two goals. From a definitive standpoint, the ultimate goal is the glory of God, as intimated in such phrases as "to the praise of the glory of his grace" (Eph 1:6), "to the praise of his glory" (Eph 1:12), and "to the glory and praise of God" (Phil 1:11). From a progressive standpoint, the proximate goal of sanctification is the perfection of the believer as found in the ongoing conformity to and ultimate likeness of Christ. In God's conception, his delight for his children moves him to transform them over time into the likeness of his Son, with the ultimate outcome being sinless perfection. In other words, this "higher destiny" for the believer is higher in the sense that it entails final and complete transformation into the image of God over such things as personal pleasure and entrance into heaven.[26]

But, does this view really explain the process? Granted, the process is supernaturally driven and spiritually effected, however, the Reformed view is fairly ambiguous in describing the actual transformational process. Is the obedience of the believer really designed to express gratitude, or is there a deeper intrinsic need that obedience satisfies and fulfills in the process itself?

In addition, as with the Wesleyan view, the Reformed view is highly individualistic. Whereas the Wesleyan view focuses more on the Holy Spirit's role, the Reformed view emphasizes a balanced partnership between the Holy Spirit and the individual believer, and what the believer is capable of doing alone with the Holy Spirit. As a result, very little is said in either view regarding the role of the community in the process of sanctification. Sinclair B. Ferguson touches on the community by explaining that the community is "the context in which sanctification matures." He goes on to explain that the community is in a sense the means for the deployment of sanctification.[27] In other words, our sanctification is "tested" in community to demonstrate that it is occurring. But, does this really address the role of the community? Is the community simply the bystander in the maturing process or is there a deeper and more essential role that community plays?

Finally, the emphasis on the Word and faith tends to have the effect of overlooking experience. Is it the "exercise of faith" that allows the believer to experience the realities of Christ's accomplishments? It seems that the community is somehow more involved in turning Christ's accomplishments into life-changing realities than demonstrated by the Reformed view.[28] Reformed theology is correct in placing a heavy emphasis on the Word and faith, but may be negligent in assessing the transformational process and how people are involved in that process. In other words, God may have designed the process so that it takes more than the Word and faith to motivate believers to godliness and experience genuine life-change.

Pentecostal Views

Pentecostal beliefs about sanctification have their roots in Wesleyan theology.[29]

A review of the history of Pentecostal theology reveals spiritual growth involving tension and conflict that seem to be rooted as much in experience with the Holy Spirit as in clear biblical study. Because of the experiential aspect of the Pentecostal movement, its theological and philosophical guidelines are less easily discerned and therefore less definitively agreed upon among the movement's constituent groups. And yet, it appears that a consistent effort has been recently applied by Pentecostal theologians to attempt to understand biblical teaching in light of the various experiences of the groups involved.

Pentecostals, with all of their differences, have several things in common. They place a great emphasis on the Holy Spirit and the contemporary relevance of the gifts of the Spirit. They zealously seek personal spiritual renewal through their relationship with the Spirit. They emphasize a life of holiness through the empowerment that comes from the Spirit. Finally, they seek a dynamic and deeply worshipful experience in their gatherings (p. 134). In contrast, they are highly individualistic in their spirituality; that is, spirituality in Pentecostalism deals with quality of individual piety as it relates to the things of the Spirit, especially in an extraordinary, or supernatural, sense (p. 140–41). With these things in mind, the following discussion presents the more significant concepts impacting the current study where some form of theological agreement is found.

The first concept involves the importance of holy behavior in the sanctification process.[30] There seems to be widespread agreement among Pentecostals that progressive sanctification involves a strong and committed separation from sin and the world. Myer Pearlman, in discussing sanctification and purity states, "Things devoted to Him [God] must be clean. Cleanliness is a condition of holiness, but not the holiness itself, which is primarily separation and dedication."[31] Similarly, William Menzies and Stanley Horton explain that God and the believer each have a part to play in the process of sanctification.

The believer's role centers on yieldedness to the Holy Spirit and the rooting out of sin. Using the warning passages in Hebrews as the major texts, Pentecostal theologians point out that failure to accomplish this will "lead to a hardened, settled rebellion against God, resulting in the final loss of one's salvation."[32] Guy Duffield and Nathaniel Van Cleave note that the aspect of sanctification involving the cleansing and purifying of the believer is both a crisis and a process.[33] They go on to explain,

> The definite surrender of the life to God constitutes the supreme condition to practical Sanctification. This involves the yielding of all our members to His will... How many times we have prayed, 'Lord, purge me.' Perhaps if we would listen carefully we might hear Him say, 'Purge yourself!' (p. 245)

Timothy Jenney explains that what God is about in the world today is the gradual and continual cleansing of all things from "any taint of sin or uncleanness,"
and at the end of time, everything not cleansed will be consigned to the fire.[34]
Finally, Ernest Williams explains this as a "cutting loose" from the world and
sin.[35]

A second concept important to Pentecostalism involves a post-regeneration
"crisis" experience with the Holy Spirit.[36] As Pentecostalism has developed, the
treatment of this second experience has differed widely, both in its definition
and application. Within almost every line of theology in Pentecostalism, however, this experiential event ultimately involves a supernatural baptism in the
Holy Spirit.[37]

Thirdly, Pentecostal theology teaches that sanctification involves the whole
person, and the means given by God are the blood of Christ, the Holy Spirit,
and the inspired Word of God. The blood of Christ is effective in "instantane-
ous" or positional sanctification, while the Holy Spirit and Word of God are
effective in progressive sanctification.[38] While sanctification is made possible by
the blood of Christ, it is the Holy Spirit who makes it personal to the believer.[39]
For their part, believers must maintain "unbroken communion" with Christ
during their sojourn on the earth.[40] This teaching clearly has the believer's life
of holiness in mind. True sanctification occurs when a believer obeys God and
does whatever work God gives him to do (p. 125–26).[41] This partially explains
the significance of the experiential life with the Spirit in Pentecostal thinking.

For the purposes of the current study, it is important to understand that
Pentecostal theology distinguishes between the sanctifying work of the Spirit
and the empowering work of the Spirit. The baptism in the Spirit is an empowering work and not a sanctifying work.[42] Within this context, the Pentecostal
view of sanctification places a heavy emphasis on works. In other words, sanctification is defined in terms of the believer accomplishing "works of service."
This partially explains why the baptism in the Spirit becomes such an important
theological necessity. The believer is not able to accomplish these works without the empowering baptism of the Spirit. As such, the various Pentecostal
groups have placed the focus more on behavior as defining godliness, and less
on life-change and growth in character.

But does this adequately account for the biblical data regarding transformation and growth? With such a strong emphasis on the second work of the Spirit,
there is very little room for the believer who is not completely devoted. What
happens to believers who do not experience the Spirit in such experiential and
enthusiastic ways? The all-or-nothing approach to sanctification seems to
minimize varying degrees of devotion to the Lord on the part of the believer.
The Pentecostal attempt to downplay human involvement in the second work

and play up God's power and glory is commendable, but questionable if genuine sanctification is defined in terms of life-change. As a result, the believer's motivation is in danger of being oriented toward guilt, rather than a fascination with God and his grace in the believer's life.

The Pentecostal view is largely individualistic and does not adequately account for the role of the community in the process of growing in Christ. This focused individualism combined with an emphasis on works tends toward a legalistic environment. As a result, the community, rather than being a primary source of relationship and encouragement, is actually in danger of being seen as spiritual watchdogs.[43] And the believer is left to fight the battle alone, with only the help of the Spirit. While not downplaying the role of the Spirit, this view overlooks significant biblical texts regarding the importance of community in the spiritual battle.

The Lutheran View

At the beginning of his discussion on sanctification, Gerhard Forde provides an interesting definition of sanctification, "If it is to be spoken of as something other than justification, [it] is perhaps best defined as the art of getting used to the unconditional justification wrought by the grace of God for Jesus' sake."[44] He goes on to point out the "disastrous" result of arguing for a distinction between justification and sanctification, noting that sanctification is just as much a part of the Spirit's work as justification. If the distinction is too great, the believer enters into a "moral life" where some degree of holiness is sought after, thus giving the "old being" inordinate control in the process. This then leads to erroneous discussion about being sanctified according to some "moral scheme." He questions how this can happen if God is truly in control (p. 14–15).[45]

The Lutheran view of sanctification, therefore, frames the discussion within the context of gospel and law.[46] In other words, the "old man" continues to pursue a righteousness of its own in an attempt to keep the law. Granted, the attempt might be more morally or piously pursued, nevertheless, it is still in contradistinction to grace. The Lutheran concept involves the death of the "old man" and the resurrection of the "new," rather than the continuation of the "old."[47] This theological understanding and approach has consistently led Lutheran theologians to emphasize the inseparable nature of justification and sanctification.

The law, which represented the conditional promise, did not effectively deal with sin; it only made it worse by exposing it. And since the law exposes sin, it essentially prepares the way for the gospel and subsequent conversion.[48] And where sin abounded, it is pointed out, grace abounded still more. This linkage is what led Paul to ask the rhetorical question about whether a believer should continue in sin so that grace might abound. The answer to the sin problem, it is argued, is not the keeping of the law nor even sanctification, but the death of the "old man" and resurrection of the "new man." And this is found in the finished work of Christ as accomplished through the believer's justification.

Given this, there is the still the problem of being just and sinner at the same time. Emphasizing the unconditional promise of justification, it is at this point in Lutheran theology that sanctification enters the discussion. The beginning of sanctification is the realization of the truth of what Christ accomplished through the individual believer's justification. It is a "psychic process" in which God uses "man's intellectual, emotional, and volitional abilities" to teach, move and convert the heart to understand truth.[49]

It is not to be tied to the "schemes of the law" or "progress thinking" (p. 23). In Lutheran theology this is mutually exclusive with a true understanding of justification by faith alone. In realizing the truth of what Christ accomplished, it is necessary for the believer to acknowledge fully their total depravity. This prevents the believer from relying on their own devices and allows the justifying act of God to stand alone in its accomplishment. "Sanctification is thus included in justification as a total state" (p. 27).

Bringing the discussion back to the beginning, sanctification, in a progressive sense, is more related to becoming aware of ("used to") God's grace, rather than an actual change in holiness. It is a growing in grace that captures the believer more and more as they focus on what God has accomplished. After all, "Where can there be more holiness than where God is revered and worshiped as the only Holy One?" (p. 27)

The progressive aspect involves the concept of daily "starting again" in understanding anew the totality of God's accomplishment.[50] It is at this point that the distinction between law and grace surfaces again. This is something the believer never really accomplishes or grasps, therefore it is refreshing every time it occurs. As a result, the believer never achieves any further development or advanced stage of maturity. Rather what changes is the awareness of reality: a resurrected new man.[51]

Edward Koehler argues at this point for faith in the sanctifying process. He sees faith as the distinguishing feature that allows the Christian to continue believing, resulting in daily sanctification. As faith wanes, it is reflected outwardly in the life of the Christian. "As faith weakens, love waxes cold, and good works decrease in number and quality. To achieve a greater sanctification of life, there must be a stronger faith and a deeper appreciation of the goodness of God."[52]

Lutheran theologians are, therefore, reluctant to talk about "progressive" sanctification. They see the sanctifying work of God as better expressed in daily and discrete starting points, rather than progress or growth. The dynamic movement of God in the believer's life is expressed in terms of the goal moving closer to the believer as they grow in awareness, rather than the believer moving closer to the goal. It is argued that this idea is conceptually closer to the eschatological language of the New Testament where Christ taught that the kingdom is coming "upon" believers, rather than the reverse. Practically, this means the believer is more and more moving away from self and growing in awareness of the justifying work of God; a "revival of true human living."[53]

The emphasis on the inseparability of justification and sanctification orients the sanctification discussion around the sin problem and depravity, rather than changed character. The issue is that orienting the discussion in this fashion seems to overlook significant portions of scripture wherein changed character is still a necessity as well as a priority. The tension that develops with a redemption that requires further transformational work seems to account better for the biblical data and is a real problem that must be addressed. This is the basis for the various views of progressive sanctification. Allowing for a both-and approach, the sin problem was dealt with positionally while the necessity for growing in Christ-likeness is being dealt with progressively. Both can be true and in tension at the same time.

In addition, the Lutheran distinction of growing in awareness rather than maturity is ambiguous and does not adequately address the passages that seem to reflect a dynamic movement on the part of the believer under the guiding and empowering influence of the Holy Spirit. While growing in awareness of our state in Christ is certainly biblical, growth in maturity is also biblical. In short, the Lutheran view emphasizes the solution to the sin problem to the exclusion of the passages and imagery (not to mention experience) dealing with the progressive nature of growing in godliness and holiness.

The Keswick View

The Keswick Convention began formally in 1875 in England by "leaders who had become increasingly frustrated with their own low-level (albeit average) Christian experience and who longed for a life lived in the power of the Holy Spirit."[54] The movement was rooted in the core belief that the Christian life should have a more abundant aspect than was being experienced by the average Christian. Quoting from the first issue of *The Christian's Pathway of Power*, Steven Barabas cites the original idea.

> We believe the Word of God teaches that the *normal* Christian life is one of uniform sustained victory over sin;… the normal experience of the child of God should be one of victory instead of constant defeat, one of liberty instead of grinding bondage, one of 'perfect peace' instead of restless worry.[55]

Keswick history begins even earlier in 1873 with Robert Pearsall Smith from Philadelphia, who came to London on sick leave. Smith

> found evangelicalism dominant yet slowly suffocating in an atmosphere of introspection and gloom; a world of crepe and wails and preoccupation with death; of sanctions and inhibitions. Fervent Christians groaned and gloried in unceasing inner conflict. Many were afraid to be happy: happiness would be sapped by lurking sense of guilt.[56]

During this sick leave, Smith began meeting with clergy and discussing his observations and his own life which he felt outpaced the average Christian with grace and joy. Soon, conventions were being held in which he and his wife were the guest speakers. The response was so great that the first convention was held in 1875. From this beginning, the Keswick movement sprang up (p. 12–17).

This history is significant in that the Keswick movement is not associated with any denomination. Rather, it represents a cross-section of evangelical believers that are attempting to both understand the sanctified and abundant life and are trying to experience it in real and refreshing ways. It may be that this is the key distinctive of the Keswick movement.[57] This combined desire to understand with a quest for experience is accomplished at the annual conventions. Over a five day period the participants are exposed to a progressive series of topics that move them from an awareness of their sins to a commitment to service.[58] This very process reveals a great deal about the theology of the Keswick movement.

Rather than seeing the Convention as a Bible conference, the participants see it as a spiritual clinic whereby the Lord identifies, diagnoses and heals spiritual ailments. Day one emphasizes sin and is a day "of deep heart-searching, when the searchlight of God's Word is turned upon the inmost recesses of the soul, and sin is laid bare."[59] Day two emphasizes God's provision for living a victorious Christian life wherein integrity is highlighted and reflected upon (p. 69–84).[60] This day is designed to focus the believer on God's provision as found in his Son and his Spirit. Day three emphasizes entire consecration of the believer to God. The goal of the spiritual life is a dedicated spiritual wholeness that results in a "practical walk in the Spirit and the daily doing of God's will" (p. 108). Day four emphasizes the abundant life found by living in the Spirit, and a distinction is made between fullness and lack of fullness and the ensuing impact on the believer's ability to enjoy the spiritual life. Day five emphasizes the outward focus of service to others. The sequence of daily teachings to this point have all been designed to get the believer to a "state of spiritual health," while this last day focuses outward on ministry (p. 148–51).[61]

It seems from this discussion that at the heart of the Keswick movement is the commitment to sanctification. As with other theological systems, Keswick theology[62] holds to a basic definition of sanctification that involves the holiness of God and the believer's being set apart unto holiness. However, their emphasis is on the loving nature of God to restore believers to a "full, loving fellowship with Himself." The problem is the barrier presented by sin. Living in perfect unity with God requires that the sin barrier be removed. This is the process of sanctification (p. 158).

At this point Keswick theology differs from Wesleyan theology. Both hold that people are sinful by nature and in need of the work of Christ. In addition, both hold that sanctified believers continue to grow in grace as long as they live and that they experience a second event involving the Spirit and grace. Where they differ is not in their experience, but in their understanding of what takes place at that moment. Whereas Wesleyan theology teaches that the believer is delivered from sin, Keswick theology holds that the believer is enabled to choose correctly and enjoy victory in a deeper way.[63]

Keswick theology holds to the traditional three-fold view of sanctification, that is, positional sanctification (justification), "experiential" sanctification, and complete and permanent sanctification (glorification). It seems that it is in the second aspect that the Keswick movement has gained a following and interest. The beginning point in understanding and appropriating this "experiential" sanctification lies in the inner working of the Holy Spirit. While Christ secured our justification, it is the Spirit who sanctifies the believer. He is the one who counteracts the daily effects of sin. While not removing the believer's choice and "susceptibility" to sin, the Spirit does enable believers to surrender to him and trust him, against their natural inclination.[64]

Keswick theology teaches that the answer to the sin problem is faith. They emphasize that by faith it is possible to live an abundant life in the Spirit and not give in to the sinful desires of the old nature. They point out that the Bible consistently points back to the original saving event with the added exhortation to believe that experience. J. Robertson McQuilkin goes so far as to say, "I know of no exception to the consistent teaching of New Testament authors that the solution for defeated, failing, sinning Christians is to return to what took place at salvation" (p. 166). This is what they refer to as "supernatural" living.

Living a supernatural life involves being transformed into Christ-likeness. The way this occurs involves a carefully balanced integration of free will on the part of the believer and a new relationship with God in which he indwells the believer. The free will aspect involves the believer's ability to choose to do right since they are no longer under the control of sin. Because of the work of Christ and the regenerating work of the Spirit, the believer is given the ability to obey and serve God. This does not mean that sin is absent. On the contrary, Keswick theology teaches that the very fact that the believer remains under the influence of the "sinful disposition" means that it is a process and more than an accomplishment. Even then, this choosing to do right can only be accomplished by the strength supplied by God. This is found in the indwelling Spirit (p. 174).

The indwelling Spirit and the ensuing relationship is the key to transformation and the victorious life. McQuilkin further explains that this indwelling involves being filled with the Spirit, which he defines as,

> A figurative, poetic expression that refers primarily to the relationship between two persons in which one is in charge, a relationship that began as a specific event that was intended to initiate a continuing condition. The relationship normally results in a glorious sense of the divine presence and certainly results in a transformed life. (p. 177)

Charles Inwood describes it as "a new, overwhelming sense of God, the consciousness, the awful and yet glorious consciousness, that God is at last in actual and undisputed possession of the whole temple of one's being."[65]

The result is a new basis for growth, both in the "inner mind" and in "outer behavior." As believers are filled with the Spirit their thought process is gradually and consistently changed. This results in a transformed mind, followed by changed behavior. This process results in gradual character change from worldliness to Christ-likeness.[66]

To accomplish this, there are four means of grace which are, in actuality, "conduits of divine energy." In addition, these means of grace require active participation between God and the believer. The first means of grace is prayer. Prayer is the means by which believers intensify their relationship with God, especially at the moment of temptation. Prayer in the midst of temptation brings victory.[67] The second means of grace is scripture. It is in the Word that both God's character and will are revealed to the believer. The third means of grace is the church. As McQuilkin states, "The congregation of God's family is indispensable for spiritual growth." Grace is dispensed in the "united" gathering of God's people as they join in all of the various aspects of church life. The fourth means of grace is suffering. Suffering is the means by which God distinguishes himself in glory. In other words, it is in the midst of terrible circumstances that God often is revealed most clearly to the believer who chooses to respond rightly.

When the believer is filled with the Spirit, the resulting relationship brings a "delightful personal companionship." This new relationship has many facets to it. The Spirit comforts the believer when discouragement sets in and, through his Word, makes the believer sensitive to ethical and moral dilemmas. There is a real sense in which the Spirit is present with the believer, thus providing real strength in weakness. His counsel through his Word clarifies issues for the believer. He consistently works to change the believer's thought patterns to be more like Christ. Finally, he controls external circumstances for the long-term good of the believer (p. 175).

The Keswick movement has produced an emphasis on the experiential and qualitative aspect of sanctification that moves one to believe that there is more to the Christian life than is found in day-to-day experiences. In this regard, Keswick theology seems to have produced an enthusiasm among its constituents that results in a commitment to grow in the Lord.

However, several issues arise when the theology, as well as the practice, is examined. Is it necessary to be at a convention for this work of the Spirit to occur? Even though there are several significant differences between Keswick theology and Wesleyan theology, it nevertheless has a strong second work of grace aspect. What about life between conventions and those who are unable to attend the conventions? It seems that this approach, while resulting in a high degree of enthusiasm, communicates that the rest of the Christian life is somehow sterile or superficial.

Is it possible that what occurs at the conventions is, in reality, what should be occurring at each local church? Although Keswick theologians would probably agree that this increased level of enthusiasm and commitment should routinely occur in the local church, the literature suggests that the conventions are necessary precisely because it rarely occurs at this level. In addition, rather than reflecting a second work of grace aspect, perhaps the experience is more the result of focusing on the guiding influence of the Spirit in community. While giving credit to the church as a means of grace, Keswick theology has done very little to explore the role of the believing community in the experience.

Recent Contributions

Larry Crabb

Larry Crabb's[68] works often deal specifically with sanctification since he is addressing the problem of self-centeredness and growing in Christ-likeness. However, he spends very little time defining sanctification from an exegetical or biblical perspective.

> Sanctification includes abandoning every agenda that aims toward recovering or enhancing our own intactness, and pursuing God with not our wholeness, but with his glory in view, with the confidence that his agenda includes satisfying every longing in our hearts.[69]

For Crabb, growth to maturity involves the "path of righteousness," by which the believer is moving from justification to glorification. This path involves God completing what he has declared to be true; that the believer is totally acceptable to God. For Crabb, the problem is that the believer does not believe God and, therefore, must grow in their understanding. At this point the path to righteousness enters the discussion. Between justification and glorification the believer is to engage in acts of obedience. "Christian maturity involves becoming more and more like the Lord Jesus through increased obedience to the Father's will."[70]

At the heart of his sanctification model is the idea that true change does occur unless it is effected at a level that he identifies as being "below the water line."[71] He feels most counseling methods center on some form of behavior modification rather than transformation. He is clear that sanctification cannot occur without divine intervention and is therefore unavailable to the unbeliever; yet the majority of his method is focused on the internal issues and relational methods of exposing these internal problems.

Crabb sees the image of God as related to the individual. As such, the image of God is defined in terms of four capabilities. First, people are personal beings with deep and personal relational longings. Second, people are rational beings who think and are capable of evaluating the world around them. Third, people are volitional beings capable of willfully choosing a certain direction. Finally, people are emotional beings whose experiences in the world involve feeling. This leads Crabb to locate the nature of personhood in relational terms, rather than anthropological or christological terms. In other words, image-bearing is more related to how we relate, rather than what we are in our present state. This means that the ultimate devastation of sin lies in the breakdown of relationship, both with God and with man.[72]

In order to understand his concept of sanctification, it is important to explore each element in his view of people. First, people are personal beings. People, in their innermost beings, are like God in that they are capable of deep longings for something intensely personal. Crabb believes this deep longing involves two factors. People have a deep longing for relationship. As the Trinity enjoys deep relationship with each other, so people were created with this same desire. Similarly, people have a desire for impact. He defines this as, "*a desire to be adequate for a meaningful task, a desire to know that we are capable of taking hold of our world and doing something valuable and well*" (p. 114). People are not machines, but persons and, therefore, like God.

Second, people are rational beings capable of thinking. Attempting to explain Paul's exhortation to be "transformed by the renewing of your mind" (Rom 12:2), Crabb differentiates between "images" and "beliefs." Images are how people experience the world. A series of images that form a pattern result in deeply held beliefs and perceptions about the self (p. 137).[73] The problem lies in how the beliefs are formed. If they are formed based on life experiences, rather than the truth of God's Word, then the belief ultimately leads to a commitment to make life work without God. "Real change from an unhealthy person who lives for himself to a healthy person who loves and lives for God requires a change in that belief" (p. 138).[74] In other words, genuine transformation involves a change in beliefs from independence (no need for God) to dependence (a total need for God).

Third, people are volitional beings capable of willfully choosing a certain direction. Crabb holds to what he calls a "personal teleology," by which he means that every behavior has a goal. The concept of personal choice is inextricably bound up with purpose. When sinful people exercise choice with a sinful purpose in mind, a sinful goal or outcome is in view and achieved. This teleological view of choice is significant in that it explains the core issues surrounding motivation. The goals that control, direct or influence behavior are derived at a deep level from the belief structure of the individual. The behaviors, then, are often the result of subconscious goals designed to protect the self and achieve whatever form of "happiness" the person feels is needed (p. 159).[75]

Finally, people are emotional beings whose experiences in the world involve feeling. God made people to enjoy him and experience what it feels like to live with him. However, sin has significantly affected our ability to feel the way God intended. Since humanity was not created for sin and its devastation, it seems obvious that the reactions generated by sinful experiences can be "good" or "bad." When people make choices based on their goals and beliefs, they experience consequences. These consequences in turn generate the "good" or "bad" responses. He classifies these two responses as "constructive" and "destructive" emotions (p. 175). The basic distinction between the two involves control and responsiveness. Does the emotion interfere with what God has outlined as the righteous response or does it provoke the person to explore his own sinfulness and respond in a godly fashion?

In Crabb's view of sanctification, while evaluating behavior is important, evaluating emotions is just as important. Emotions become the "window into the soul." If the believer is willing to take the time, exploring the emotions resulting from decisions made will have a profound impact on understanding the sinful and subconscious strategies that control the way we think and act. Only at this point can genuine transformation begin to occur (p. 176–77).

This view of people has significantly influenced Crabb's view of the sanctifying process. At the heart of growing in maturity is the ability to love people genuinely. It is the very evidence of maturity (p. 195). When character development is measured by standards, change is usually dealing with issues that are "above the waterline." In his model, the process from viewing patterns of images to developing subconscious goals represents thinking that is "below the waterline" and the corresponding behaviors and resulting emotions represent the external and visible portion that is "above the waterline." Obviously, the belief structure is below the waterline. Crabb believes that genuine change requires transformation "below the waterline" (p. 204). Thus, many approaches taken by churches employ some form of behavior modification.

If people are to change, below-the-waterline analysis and reflection need to occur.[76] This requires two essential elements. First, the true issues of the heart need to be exposed so that change can begin to occur. Second, this is best accomplished in genuine relationship and community. He calls this model "Character Through Community."[77] But even then, this does not guarantee genuine change and transformation. What needs to occur in the heart of the person is what he calls true repentance and a desire to change. This repentance leads to forgiveness and involvement. Repentance reveals that the person has recognized a sinful way of thinking that leads to a sinful behavior or attitude. Forgiveness frees the person from harboring controlling resentment toward others who have sinned against them. Finally, involvement represents a renewed emphasis and movement toward others, especially those who have the greatest need for love (p. 142–52).

Crabb has come under severe scrutiny and criticism from a variety of theological camps. His "needs based" model of sanctification has been criticized as originating from non-Christian thinkers such as Sigmund Freud and Abraham Mazlow. Is it helpful to define human needs in non-biblical terms such as "deep longings," rather than in theological or biblical terms such as "salvation," "total depravity" and "God's love?"

In addition, locating the nature of personhood in relational terms, rather than anthropological or christological terms is distinctive, given the systematic theological approaches in recent history. This clearly impacts the theological concept of image-bearing by defining it in teleological terms, rather than ontological terms. This has led Crabb to have a much more relationally oriented approach to sanctification and transformation. If it is correct to define image-bearing capacity in teleological terms, then the role of the community plays a much more significant part than previously evaluated in the history of the church.

Stanley Grenz

Stanley Grenz's concept of progressive sanctification begins with a concept of an "eschatological community" in which all believers belong and participate. In terms of anthropology, we exist in a state of "openness" to the world, by which he means our significance and fulfillment are found outside of creation. In other words, "humans can find no permanent home in the world but are dependent on God for ultimate fulfillment."[78] In Christianity this is immediately and ultimately found only in God (p. 130–31).

Thus, he sees God's image as "a reality toward which we are moving" (p. 173). The believer's image-bearing capacity, therefore, is a dynamic concept rather than a state resulting from creation. This leads Grenz to locate the nature of personhood in eschatological terms, rather than anthropological or christological terms (p. x). Image-bearing is more related to what we are becoming, rather than what we are presently. This means that the ultimate devastation of sin lies in the breakdown of relationship within community and humanity's inability to live in relationship as God intended (p. 187).

Given this, Grenz defines progressive sanctification in terms of conditional sanctification—"our movement from imperfection and immaturity to increasing conformity to the standard, which is Jesus Christ" (p. 443). It is closely connected to holiness and, in fact, represents the believer's "quest for holiness."[79]

Conditional sanctification involves the subjective and experiential. It is the transformation that occurs in the life of the believer who has by faith experienced "positional sanctification," or, a new standing in which righteousness is extended by God to the believer. This new standing of the believer defines the relationship with God and serves as the "fountainhead out of which the Christian life emerges."[80] It refers to the believer's character and conduct, and it is a necessary action on God's part. It is derived from "his purpose in calling out a people to be his own" (p. 442).

Paramount in Grenz's conditional sanctification is the involvement and working of the Holy Spirit. It is the Spirit that is at war with the sinful nature. In addition, it is the Spirit who provides the power and ability for overcoming temptation and sin. And yet, while foundational, the Holy Spirit is not alone in the process. It also requires the believer's personal cooperation. It requires the believer to be diligent to obey the commands of God, as well as fight the spiritual battle and engage in fervent prayer (p. 444). It begins with the believer's "frame of mind" and, as such, is observable. In other words, the believer should be able to see quantitative and qualitative growth in their life.[81]

It is interesting that, while one of the central organizing facets of Grenz's theology is the community of God, he spends little time locating conditional sanctification within that community. For Grenz, the community is eschatological in nature and focus and, therefore, it seems that his theology revolves around how all believers end up in that community, rather than how the community is involved in helping the believer grow in Christ-likeness.[82]

Similar to Crabb, Grenz orients image-bearing capacity in teleological terms rather than ontological terms. However, whereas Crabb moves to a relationally based sanctification model, Grenz's theology focuses more on the eschatological outcome rather than the means of sanctification. While an eschatological view of community and sanctification is attractive and treats the community texts with a fresh perspective, it does not adequately address the present process of growth in which the individual is involved with and in the believing community.

David Peterson

David Peterson has recently entered the discussion because he sees conflicting theologies of sanctification and holiness. In his view, the various approaches to sanctification have generated confusion between sanctification, renewal and transformation. In the various theological camps and approaches to the sanctification issue, the foundation for holy living has been inappropriately located in either the progressive aspect or the second work of grace experience. For Peterson, the proper location is the definitive aspect of sanctification. Sanctification is a one-time event that has process implications in life and is expressed in such terminology as transformation and renewal. The believer is holy and must learn to live that way. However, the primary basis for holy living is the finished work of Christ and the ongoing work of the Holy Spirit. In other words, definitive sanctification is the primary biblical motivation for holy living.[83]

In the Old Testament concept of holiness, there are four considerations he believes to be foundational to a proper biblical understanding of sanctification. First, sanctification is inherent in the redemptive work of Christ. It was in God's saving activity in the Exodus that Israel was declared and commanded to be holy. Similarly, in the New Testament, holiness is "regularly portrayed as a once-for-all, definitive act and primarily has to do with the holy status or position of those who are in Christ" (p. 24).

Second, "Christians are sustained in holiness by the ongoing presence of the Holy Spirit and the trust that he gives in the finished work of Christ" (p. 24). He bases this on God's continual presence with Israel in the form of the tabernacle and, later, the temple, and the provisions of the priesthood and covenant rituals. It was in this presence and through the provisions of the priesthood and rituals that God maintained Israel as a holy people unto himself. In the New Testament God again is present with believers through the indwelling Holy Spirit. In addition, Christ fulfilled all of the priesthood and ritual requirements of the law.

Third, "Christians are called to live out the practical consequences of knowing God in Jesus Christ and of being consecrated by his saving work." Similarly, there were "lifestyle implications" in the Old Testament for the Israelites who "were convinced that they belonged to [God] in an exclusive way" (p. 24)

Finally, "sanctification in Christ has to do with a profound re-orientation of values and behaviour" (p. 25). This is what he refers to as transformation. He believes it is brought about by involvement with God's Word and God's Spirit. The Old Testament parallel is that Israel was to be separated from the beliefs and practices of the surrounding nations. In addition, just as Israel was to reveal God's holiness to the surrounding nations, so also Christians are to reflect God's holiness to the world.

In light of these four concepts, rather than seeing sanctification as a process, Peterson believes it refers primarily "to God's way of taking possession of us in Christ, setting us apart to belong to him and to fulfil his purpose for us" (p. 27). In the New Testament, the sanctification terminology regularly emphasizes the saving work of Christ applied to the believer through the ministry of the Holy Spirit. This is what brings about a consecration to God. Similarly, the consecration rituals identified in the Old Testament are replaced by the consecrating work of Christ in his death and resurrection. The terminology related to his sacrifice and role as High Priest provide the continuity between the ritual practices and the work of Christ.

He makes several conclusions as a result of his position. First, "Our essential identity as Christians is formed by Christ and the gospel, not by our own personalities, backgrounds or achievements" (p. 47–48). Christians enjoy a "distinctive" and "exclusive" relationship with God based on the work of Christ. This is the basis for developing self-identity as a believer. Because of the work of Christ, the Father draws believers into an intimate and pleasing relationship with himself.

Second, "Although God calls upon us to express the fact that we have been sanctified by the way we live, our standing with him does not depend on the degree to which we live up to his expectations. It depends on his grace alone" (p. 48). This should be the primary form of encouragement for believers who are struggling and tempted to give up. God promises mercy and grace to help the believer who comes to him with boldness (Heb 4:16).

Third, believers must continue to see themselves from God's perspective as sanctified based solely on the work of Christ. Often, life experiences suggest to the believer that the opposite is true. Part of growing in maturity is disciplining ourselves to continue to focus on the truth (reality) about our standing in Christ and not on our perceived reality.

Fourth, Christians are to view one another as those who are already sanctified in Christ. Peterson believes this would increase the patience between believers in daily relationships, especially where sin is present. This also has impact on how new believers coming into the church who continue to struggle with sin are treated by others. Emphasizing conditions and requirements at the expense of this basic truth involving our sanctification too often results in discouragement, disillusionment and failure. A proper view in relationships would go far to correct this.

Peterson's approach does not discount growth. Indeed, he spends an entire chapter discussing the pursuit of holiness and what it entails for the believer. Aside from desiring to present an accurate and biblical view of sanctification, he is also interested in refuting the problems that arise from a "progressive" view of sanctification in which a believer can grow in holiness over their lifetime. "Such an approach creates unrealistic expectations and is capable of producing guilt and despair in those who do not perceive the evidence of such progress in their lives" (p. 70).[84] Rather, sanctified living has more to do with living daily in the reality of what Christ has already accomplished and living out that reality in our obedience. In this regard, the language of renewal, transformation and growth are more regularly employed by the New Testament to describe the process of growing in maturity.

Peterson's analysis has highlighted an oversight in recent critical approaches to sanctification. The traditional emphasis on process has shifted the focus away from the definitive nature of sanctification and the finished work of Christ on the cross. This has resulted in a variety of approaches to determine how to grow in holiness. If sanctification is addressed in its entirety at the cross, then this focus has caused much confusion and even misunderstanding of Christ's accomplishments on behalf of the believer.

The implications to this are tremendous. Peterson's study has shifted the question from one involving the progression toward holiness to one involving the believer's understanding of their present holiness in Christ and learning to live with this simple truth. It is no longer a matter of becoming something that we are not. Rather, it is a matter of understanding and growing into what we are already declared by God to be, namely, holy.

Peterson's work did not account for the role of the community in this transformational process of growth. Later, definitional work is done regarding sanctification in both the Old Testament and the New Testament. It will be apparent there that Peterson's work has largely been incorporated into this study. Providing clarification between definitive sanctification and transformation and growth allows for a more clear and cohesive understanding of the community texts, since they frequently are related to the progressive aspect that results from our sanctified position in Christ.

Summary

The process of growth to Christian maturity is viewed very differently in different parts of the church and throughout church history. Peterson notes, while some understand sanctification in either "ritual terms" or some form of asceticism or heightened self-discipline, the more common understanding has been explained as "*a process of moral and spiritual transformation,* flowing from justification by faith" (p. 15). But, as Peterson has pointed out, does this accurately reflect the growth and community texts?

In summary, based on the above discussion, the following common points are identified among the positions analyzed. First, sanctification is first and foremost the work of the triune God, specifically in the person of the Holy Spirit. Second, aside from the positional and ultimate fulfillment aspects, it involves a progressive element wherein the believer is somehow being transformed into the image of Christ and is enabled to mature and effectively deal with sin. At its core, sanctification involves holiness and is essential for growth to maturity. Third, this progressive aspect of sanctification is not a point-in-time event but can be viewed from a daily perspective as the believer lives life. Fourth, the ethical aspect, or obedience to God, is a result of the process, not the cause of it. This last point includes the relationship between believers. The way believers relate to one another is traditionally viewed as a result of the sanctification process, not an essential element in producing it. In other words, the community of believers is seen as a place to carry out the commands of the New Testament, not as a causal factor leading to maturity. This study takes an opposing viewpoint in this regard. The primary thesis is that the redeemed community and associated imperatives are both a cause and a means leading to maturity.

Whereas the various views have common features, there are significant differences as well.[85] The question of how we are transformed into the image of God has historically not been presented in the sanctification arguments. Rather, it seems that the various views have developed with an ontological perspective at the center. This seems to lead to a view of growth oriented more toward individualism and obedience. In contrast, the current trend is moving more toward a teleological perspective of image-bearing which is oriented more toward relationship and community. While Peterson's sanctification view is more definitive, his perspective on growth and transformation is much more teleologically oriented. This allows for greater emphasis on the progressive aspect, but as it relates to transformation, rather than sanctification.

Based on this, the current understanding is much more community oriented than previous views. Whereas Crabb's view is more relationally oriented, Grenz's view is more eschatologically oriented. Nevertheless, current research on this topic takes the community much more into account. In contrast, a consistent weakness in each view analyzed was the failure to account adequately for the role of the community as it relates to the process of growth to Christian maturity. This is the primary concern of this study.

NOTES

1 This section summarizes the major current authors who have written to articulate the common essentials of Wesleyan theology in order to provide a basis for analysis.

2 Marvin E. Dieter, "The Wesleyan Perspective," in *Five Views on Sanctification* (Grand Rapids: Zondervan, 1987), 21.

3 *The Works of John Wesley*, vol. 6 (London: Wesleyan Methodist Book Room, 1872; reprint, Grand Rapids: Baker, 1978), 66; Dieter, "Wesleyan," 22–23.

4 Wilber T. Dayton, "Entire Sanctification: The Divine Purification and Perfection of Man," in *A Contemporary Wesleyan Theology: Biblical, Systematic, and Practical*, ed. Charles W. Carter, R. Duane Thompson, and Charles R. Wilson (Grand Rapids: Francis Asbury, 1983), 1:524.

5 Dieter, "Wesleyan," 22–23.

6 True freedom is not release from the demands of the law, but the ability and responsibility to love. Whereas all believers are released from the curse and obligation related to the law as a means of acceptance, they are obligated to keep the law on the basis of faith. Thus, Wesleyan theology heavily emphasizes the ethical aspect of obedience in the process of sanctification. See also Harald Lindström, *Wesley and Sanctification: A Study in the Doctrine of Salvation* (Grand Rapids: Zondervan, 1980), 123–25, 205–15; José Míguez Bonino, "Wesley's Doctrine of Sanctification from a Liberationist Perspective," in *Sanctification and Liberation: Liberation Theologies in Light of the Wesleyan Tradition*, ed. Theodore Runyon (Nashville, TN: Abingdon, 1981), 62.

7 Dayton, "Entire Sanctification," 525.

8 Dieter, "Wesleyan," 28.

9 Laurence W. Wood, "The Wesleyan View," in *Christian Spirituality: Five Views of Sanctification* (Downers Grove, IL: InterVarsity, 1988), 96; John R. Tyson, *Charles Wesley on Sanctification: A Biographical and Theological Study* (Grand Rapids: Zondervan, 1986), 165–66. This restoration is not so much concerned with moral infallibility as it is with moral restoration, which overcomes human sin and brokenness. This is in contrast to absolute perfection, which will be accomplished in eternity. See Dayton, "Entire Sanctification," 537, who argues that the distinction between Christian perfection and absolute perfection lies in the difference between the inner and outer man and the difference between process and completion. Whereas absolute perfection includes the entire man, Christian perfection addresses only the heart condition. See also, Dieter, "Wesleyan," 30, who further argues that this concept of holiness, expressed in love, is foundational to Wesleyan theology and "sets the hermeneutical agenda for understanding God's purpose in all of His work of redemption in His Son Jesus Christ."

10 Dieter, "Wesleyan," 40–41.

11 Dayton, "Entire Sanctification," 521.

12 It is interesting in this verse that the goal of loving others arises as much from Paul's instruction as it does the work of the Holy Spirit. Granted, it is clear from Paul's writings that

he views the Holy Spirit as the ultimate source; nevertheless, at this point in his instructions to Timothy, he emphasizes the instructional aspect.

The concept of progression and process is latent throughout the entire Pauline corpus, as will be developed later. For example, it is difficult to understand the three-fold Pauline imagery of 1 Timothy 2:1–7 (suffering, competing, and farming) outside of the concept of process and endurance. The Wesleyan shift in focus from a point-in-time experience to a dynamic and growing experience reflects, in part, recognition that process plays a much larger part than originally articulated.

13 Anthony A. Hoekema, "The Reformed Perspective," in *Five Views on Sanctification* (Grand Rapids: Zondervan, 1987), 61–62.

14 G. C. Berkouwer, *Faith and Sanctification*, trans. John Vriend, Studies in Dogmatics, (Grand Rapids: Eerdmans, 1952), 102.

15 Sinclair B. Ferguson, *Know Your Christian Life: A Theological Introduction* (Downers Grove, IL: InterVarsity, 1981), 92–101.

16 Sinclair B. Ferguson, "The Reformed View," in *Christian Spirituality*, ed. Donald L. Alexander (Downers Grove, IL: InterVarsity, 1988), 51.

17 Louis B. Smedes, *Union with Christ: A Biblical View of the New Life in Jesus Christ*, rev. ed. (Grand Rapids: Eerdmans, 1983), 93–94.

18 Ferguson, "Reformed View," 54.

19 Hoekema, "Reformed Perspective," 63–65.

20 Berkhof, *Systematic Theology*, 537; Hodge, *Systematic Theology*, 245–47, 250–58.

21 Hoekema, "Reformed Perspective," 88.

22 Smedes, *Union with Christ*, 145.

23 Berkouwer, *Faith*, 106.

24 Hoekema, "Reformed Perspective," 74. The existence of both indicative and imperative moods in the various biblical passages that describe sanctification reveals that there is a partnership aspect to this process. While the Holy Spirit is powerfully taking the believer through the process, the believer is obligated to cooperate with him through obedience (pp. 66–68). See James I. Packer, *Keep in Step with the Spirit* (Old Tappan, NJ: Fleming H. Revell, 1984). This represents an extended treatment of holiness and the role of the Holy Spirit in the process of believers living holy lives.

25 Ferguson, "Reformed View," 64. This is what is known as "mortification" of sin. Whereas progressive sanctification begins with understanding the truth about one's relationship with the risen Christ, it is also necessary to "mortify," or put to death the sins that are controlling. This mortification involves rigorously dealing with sin and eliminating all sources of temptation, and it is the outworking of the believer's union with Christ. Without it, there is no holiness. Ferguson, *Christian Life*, 98–99, goes on to argue here that this is the "one condition" for the believer to experience union with Christ.

26 Hoekema, "Reformed Perspective," 88–90.

27 Ferguson, "Reformed View," 72.

28 While this study is not oriented toward counseling, telling a person who is the victim of child sexual abuse to "think correctly" does not begin to address the intricate and intrinsic

issues that have developed as a result of this heinous sin. And yet, thinking correctly is part of the process leading to transformation and growth.

29 Russell P. Spittler, "The Pentecostal View," in *Christian Spirituality*, ed. Donald L. Alexander (Downers Grove, IL: InterVarsity, 1988), 136.

30 Stanley M. Horton, "The Pentecostal Perspective," in *Five Views on Sanctification* (Grand Rapids: Zondervan, 1987), 109–14.

31 Myer Pearlman, *Knowing the Doctrines of the Bible* (Springfield, MO: Gospel Publishing House, 1937), 250.

32 William W. Menzies and Stanley M. Horton, *Bible Doctrines: A Pentecostal Perspective*, ed. Stanley M. Horton (Springfield, MO: Logion Press, 1993), 153.

33 Guy P. Duffield and Nathaniel M. Van Cleave, *Foundations of Pentecostal Theology* (Los Angeles: LIFE Bible College, 1983), 238.

34 Jenney, "Holy Spirit," 399.

35 Ernest Swing Williams, *Systematic Theology* (Springfield, MO: Gospel Publishing House, 1953), 2:256.

36 The issues surrounding the spiritual gift of speaking in tongues are not addressed here, since they do not directly impinge on the current study. As with the baptism in the Spirit, there are widespread differences regarding the purpose and timing of this gift. Agreement is found, however, in the supernatural aspect and post-regeneration timing of the gift, as well as the grounding of the theology in both experience and the Word of God. For further study in this area, see John W. Wyckoff, "The Baptism in the Holy Spirit," in *Systematic Theology: A Pentecostal Perspective*, ed. Stanley M. Horton (Springfield, MO: Logion Press, 1994), 425, 428; David Petts, "The Baptism in the Holy Spirit: The Theological Distinctive," in *Pentecostal Perspectives*, ed. Keith Warrington (Cumbria, UK: Paternoster, 1998), 99; Spittler, "Pentecostal View," 141–42.

37 Horton, "Pentecostal Perspective," 108–9. Holiness groups such as the Church of God of Cleveland, Tennessee, and the Pentecostal Holiness Church teach a crisis experience involving sanctification as a second work of grace that necessarily precedes the baptism. They view justification and sanctification as two distinct events that precede the baptism in the Spirit. Thus, a sanctification experience is necessary to prepare the believer to receive the Holy Spirit. God's pardon at regeneration is not enough to root out sin and corruption and therefore a second work of sanctification is necessary to keep the believer from going to hell. As a result, all of this must occur before the believer can begin to experience the abundant life talked about in the Bible. All of these events are supernatural in nature and involve the believer's yieldedness to the Spirit. Failure to experience these events is evidence that the believer is significantly lacking in spirituality. In contrast, the Assemblies of God see faith and the cleansing of the blood of Christ as the only prerequisite to baptism in the Spirit. They reject the idea that a believer may be justified without being sanctified, at least in a positional sense. And yet, even though they reject the second work of sanctification on theological grounds, there is still a strong emphasis on consecration of self and separation from the world in anticipation of the baptism (cf. ibid., 111; Pearlman, *Doctrines*, 253).

38 Steven J. Land, *Pentecostal Spirituality: A Passion for the Kingdom*, Journal of Pentecostal Theology Supplement Series, ed. John Christopher Thomas, Rick D. Moore, and Steven J. Land, vol. 1 (Sheffield: Sheffield Academic Press, 1993), 175. Land represents in some sense a mitigating voice within Pentecostalism. He sees the Spirit as the one who "forms persons in

accordance with the requirements of the kingdom." This is accomplished through the believer's "gratitude, compassion and courage" in walking in holiness.

39 Horton, "Pentecostal Perspective," 119.

40 Land, *Pentecostal Spirituality*, 175. "To live before and in the presence of God through Christ is absolutely necessary if all is not to be in vain and fruitless."

41 Albert L. Hoy, "Sanctification," *Paraclete* 15 (fall 1981): 5.

42 Horton, "Pentecostal Perspective," 131. It is that act by which Christ uses the Spirit to empower the believer for works of service. The believer is then enabled to evangelize with great power, to enjoy a deepened relationship with the triune God through dynamic spiritual worship, and to enjoy and utilize the spiritual gifts fully. Cf. Wyckoff, "Baptism," 449; Menzies and Horton, *Bible Doctrines*, 126.

43 For a more recent and balanced view see Land, *Pentecostal Spirituality*. His mitigating tendency may represent a modern trend within Pentecostalism. Even so, his emphasis remains on obedience and the necessity of avoiding sin.

44 Gerhard O. Forde, "The Lutheran View," in *Christian Spirituality*, ed. Donald L Alexander (Downers Grove, IL: InterVarsity, 1988), 13.

45 Paul R. Raabe, "The Law and Christian Sanctification: A Look at Romans," *Concordia Journal* 22 (April 1996): 178. Raabe similarly points out that, within Lutheran circles, there has been consistent debate on the relationship between justification and sanctification. The debate has revolved around emphasizing sanctification and therefore obscuring the core belief of justification by faith alone or emphasizing justification and therefore denying sanctification and progression toward holiness in the believer's life. One extreme is in danger of leading to legalism, or an emphasis on obedience, while the other is in danger of leading to antinomianism, or a disregard for obedience.

46 Francis Pieper, *Christian Dogmatics*, vol 3. (Saint Louis, MO: Concordia, 1953), 18–19. "The Gospel is the means of renewal and sanctification." In contrast, "The Law continually prepares the way for the Gospel." The law "multiplies" sin and the gospel "dethrones" sin. This is the means by which sanctification is effected.

47 Forde, "Lutheran," 15.

48 Edward W. A. Koehler, *A Summary of Christian Doctrine: A Popular Presentation of the Teachings of the Bible*, 2d ed. (St. Louis, MO: Concordia, 1971), 130.

49 Forde, "Lutheran," 129, 131.

50 Pieper, *Christian Dogmatics*, 14. While growing in sanctification involves a new awareness, Pieper is clear that the Holy Spirit is the one who effects sanctification. "However—and let this be clearly understood—the working of God and the working of the new man are not co-ordinate... but the activity of the new man is always and fully subordinated to God's activity; it always takes place *dependenter a Deo*. In other words: it is the Holy Ghost who produces the activity of the new man; the new man remains the organ of the Holy Ghost."

51 Forde, "Lutheran," 28. Cf. Robert Kolb, *The Christian Faith: A Lutheran Exposition* (St. Louis, MO: Concordia, 1993), 253, who argues that, whereas the law condemns daily, the gospel renews daily as well. He places a heavy emphasis on the balance between these two and the necessity of daily staying in the scriptures.

52 Koehler, *Summary of Christian Doctrine*, 157–58. Cf. Edmund Schlink, *Theology of the Lutheran Confessions*, trans. Paul F. Koehneke and Herbert J. A. Bouman (Philadelphia: Fortress,

1961), 105–07. He similarly argues that the Holy Spirit uses faith to generate a powerful work in the heart, enabling the believer to gain confidence in what God has accomplished. As a result, faith is "certainly" followed by love and obedience; a desire to produce good works and grow in grace.

53 Kolb, *Christian Faith*, 244. Cf. Timothy Wadkins, "Christian Holiness: Positional, Progressive and Practical: Martin Luther's View of Sanctification," *TJ* 7 (spring 1978): 57–59. Wadkins notes that this strong theocentric aspect is deeply rooted in Martin Luther's teachings and was at the core of his disagreement with Catholic theology. Luther, like most other theologians, wrestled with the twin facts of being made righteous at conversion while concurrently in need of transformation to become holy and Christ-like. This formed the basis for his famous description of the believer as a person in contradiction.

54 J. Robertson McQuilkin, "The Keswick Perspective," in *Five Views on Sanctification* (Grand Rapids: Zondervan, 1987), 153.

55 *The Christian's Pathway of Power*, February 1875, p. 1, 6, as quoted by Steven Barabas, *So Great Salvation: The History and Message of the Keswick Convention* (London: Marshall, Morgan & Scott, 1952), 84.

56 J. C. Pollock, *The Keswick Story: The Authorized History of the Keswick Convention* (Chicago: Moody, 1964), 12.

57 W. Graham Scroggie, "Abounding Life," in *Life More Abundant: Spirit-Filled Messages from the Keswick Convention*, ed. Herbert F. Stevenson (Grand Rapids: Francis Asbury, 1987), 13–14.

58 McQuilkin, "Keswick Perspective," 154–55.

59 Barabas, *So Great Salvation*, 39. The placement of this topic on the first day is because most Keswick participants believe that the church's testimony is weak because its view of sin is weak. The church takes sin for granted and often overlooks, or treats as non-sinful, acts of sin clearly spelled out in the Word.

60 In attempting to discover why so many believers live a defeated life, the Keswick speakers have identified several "unscriptural" principles used by the church involving sanctification. First, the view that sanctification is a matter of "due course" is wrong and does not take into account the countless passages that deal with believers who struggle and give in to sin. Second, the view that sanctification is a matter of gradual, steady growth with no change in the rate of growth is wrong and leads to believers who accept the "status quo" and, therefore, have suppressed expectations regarding the abundant life. Third, it is wrong and dangerous to assume that it is possible to eradicate the "sin principle" in this life, either instantaneously at regeneration or through some subsequent work of the Spirit, or progressively through the maturing process. Fourth, the view that sanctification can be gained through the believer personally attempting to suppress the flesh is wrong and leads to legalism.

61 It is on this day that the participants are challenged to discern what God is doing in their hearts with regard to service. In order to answer this question, Keswick teachers have identified four ways that the Lord guides the believer. First, he guides through his Word and the truth that is revealed in study. Second, he guides through circumstances and the focus is placed on what God is doing in the life of the believer. Third, he guides through the believer's conscience with a heavy emphasis placed on education by the Spirit in his Word. Finally, he guides directly by the ministry of the Spirit in the heart of the believer. These four principles are designed to act in concert with each other in a sort of check-and-balance manner, to protect and guide the believer properly.

62 If it can be called "Keswick theology." The Keswick movement represents a group of

cross-sectional evangelicals who have "common" beliefs. However, there has been no systematic attempt to streamline those beliefs into any form of systematic theology. As J. Robertson McQuilkin points out, this has led to what he calls "marginal ambiguities" in the areas of the believer's ability not to sin and the identification and reality of the old nature. Since the Keswick movement is not designed to be a denomination with identified beliefs, he allows for these ambiguities as he attempts to construct a theological system that best explains the common beliefs. McQuilkin, "Keswick Perspective," 156–58.

63   W. Ralph Thompson, "An Appraisal of the Keswick and Wesleyan Contemporary Positions on Sanctification," *Wesleyan Theological Journal* 1 (spring 1966): 14.

64   McQuilkin, "Keswick Perspective," 155.

65   Charles Inwood, "The Fullness of the Spirit," in *Life More Abundant: Spirit-Filled Messages from the Keswick Convention*, ed. Herbert F. Stevenson (Grand Rapids: Francis Asbury, 1987), 73. At the heart of this definition is the concept of relationship with God which is intimate, full and powerful. The distinction between Spirit-indwelt Christians and Christians who are filled with the Spirit comes into focus at this point. While all Christians are Spirit indwelt, not all Christians are filled with the Spirit. This is an experience that occurs as the believer yields himself or herself to God and God responds in a powerful and intimate way to "carry" the believer through to triumph.

66   McQuilkin, "Keswick Perspective," 179–80. See also Paul S. Rees, "Adequacy for Life and Witness," in *Life More Abundant: Spirit-Filled Messages from the Keswick Convention*, ed. Herbert F. Stevenson (Grand Rapids: Francis Asbury, 1987), 85–87.

67   McQuilkin, "Keswick Perspective," 180–81. The following means of grace are taken from McQuilkin's discussion on page 181.

68   These contributors were selected because of their recent and significant contribution to the discussion of sanctification. They provide insight into how the argument is progressing in recent times beyond the traditional denominational lines and various theological positions.

69   Larry Crabb, *Men & Women: Enjoying the Difference* (Grand Rapids: Zondervan, 1991), 114.

70   Lawrence J. Crabb Jr., *Effective Biblical Counseling* (Grand Rapids: Zondervan, 1977), 25.

71   Larry Crabb, *Understanding People: Deep Longings for Relationship* (Grand Rapids: Zondervan, 1987), 204. Crabb has developed his thinking regarding how people process through the maturing process, however his basic sanctification model remains intact throughout his writings. See also Larry Crabb, *The Safest Place on Earth: Where People Connect and Are Forever Changed* (Nashville, TN: Word, 1999). Here, he uses the analogy of two rooms; the lower room and the upper room.

The lower room is the one built by the self that is familiar yet lonely. It is characterized by (1) the "corrupted *image of God* that fills us with a *passion for self*," (2) the "corrupted *resources* we've been given as human beings that fill us with a *passion for control*," (3) "pleasurable and painful *life experiences* that we corrupt by responding to them with a *passion to define life* and *death*," and (4) "the corruption of *God's holy law* that was given to reveal our need but now stimulates a *passion to perform* that literally drives us mad" (p. 87).

The upper room represents the new room Christ gives to the regenerated believer. It represents the true room we were created for. It is the room we long to live in. It is characterized by (1) a new purity which involves a deeper passion to worship, (2) a new identity with a renewed passion to trust God, (3) a new inclination with an enabled passion to grow, and (4) a new power with a new passion to obey (pp. 110–11). Through the use of a building analogy, Crabb seems to be exploring the traditional concept of the old man – new man.

His language, while different, does not contradict his earlier views of below-the-waterline thinking. His below-the-waterline thinking is now explained in terms of the lower room furnished with what he calls "Flesh Dynamics" (p. 94). The question for Crabb now centers on how the self moves into the upper room, the room built and furnished by Christ, to enjoy its genuine peace and relationship with others.

72   Crabb, *Understanding People*, 93–96.

73   For example, an isolated angry outburst from a father to a son may not create a poor misconception of self, whereas a consistent pattern of angry outbursts during the formative years clearly leads to a poor self-image.

74   Crabb's understanding of belief has a strong controlling element to it. In North American thinking, belief is a loose term with a wide range of meaning. Its usual meaning has more to do with cognitive acquiescence, rather than deep conviction controlling life's decisions. His concept of belief falls more in line with deeply held values that dictate how a person thinks and acts.

75   To follow the earlier example, the son, whose poor self-image derived from an abusive father, may develop a goal of self-protection or needed personal acceptance. Worked out in behavior, this may lead the son to a life-time of actions designed to gain approval or acceptance.

76   Larry Crabb, *Inside Out* (Colorado Springs, CO: NavPress, 1988). This entire book is devoted to the process of transformation. Crabb's below-the-waterline analysis can be clearly seen in his statement, "Although an inside look can be overwhelming (and indeed must be if the core direction of our life is to really shift), still there must be more to it than a journey into darkness. We are children of light. Even in the midst of darkness, we know where we are headed. We have a lamp that always reveals the next step and a hope that keeps us moving even when the lamp seems to go out" (p. 201).

77   Crabb, *Understanding People*, 205.

78   Stanley J. Grenz, *Theology for the Community of God* (Grand Rapids: Eerdmans, 1994), 178.

79   Stanley J. Grenz, *Created for Community: Connecting Christian Belief with Christian Living* (Wheaton, IL: Victor/SP Publications, 1996), 198.

80   Grenz, *Theology*, 443.

81   Grenz, *Community*, 198–99.

82   Grenz, *Theology*, 446. In his critique of Wesley's doctrine of "entire sanctification" he highlights the Wesleyan focus on loving one another and resulting "anticipation of community" that this produces. "It reminds us that the Spirit's work leads to the establishment of community—our enjoyment of fellowship with God, with one another, and with all creation."

83   David Peterson, *Possessed by God: A New Testament Theology of Sanctification and Holiness*, NSBT, ed. D. A. Carson (Downers Grove, IL: InterVarsity, 1995), 11–14.

84   Similarly, "The call to 'be holy' can so easily degenerate into a moralistic and perfectionistic programme for believers to pursue. In New Testament terms, we are to live as those who have been brought from death to life, discharged from the law to belong to Christ, led by the Spirit in a continuing struggle with the flesh" (p. 137).

85   Aside from the obvious denominational differences, the differences presented here relate primarily to the current study.

CHAPTER 3

Definitional Considerations

Before examining the central thesis in the Pauline literature, it is necessary to define certain aspects of sanctification. Various definitions have been provided by theologians throughout the history of the church; some lengthy and complex and some simple and concise. While it is outside the scope of the current study to define sanctification, it is appropriate and helpful to look at some definitional considerations, especially as they relate to the present study.

Old Testament Concepts

The concept of sanctification in the Old Testament begins with the idea of distinctness.[1] It is consistently presented in contrast to what is common or unclean. This is seen clearly in Lev 10:10,

> Do not drink wine or strong drink, you and your sons with you, when you enter into the tent of meeting so that you do not die, which is a perpetual statute throughout your generations, as well as to distinguish between the holy and the common, and between the unclean and the clean...

In the Old Testament, by far, the most common usage of the concept of holiness is in relation to God. The word group קדשׁ is most consistently presented in terms of who God is and who the rest of creation is in relation to God. Of God, it is used of God himself (Exod 15:11), his Spirit (Isa 63:10), his name (Lev 20:3), his arm (Isa 52:10), and his ways (Ps 77:13[14]). Of the rest of creation, it is used of priests (Lev 21:6), Levites (2 Chr 23:6), offerings (Exod 29:33), gifts (Exod 28:38), sanctuary furniture (1 Kgs 8:4), priestly clothing (Exod 29:29), sanctuary treasury (Lam 4:1), tabernacle and temple items (Num 35:25; Exod 30:35), Jerusalem (Isa 48:2), heaven (Deut 26:15), and the Sabbath (Exod 31:14–15).[2]

Holiness is Intrinsic to God

There are several attributes associated with the concept of holiness in the Old Testament. Holiness is not inherent in creation. Only God is intrinsically holy. This is made clear in Hannah's prayer in 1 Sam 2:2, where she exclaims, "No one is holy like the LORD! There is no one other than you! There is no rock like our God!"[3] In all of the verb stems the root idea inherently includes becoming something that did not exist previously.[4] For example, in Lev 11:44, the Israelites were told to sanctify themselves and be holy for God is holy.[5] In other words, central to the meaning is a contrast between what is holy and what is not; that is, what is clean and uncommon and what is not. This is clearly seen in Exod 29:37 where, once the altar has been "sanctified," anything that subsequently touches the altar will be declared holy as well. Similarly, whenever something is declared to be holy, it is to be treated as holy from that point in time forward. The concept of holiness does not include a reversal to the unclean or common.[6] This is in view in all the passages dealing with the cultic restrictions and rituals. The people were consistently told not to defile themselves (Lev 11:44) and were punished or even killed when they did (Lev 19:8; Num 4:20).

Holiness Indicates Uniqueness

Similarly, holiness reveals a unique status when compared to the common and unclean.[7] This is revealed to Moses when God commands him to remove his sandals at the burning bush because he was standing on holy ground (Exod 3:5). It seems that that particular plot of ground was not of equal status with the surrounding ground. Exod 28 reveals that holy clothing was made for Aaron and his sons for when they were ministering in the temple. Along with the idea of distinctness, these clothes were of a different status and were not equal with Aaron's common clothes. Exod 31:14–15 reveals that the Sabbath was a holy day unequal to the remaining days of the week. It was on this day that the Israelites were to rest, because God had rested on the seventh day of creation. The punishment for working on this day was death. Lev 23 reveals the various times the nation was to gather for holy assemblies. These events are set apart from the rest of the year and reveal how unique they were when compared with the common everyday work and life of Israel.

Holiness Refers to the Deity of God

Holiness speaks about God, almost as a synonym of deity in many places.[8] The psalmist cries out, "give thanks to his holy name" (Ps 30:4[5]; 97:12). The various places pictured as God's dwelling are all called holy. He dwelt in the Holy of Holies (Exod 26:34; 1 Kgs 8:10; Ps 11:4). His heavenly dwelling is called holy (Deut 26:15; Ps 20:6[7]). He calls Zion his holy hill (Ps 2:6). He is pictured as answering the psalmist from his holy hill (Ps 3:4[5]). The psalmist asks who can live on God's holy hill along with him (Ps 15:1). He is pictured as living on his holy hill (Ps 43:3).

In these uses, two aspects come into view. In each of these uses there is an inherent power that comes from the sovereign Lord who is holy. This includes his name, his dwelling and his answering from on high. In addition, in each of these uses there is an inherent quality of his character that comes to the fore-front. The fact that these different aspects of holiness are applied to him reveals that his character is different from every other's character.[9] This is seen clearly in all of the cleansing and purification rituals. The repeated commands to keep holy objects clean and separate from common use become practical everyday pictures that reveal that God's holy character is also clean and pure.[10] This then becomes the basis for trust in the Lord. Because God is intrinsically holy, he can be trusted (Ps 33:21).

Here the idea of distinctness comes into view. The holiness terminology applied to God reflects his "otherness" such that his holiness is associated more with his majesty, sovereignty and awesome power. He is distinct and different from everything he has created. Therefore, he is beyond comparison. It is not possible to compare him adequately with "the gods of human imagination" or to judge him by human standards. "God alone is holy in himself."[11] In other words, he is not holy because of any comparison with his attributes, qualities or actions. He is holy because of who he is. This becomes the basis for under-standing the concept of holiness in the Old Testament, both as it relates to God and as it is applied to Israel.

Holiness Reveals Humanity's Separateness from God

Holiness reveals how far humanity is from God. All of the rituals and acts of consecration were designed to reveal the impossibility of achieving, much less maintaining, holiness.

> As purity is the proper characteristic of everything that is holy, it is the duty of every-one who takes part in the cultus to be pure (to sanctify oneself). Whoever is unclean must quickly take steps to purify himself.[12]

It is interesting that, while the "realm of the holy was conceptually distinct" from everyday common life, it could function within the realm of the sinful world as long as its boundary was maintained. It was the maintenance of this boundary that seemed to form the basis for the Israelite rituals.[13] Indeed, it was this boundary which protected people. Anyone could come into contact with the holy God through certain places, objects, occasions or events. If done inappropriately, this contact resulted in awesome and terrifying experiences (1 Sam 6:19–20).[14] It is this holy God that brings judgment to those who would stand against his purposes and salvation to those who would trust in him.[15]

This same boundary between the holy and the common is in view when God commands the Israelites to be holy (Lev 19:2). Their propensity to sin consistently prevented them from serving God and enjoying his presence. This is clearly seen in the way God dealt with Israel after they sinned with the golden bull while Moses was on Mt. Sinai. The revelation of his holiness to Israel at Mt. Sinai made him appear threatening and unapproachable (p. 18). And yet, after God introduced himself to Israel in such frightening fashion, Moses declares, "Do not fear, for God has come to test you, that the fear of him may be before you so that you do not sin" (Exod 20:20). Here his love for Israel surfaces.[16]

The golden bull event comes after the Mt. Sinai experience. It seems that Israel did not completely grasp the message at Mt. Sinai. Their recent experience with God and resulting "fear" was not sufficient to prevent them from making the golden bull. In his discussions with Moses after the sin, God commands Moses to take the people up to the Promised Land. God said that he would send an angel to accompany them, but he, himself, would not go up because he would destroy them on the way, because of their sin (Exod 33:2–3). In this way, God communicated the boundary between his holy character and their "commonness" and how their sin separated them from him.

Because God is holy and people are not, there is necessarily an impossible gap between God and people. In light of this, the rituals and commands of the Mosaic Law designed to preserve this holy realm can be seen as God's redemptive love. It was redemptive in that it revealed that it was impossible to achieve any state of holiness. It was redemptive in that it provided the route for unholy people to experience relationship with a holy God and with each other. It was also redemptive in that it proved that holiness could never be sustained for any length of time, hence the reason for the continual and unending rituals. Finally, it was redemptive in that woven throughout the various rituals and commands was the far-off hope and belief that God would someday move powerfully to unite his people permanently with him in his holiness.[17] As such, the giving of the law was "an expression of his mercy and grace and a sign of his intention to dwell among his people as 'the Holy One.'"[18]

It was this understanding that prompted David to exclaim, "I rejoice in the lifestyle prescribed by your rules as if they were riches of all kinds" (Ps 119:14), and "Look, I long for your precepts. Revive me with your deliverance!" (Ps

119:40). One has to look long and hard in the Old Testament to find where God's redeemed find fault with the law. It is just the opposite. His redeemed always look to the law with praise and thanksgiving. Perhaps they viewed the law as God's purposeful movement toward mankind to redeem them from the earth, or at least show them the way to live in right relationship with him and each other. They realized through his actions and the law that he had done the inconceivable; he had separated them from the nations to himself and prized them above all others (Lev 20:26; Deut 7:6).[19]

God is the Source of Holiness

To this end, God is considered to be the source of holiness and only in relationship with this holy God could holiness be found.[20] If he declares his people to be holy, this implies ownership. Just before entering the Promised Land, Moses explains that God had declared Israel to be his special people because they had committed to keep the entire law (Deut 26:16–18). It was the law that distinguished Israel from the rest of the world. Moses continues, "…so that he may elevate you above all the nations he has made as a cause of praise, as a name, and as an honor, and so that you may be a holy people to the LORD your God, as he has said" (Deut 26:19). God's elevation of Israel clearly has ownership in view, with the result that they would be called "holy."[21]

Holiness is more than separation from something bad. It is also dedication to something good. When asking the question about who could go up to God's holy dwelling place, David cries out, "The one whose deeds are blameless and whose motives are pure, who does not lie, or make promises with no intention of keeping them" (Ps 24:4). Here, hope surfaces in that a person could look with anticipation toward the possibility of having right attitudes and behaviors. David continues, "Such godly people are rewarded by the LORD, and vindicated by the God who delivers them. Such purity characterizes the people who seek his favor…" (Ps 24:5–6). This suggests that the concept of holiness was concerned with "one's way of life" more than rituals and practices.[22]

Holiness Involves Separation from the Unclean

Similarly, the phrase "the holy people" reveals that God's people are holy to him. As such, "their separation from the practices and cult objects of foreign religions" was paramount.[23] Moses, in giving the law at the end of the wilderness wanderings, warns strongly in this regard when he says,

> Make no covenant with [the foreign nations] nor show them compassion! You must not intermarry with them. Do not give your daughters to their sons nor take their

daughters for your sons, for they will turn your sons away from me to worship other gods (Deut 7:2–4).

This reveals a consistent exhortation regarding holiness which involved avoiding the religions of the foreign nations. Coming out of Egypt, it seems that this was a significant weakness of the Israelite cultural mentality. They struggled with following after foreign gods throughout their history. Moses continues,

> You must tear down their altars, shatter their sacred pillars, cut down their sacred Asherah poles, and burn up their images. For you are a people holy to the LORD your God. He has chosen you to be a people prized above all others on the face of the earth (Deut 7:5–6).

Here the connection between holiness and avoidance of evil is made.

Holiness Involves Ministry and Outreach

Israel's declared holiness by a holy God carried with it immense responsibilities. One of the reasons for their separation was ultimately to demonstrate to the world what it means to live directly under the rule of God. In the early part of the Mt. Sinai experience God said to Moses, "And now, if you will diligently obey me and keep my covenant, then you will be my special possession out of all the nations, for all the earth is mine. And you will be my kingdom of priests and a holy nation" (Exod 19:5–6). The three terms God used to describe Israel's vocation all carried the idea of distinctness. They were to be a "special possession," "kingdom of priests" and "holy nation." The context reveals that this distinctness was set in contrast to the whole world (which belongs to God) and the other nations. In the unfolding plan of God's redemptive program, here we begin to see one of the purposes for God choosing Israel; namely, "to be the means by which God's original promise to Abraham of bringing blessing to all the nations would be enacted" (Gen 12:1–3). As such, "they were to serve the Lord exclusively and thus be a people through whom his character and will might be displayed to the world."[24]

The fact that Israel's priestly role is set in contrast to the nations reveals a portion of their vocation that relates to holiness. The Levitical priesthood had already been established and was functioning. The priest played a significant mediatorial role in the life of another, especially as it related to the sanctifying process of consecrating or preparing the person to carry out their ritual functions before God. This was reinforced in the sanctifying process of preparing the people to meet God in the Mt. Sinai experience. It was necessary to consecrate the people as well as the priests (Gen 19:10, 14, 22). Here the cultic rituals again seem to serve the purpose of preparing the people and educating them that "mediation was necessary to prevent the Israelites from being destroyed by God's holiness" (p. 20).

In God's plan, Israel, as God's "holy people," was somehow to be involved in a priestly role before the nations. Just before entering the Promised Land, Moses alluded to this again when he said,

> And today the LORD has declared you to be his special people (as he already promised you) so that you may keep all his commandments, so that he may elevate you above all the nations he has made as a cause of praise, as a name, and as an honor, and so that you may be a holy people to the LORD your God, as he has said (Deut 26:18–19).

Inherent in this priestly role and being a chosen people was the demand for sanctification as a way of life (p. 20–22). It was not enough to be chosen and assigned functionality. Israel was to maintain that relationship throughout their sojourn on the earth. This was emphasized in every aspect of the law. The priests had elaborate instructions given for consecration (Exod 28:3, 41; 29:1, 21, 27). Similarly, as pointed out earlier, the various articles of the tabernacle were to be consecrated (Exod 30:26–30). The placement of the tabernacle was intentional to represent God's presence with his chosen people and their need for him. Finally, the law itself involved a series of rituals designed to provide for the people a way to enjoy relationship both with God and with each other.

This is especially significant since they had come out of Egypt with a pantheon of gods who were dead. As they entered the Promised Land, they were confronted with other pantheons comprised of dead gods. It is impossible to overstate the impact on Israel of God's "irruption" into human history during the Exodus in such dramatic, powerful, salvific, and therefore relational ways. Beginning with the Exodus and continuing throughout the conquest, Israel struggled with following after false gods. As such, they struggled deeply to embrace the true and living holy God who consistently initiated toward them in love. The placement of the tabernacle within the center of Israel represents God's awareness of those struggles and his desire to move them into a deeper relationship with him. It was this placement combined with such an incredible demonstration of his power that makes this accomplishment so vivid and real.

Summary

Based on the above discussion, being a "holy people" involved several facets. The people were to separate themselves from everything evil and foreign because they were a people chosen by God to be holy or distinct from the rest of the world. It is in this context that they enjoyed this sense of holiness and relationship. Inherent in this relationship was an outward focus that impacted the other nations. It was God's plan from the very beginning to reach the world. His choice of Israel involved their sanctification so they could be his instrument in reaching the other nations.

This outward reaching purpose is captured by the various Psalms. God is declared to be a "great God, a great king who is superior to all gods" (Ps 95:3). Again, in Psalm 96 the entire earth is encouraged to "sing to the Lord" (96:1) and Israel is encouraged to "Tell the nations about his splendor! Tell all the nations about his amazing deeds!" (96:3). They are to proclaim among the nations, "The Lord reigns! The world is established, it cannot be moved. He judges the nations fairly" (96:10). In Psalm 97 we are told, "The Lord reigns! Let the earth be happy!" (97:1) and "the sky declares his justice, and all the nations see his splendor" (97:6). This sampling reveals a consistent outward reaching theology in which Israel was to be involved in declaring God's glory and bringing the nations before a holy God.

These considerations set the stage for surveying the concept of holiness in the New Testament.

New Testament Concepts

When the concept of holiness is explored in the New Testament, two distinct differences from the Old Testament must be noted. First, the emphasis on the holiness of God, while present, is significantly decreased in proportion to the attention given in the Old Testament (Luke 1:49; John 17:11; 1 Pet 1:15; Rev 4:8; 6:10).[25] Whereas the New Testament spends less time expounding the holiness of God, it is by no means absent. For example, in the Old Testament, holiness and glory combine "to express the essence of the Godhead, and a holy awe permeates the whole scene."[26] This picture is replicated in Rev 4:8, "Each one of the four living creatures had six wings and was full of eyes all around and inside. They never rest day or night, saying: *Holy Holy Holy is the Lord God, the All-Powerful,* Who was and who is, and who is coming!" Perhaps the difference lies in the fact that there is no need to provide further teaching or clarification about the holiness of God over and above the Old Testament teaching.

Second, the realm of holiness is transferred from the cultic rites, places and objects to the life produced by the Spirit. "The concept of holiness in the NT is determined rather by the Holy Spirit, the gift of the new age."[27] In addition, the New Testament reinforces Old Testament teachings about the holiness of things declared so by God. His covenant is viewed as holy (Luke 1:72). His angels are called holy (Mark 8:38; Luke 9:26). The prophets are viewed as holy (Luke 1:70). The scriptures are called holy (Rom 1:2), including the law (Rom 7:12).

Holiness Indicates Uniqueness

In spite of these differences, the ἀγ* word group in the New Testament presents development in the concept of holiness.[28] In the Old Testament, holiness revealed a unique status when compared to the common and unclean and revealed how far humanity was from God. This boundary between the holy and the common remains in view in the New Testament. It is in view when Peter, quoting Lev 19:2, states, "Like obedient children, do not comply with the evil urges you used to follow in your ignorance, but, like the Holy One who called you, become holy yourselves in all of your conduct, for it is written, '*You shall be holy, because I am holy*'" (1 Pet 1:14–16).[29]

However, there is a substantive difference in that in the New Testament the holiness of humanity is accomplished by the finished and complete work of Christ. While alluded to in the Old Testament, it becomes strikingly clear in the New Testament. As in the Old Testament, because God is holy and people are not, there is necessarily an impossible gap between God and people. And since God is the source of holiness, it is necessary for him to grant holiness to humanity.

Holiness Involves Consecration

In an interesting discussion between Jesus and the Jewish authorities, Jesus pointed out that even he was sanctified by God (John 10:36).[30] Later, in his prayer to the Father, he references the fact that he will sanctify himself on behalf of the disciples (John 17:19). The use of ἁγιάζω in both of these occurrences highlights the need for Christ to be sanctified in some manner. The question is in what way did Christ need to be sanctified? In the earlier passage, it seems that his sanctification had already occurred at the pleasure of the Father.[31] In the later passage, it seems that his sanctification was related to his own action and had not yet occurred. In addition, it was somehow related to the need of the disciples.

Taking the root idea of "distinctness" with slightly different nuances, the ideas become clear. In the first passage, Jesus is being sanctified in the same sense that a prophet of the Old Testament is consecrated for his work. In this regard, the prophet is "distinct" from the common, or "set apart" by God for a special task.[32] Raymond Brown links this use to the "sequence of feasts" by which the Gospel is organized. He states, "Now at the feast of Dedication, recalling… the dedication or consecration of the whole series of temples that had stood in Jerusalem, Jesus proclaims that he is the one who has truly been consecrated by God."[33] Similarly, George Beasley-Murray explains that Jesus is described as 'he whom the Father *consecrated and sent…*' in the context of the festival commemorating the dedication or consecration of the temple is highly significant. It suggests that the meaning of the Festival of the Dedication, like that of the Tabernacles and Passover, finds its ultimate fulfillment in the mission of Jesus.[34]

Conversely, in John 17:19 the forward-looking aspect seems to be pointing to Christ's sacrifice on the cross. Here the nuance is more in line with the consecration of a sacrificial animal. In other words, Jesus is consecrating his own death as a sacrifice on behalf of the disciples (and, by extension, the rest of the world).[35] The disciples "cannot be sanctified and sent into the world until the Son of God consecrates himself to die on their behalf."[36] This is consistent with other atonement passages in the New Testament (Mark 14:24; Luke 22:19; John 6:51; 1 Cor 11:24) and becomes part of the theological basis for understanding the rest of John 17 as it relates to sanctification.

Holiness Involves Separation from the Unclean

In the Old Testament Israel was commanded to separate themselves from the practices and beliefs of the foreign nations and have nothing to do with them. In John 17, Jesus prays similarly for the disciples (and other believers) that they may be separate from the world. In this passage, the sanctifying of believers in the truth occurs in the context of not being part of the world (John 17:16) and yet they are sent into the world (John 17:18). Perhaps Jesus is asking God to sanctify them in *this* truth (John 17:17).[37] John 17 reveals that believers are consecrated, or set apart as distinct from the world, which is at the root of the meaning of holiness. This is accomplished by his name (John 17:11), his word (John 17:14) and his truth (John 17:17).

Holiness Involves Ministry and Outreach

Just as in the Old Testament the concept of Israel being a "holy people" involved an outward focus that had an impact on the nations around them, so in the New Testament, Jesus prays in John 17 that the disciples might be sent into the world (17:18). And Jesus himself becomes the primary example as well as the cause of this sanctification (John 17:19). His sacrifice is an act of service on behalf of the disciples that ultimately effected their sanctification. Similarly, he prays that the disciples might be truly sanctified as well. In the context, he is clearly referring to their impact in the world on his behalf. As noted by Brown, "The prayer on behalf of his disciples (9) is an extension of the prayer for his own glorification (1); for it is in the perseverance and mission of these disciples that the name of God, given to Jesus, will be glorified on earth."[38]

In the following context his prayer is applied to all believers (John 17:20–

24). And yet, the outreach focus is preceded by his request for unity in the church when he prays "that they may all be one, just as you, Father, are in me and I am in you" (John 17:21). He clarifies that this unity and the resulting glory come directly from God, "The glory you gave to me I have given to them, that they may be one just as we are one" (John 17:22). After this request Jesus states that part of the purpose of the unity of the church is outreach related; "...so that the world may know that you sent me, and you have loved them just as you have loved me" (John 17:23). Unity, while a gift from the Lord, has a visible aspect to it. What was clear in the Old Testament is true in the New Testament as well; sanctification has an outward focus to it that is designed to impact both members of the community and the world. In this passage, Jesus reveals that unity is observable by the world and it is designed to reach the world in order to demonstrate the love that he has for all people. It is correct to conclude with Peterson, "Mission is clearly the goal of sanctification in John 17."[39]

God is the Source of Holiness

In the Old Testament the phrase "the holy people" also reveals that God's people are holy to him. The New Testament reveals this same truth. Clearly the Old Testament taught that God was the one who sanctified (Lev 20:8; 21:15). Hebrews makes it clear that this is accomplished through the work of Christ (Heb 10:10, 14).[40] The following verses reveal that the New Covenant is inaugurated based on the perfection of Jesus' offering (Heb 10:11–18). Whereas the Old Testament sacrifices were inadequate, the offering of Christ was perfect and eternal. This makes possible knowing God and serving him in new ways.

This idea of the people of God being holy to him is also found in 1 Pet 1:2, where Peter addresses the recipients as "those... who are chosen according to the foreknowledge of God the Father by being set apart by the Spirit for obedience and for sprinkling with Jesus Christ's blood." Here the idea of enablement to be the holy people of God is seen in the concept of sanctification as believers are "set apart" (ἐν ἁγιασμῷ) for obedience and for sprinkling with Christ's blood in view of the fact that they are chosen (1 Pet 2:9).[41] The source given for the choosing and the sanctification is the Father and the Spirit, respectively, emphasizing the divine nature of the act.

In 1 Pet 2:4–10 Peter combines Old Testament ideas and terminology to develop further the concept that believers are the people of God. He uses language and terminology from the tabernacle, the priesthood, the sacrificial system and the Exodus. The first metaphor he uses is the metaphor of the spiritual house. Believers are being built together into this house. While he does not use the technical term for temple, the context makes it is clear that he is using temple imagery. The church has replaced the temple system as the dwelling place of

God. This reflects fulfillment of the New Covenant where God promised to put his law within his people and write it on their hearts and minds. As a result he would be their God and they would be his people (Jer 31:33). The parallel passage in Ezekiel reveals that God would sanctify his great name when he sanctifies his people among the nations (Ezek 36:23). Using the imagery of cleansing water he promised to purify them of their uncleanness and idolatrous worship with the result that they would become a new people. He would give them a new heart and put a new spirit, his Spirit, within them. Their old heart of stone would be replaced with a new living heart of flesh (Ezek 36:25–27). This is captured by the imagery of believers as "living stones."[42]

The second and third metaphors relate to the purpose behind God's sanctifying work. Believers are to be a holy priesthood who offer up spiritual sacrifices acceptable to God through Jesus Christ (1 Pet 2:5). The priesthood imagery emphasizes the direct access available to believers while the sacrificial imagery emphasizes the pleasing nature of believers before God as they perform acts of service and ministry. In other words, believers stand in God's presence concurrently ministering and pleasing God. Once again, the outreach focus discussed earlier surfaces. As with the earlier discussion on Exod 19:5–6, the imagery necessarily includes others. The church is now a "holy priesthood" to carry out God's original plan to reach the world. This development in New Testament theology emphasizes one of the primary goals of sanctification—impacting the world for God's glory.

Holiness Involves Community

The combined imagery of the spiritual house and the spiritual priesthood emphasize the community aspect of sanctification. The individual is highlighted in "whoever believes" (1 Pet 2:6).[43] But the orientation of the entire passage is the church as the people of God (p. 99–100).[44] This is captured with both the imagery of the "spiritual house" in which all believers participate as well as with the Old Testament allusions and citations in verse 9 and the quotations from Hos 1 and 2 in verse 10. God's design is that the culmination of the believer's growth must be found in community so that they together may "proclaim the virtues" of God (1 Pet 2:9).[45]

This is further supported by the final metaphor Peter uses in this passage. God has called the church out of darkness into light (1 Pet 2:9). Each of the phrases used in this verse relate to the Exodus event. In Exod 19, at the Mt. Sinai experience, God spoke to Israel and said,

'And now, if you will diligently obey me and keep my covenant, then you will be my special possession out of all the nations, for all the earth is mine. And you will be my kingdom of priests and a holy nation.' These are the words that you will speak to the Israelites (Exod 19:5–6).

It is clear from the context that the Exodus event was fresh on their minds (Exod 19:1).

During this interchange between God and his people and as part of his "introduction" of himself to his people, he is careful to lay out his expectation of them. As discussed earlier, at the theological center of this passage is his expectation that that they become a holy people devoted to him alone. The foundation for this agreement between their faithfulness to him and his response to them was the Exodus and the power he demonstrated to extricate them from Egypt and redeem them (Exod 19:4).[46] All of the ideas captured by Peter are found in this *par excellence* experience at Mt. Sinai. In a similar way to Moses, Peter ties these characteristics to the delivering and saving acts of God who calls the believer "out of darkness into his marvelous light" (1 Pet 2:9).[47]

In New Testament theology, the Exodus event prefigures the redemption of the believer and reveals the basis for the relationship between God and his people. He is trustworthy as demonstrated by his power working on behalf of those whom he has chosen. He is relational in that he draws his people to faith in him and makes them a "special possession," namely, his people.

Summary

In the Old Testament, the concept of sanctification revolves around the idea of distinctness, especially at it relates to God. God is distinct and holy from all of his creation. Only God is intrinsically holy. Holiness is not inherent to creation. As such, holiness reveals a unique status when compared to the common or unclean. It is a statement about God's character and power since he is the only one who is holy and the only one who can declare another to be holy. For God to declare something to be holy is to stake a claim of ownership, because holiness is granted only by God. The declaration of holiness implies both a responsibility to remain distinct from the unclean and a responsibility to impact the world positively for God's glory.

The New Testament continues the theme of sanctification and develops the concepts around Christ and life in the Spirit. Holiness is accomplished by the finished work of Christ. As such, the church is consecrated to God as his special possession for the purpose of impacting the world for him. Whereas the Exodus event set Israel apart in the Old Testament, the Christ-event sets the church apart today. Since the Exodus event is applied to Christ in the New Testament, Christ is the ultimate fulfillment of all that the Exodus implies. And the combined imagery of the spiritual house and spiritual priesthood reveal a community orientation. In other words, what is begun in the individual is necessarily consummated in community.

In summary, several points can be made from the study in this chapter related to the role of the community in progressive sanctification. First, sanctification, as defined above, is a major unifying theme in both the Old and New Testaments. In some respects it lies at the heart of what God is doing in his people. Second, the language of holiness reveals that part of the purpose of sanctification involves impacting others for God's glory—an outward focus. God's interaction with Israel was designed to communicate these concepts and develop them into a holy people who were his personal possession and who would carry the message of his love to the rest of the world. The New Testament continues and develops this theme. Since the law was inadequate to sanctify God's people, God sent his Son and sanctification was accomplished by his finished work—a definitive act. This means the church is consecrated to God as his special possession for the purpose of enjoying him in relationship and impacting the world for his glory.

With this as a foundation, one dimension of the concept of holiness may be described as a unique status given by God to redeemed people for the purpose of glorifying himself through them to the rest of creation. This raises a necessary question regarding the progressive aspect of sanctification. If the holiness of believers is accomplished by the finished work of Christ on the cross and is a status given by God, what is being accomplished in the ongoing life of the believer? As part of the answer to this question, it is necessary to explore two foundational theological considerations traditionally omitted from sanctification studies. In the next two chapters, the initiatory nature of God and the solidarity of the redeemed community are studied as they relate to sanctification.

NOTES

1   Jacobus A. Naudé, "קָדַשׁ," in *NIDOTTE* 3:885. He contests the idea of separateness as the root idea, claiming that "it is more its necessary consequence. Consecration is a separation to God rather than a separation from the world." Thomas E. McComiskey, "קָדַשׁ," in *TWOT*, 2:787. McComiskey explains that the concept of holiness refers primarily to "the essential nature of that which belongs to the sphere of the sacred and which is thus distinct from the common or profane." Horst Seebass, "Holy, Consecrate, Sanctify, Saints, Devout," in *NIDNTT*, 2:224. Seebass agrees with Naudé that the idea is not primarily related to separateness. Rather, in the LXX, he sees the primary idea as a "positive thought of encounter which inevitably demands certain modes of response."

2   Naudé, "קָדַשׁ," in *NIDOTTE*, 3:879.

3   See also Ps 99.

4   For example, in the Qal, קָדַשׁ "connotes the state of that which belongs to the sphere of

the sacred." Similarly, in the Piel and Hiphil it has more the idea of "the act by which the distinction is effected." In the Niphal, it may connote the concept "to prove one's holiness." McComiskey, "קדשׁ," in *TWOT*, 2:786–87.

5   It is interesting that Lev 20:26 and Deut 7:6 both reveal that the reason the people were told to be holy is because God is holy and he is the one who separated them from the other peoples to be his. Here, the "sphere" spoken of by McComiskey identified earlier comes into view. Later, in Lev 22:14–16 an intriguing situation is presented in which it was possible for the people to incur guilt because they ate "holy" offerings which the priests had mishandled. The reason given is that it is the Lord who sanctifies. It seems that cognizance was not the issue nor an excuse, but rather the mishandling of what God had previously sanctified!

6   It is interesting that the sexual unfaithfulness of the Israelite men, in giving away their "holy" semen by cohabitating with the foreign women, prompted one of the most heartfelt prayers of confession and repentance recorded in the Old Testament (Ezra 9).

7   Naudé, "קדשׁ," in *NIDOTTE*, 3:880.

8   McComiskey, "קדשׁ," in *TWOT*, 2:787. See also Naudé, "קדשׁ," in *NIDOTTE*, 3:879.

9   Otto Procksch, "ἅγιος," in *TDNT*, 1:91. He points out that God's "holy name contrasts with everything creaturely."

10   McComiskey, "קדשׁ," in *TWOT*, 2:787.

11   David Peterson, *Possessed by God: A New Testament Theology of Sanctification and Holiness*, NSBT, ed. D. A. Carson (Downers Grove, IL: InterVarsity, 1995), 17.

12   Seebass, "Holy, Consecrate, Sanctify, Saints, Devout," in *NIDNTT*, 2:226–27; Ralph A. Letch, "Sanctification in the Old Testament," *London Quarterly and Holborn Review* 180 (April 1955): 129. Letch has argued that the rituals and ceremonies were "public announcements" of a holiness already attained. "An examination of all the passages in which the verb occurs shows that in most instances God is the source of sanctification, and when men are sanctified it is almost always at His command." It must be questioned, however, whether the priest or common Israelite understood this theological concept when they went about the daily rituals outlined in the law. The treatment of the law by the Pharisees, as recorded in the Gospels, suggested that they had missed this core truth. Looking backward through the lens of New Testament theology, however, reveals that Letch has argued a reasonable and sound concept which reflects that redemptive thread woven throughout the history of Israel culminating in the far-off hope of ultimate achievement of holiness and union with God.

13   McComiskey, "קדשׁ," in *TWOT*, 2:787–89.

14   Seebass, "Holy, Consecrate, Sanctify, Saints, Devout," in *NIDNTT*, 2:224–25. And yet, even then, God is "not a destroyer or demon, even when the people had been guilty of great profanity. The Holy One intends purification through a devastating catastrophe. His purpose is not destruction, but a new future for Israel." See Procksch, "ἅγιος," in *TDNT*, 1:93, who similarly points out, "The opposition of God's holiness to Israel thus works itself out in His love which is quite incomprehensible to human nature." In other words, God's love for his people moves him to want them to share in his holiness. It seems that here the integration of his divine holiness with his incomprehensible love provides a foreshadowing of what will be accomplished in the sending of his Son.

15   Peterson, *Possessed by God*, 18.

16 This is perhaps the controlling verse that explains the concept of fearing the Lord. Moses told Israel not to be afraid of God, but to be deeply aware of his awesome power so that they would not sin. Here the idea of "reverential awe" can be clearly seen. This paradox of not being frightened by God, yet fearing who he is permeates the community texts throughout both the Old and New Testaments.

17 Naudé, "קדש‎," in *NIDOTTE*, 3:884. As Naudé points out, "it requires a special act to bring a thing or person into a state of holiness." God made Israel holy (Exod 31:13; Lev 20:8; 21:8; 22:32). In addition, he restored the holiness of Israel (Exod 37:28). He declared the Sabbath, among other things, to be holy (Gen 2:3).

18 Peterson, *Possessed by God*, 18.

19 Naudé, "קדש‎," in *NIDOTTE*, 3:884.

20 Ibid., 3:879; Peterson, *Possessed by God*, 19.

21 Seebass, "Holy, Consecrate, Sanctify, Saints, Devout," in *NIDNTT*, 2:226.

22 Ibid., 2:225.

23 Ibid., 2:226.

24 Peterson, *Possessed by God*, 20.

25 In addition, Christ is only once called holy in the same sense as God (Rev 3:7; cf. 1 John 2:20, although there is some question as to whether God or Christ is in view in the 1 John passage. See B. F. Westcott, *The Epistles of St. John* (London: Macmillan, 1883; reprint, Grand Rapids: Eerdmans, 1952), 73; John R. W. Stott, *The Epistles of John*, TNTC, ed. R. V. G. Tasker, vol. 19 (Grand Rapids: Eerdmans, 1960), 106; Glenn W. Barker, "1 John," in *Expositor's Bible Commentary*, ed. Frank E. Gaebelein, vol. 12 (Grand   Rapids: Zondervan, 1981), 325).

26 Procksch, "ἅγιος," in *TDNT*, 1:101.

27 Seebass, "Holy, Consecrate, Sanctify, Saints, Devout," in *NIDNTT*, 2:228.

28 Ibid. Indeed, it is not to say that cultic rites, places and objects are not discussed in the New Testament. There are several references to holiness in which the Israelite cultic rites, places and objects remain in view. Matthew 23:19 refers to the gold and the gifts in the temple. Matthew 24:15 refers to the holy place spoken of by Daniel. Matthew 27:53 refers to the holy city. Finally, Luke 2:23, in an allusion to Exod 13, records the presentation of Jesus to the Lord and refers to the first-born as holy. The point is that, while the New Testament authors lived in the world created by Old Testament law, they communicated that there is transference in what is considered to be truly holy from the earthly to the spiritual. In keeping with the theology of Hebrews, the temporal and tangible aspect of holiness outlined in the Old Testament becomes a foundational picture (or pattern) for understanding holiness in the true spiritual sense as presented in the New Testament. This reflects a strong eschatological development in God's plan.

29 John H. Elliott, *1 Peter: A New Translation with Introduction and Commentary*, AB, ed. William Foxwell Albright and David Noel Freedman, vol. 37B (New York: Doubleday, 2000), 360. "The notion of the believers' having been 'called' (*kaleō*) by God recurs throughout 1 Peter both as an affirmation of their special elect status before God (2:9; 5:10) and as a reason for their behavior (1:15; 2:21; 3:9)." Here, Elliott points out the linkage between holiness and behavior. Holiness is never a static idea regarding God's elect. It always has both an ontological and a teleological orientation. Cf. J. Ramsey Michaels, *1 Peter*, WBC, ed. Glenn W. Barker, David A. Hubbard, and Ralph P. Martin, vol. 49 (Waco, TX: Word, 1988), 59. He

notes, "The function of the modifier καλέσαντα is to indicate why the holiness of the God of Israel must be a model for the behavior of these Gentile Christians. Their identity rests in the fact that they have been 'called' (2:21; 3:9) by a holy God."

30 BDAG, "ἁγιάζω," 10. "God consecrates his own, incl. Christ."

31 In 10:36 the past tense idea is driven by contextual indicators, rather than the use of the aorist tense. The force of Jesus' argument is predicated on the fact that his sanctification had already occurred at the hands of God.

32 To further understand the force of Jesus' argument, note the argument in the NET Bible, SN for John 10:36. "This is evidently a case of arguing from the lesser to the greater, a common form of rabbinic argument. The reason the OT judges could be called gods is because they were vehicles of the word of God (cf. 10:35). But granting that premise, Jesus deserves much more than they to be called God. He is the Word incarnate, whom the Father sanctified and sent into the world to save the world (10:36)." See also Peterson, *Possessed by God*, 28–29 and the NET Bible, SN for John 17:19 where the use of ἁγιάζω in both 10:36 and 17:19 involves a Johannine wordplay in which slightly different meanings of the word are used to capture these two significant truths.

33 Raymond E. Brown, *The Gospel According to John (I–XII): Introduction, Translation, and Notes*, AB, ed. William Foxwell Albright and David Noel Freedman, vol. 29 (New York: Doubleday, 1970), 411.

34 George R. Beasley-Murray, *John*, WBC, ed. Glenn W. Barker, David A. Hubbard, and Ralph P. Martin, vol. 36 (Waco, TX: Word, 1987), 177.

35 Ibid., 301. Beasley-Murray adds, "That Jesus should consecrate *himself* for such a purpose is a highly unusual mode of speech, but it reflects his consciousness… of performing his service for the saving sovereignty of God by virtue of the authority given him by God." Later, he concludes that "accordingly, it represents a sacrifice of eschatological proportions."

36 Peterson, *Possessed by God*, 30.

37 Again, the use of ἁγιάζω throughout this passage clearly relates sanctification to the work of Christ and ministry. See the NET Bible, SN for John 17:17 where the "setting apart" of the disciples is in the "sphere" of truth. Just as he is set apart, or consecrated, he is asking for the disciples to be set apart as well, in the same truth as he himself was set apart. See Beasley-Murray, *John*, 300, who concurs that the disciples share in this "consecration by which the salvation of God might be conveyed to the world." He agrees that the concept of the disciples being sanctified in truth has more "in view a separation from the world's ways to God," rather than the Word of God being a means of sanctification. If so, then the primary meaning has more to do with the truth that they are not part of the world, even though they are being sent into the world. In this they share in the consecration of Christ.

38 Raymond E. Brown, *The Gospel According to John (XIII–XXI): Introduction, Translation, and Notes*, AB, ed. William Foxwell Albright and David Noel Freedman, vol. 29A (New York: Doubleday, 1970), 763. He adds, "As we have emphasized… the consecration of the disciples is directed toward their mission. This is in harmony with the OT understanding of consecration; for example, Moses, who himself has been consecrated by God, is told in Exod xxviii 41 to consecrate others so that they *may serve* God as priests. The disciples are to be consecrated so that they may serve as apostles, that is, as ones sent" (p. 765).

39 Peterson, *Possessed by God*, 30. Note also, Beasley-Murray, *John*, 294–95.

40 "The Greek periphrastic perfect points to a state or condition made possible by the self-offering of Christ in death. No further sacrifices or rituals are required to keep us in that

sanctified condition." Peterson, *Possessed by God*, 34.

41 The use of the subjective genitive (πνεύματος) by the NET Bible reinforces the role of God in securing the sanctification of the believer. Michaels, *1 Peter*, 11, concurs and notes the use of the identical phrase in 2 Thess 2:13 where the Spirit is responsible for the sanctification of the believer which results in salvation. Regarding 1 Pet 1:2, Michaels further notes, that obedience "refers to conversion from paganism to Christianity" (p. 12). He conceptually links ὑπακοὴν with ῥαντισμὸν since they are objects of the same preposition. Therefore, the concept of obedience precedes and is closely related to sprinkling. Andrew Chester and Ralph P. Martin, *The Theology of the Letters of James, Peter, and Jude*, New Testament Theology, ed. James D. G. Dunn (Cambridge: Cambridge University Press, 1994), 119, state, "His (the Holy Spirit's) task is that of making the chosen people a choice people by promoting holy living." They go on to add that this is the foundational verse that explains and precedes the later teachings on holiness in the epistle. The basis for Peter's teaching are the "cultic and ceremonial ideas" but now in spiritualized form.

42 Michaels, *1 Peter*, 98–99. Michaels notes that the phrase ὡς λίθοι ζῶντες emphasizes the relationship with Christ and "reinforces the imagery of life and growth" from the preceding context. This concept is reinforced by the change in status recorded in verse 10 where they are now called God's people and have been shown mercy.

43 This introduces a concept that is significant in sanctification studies, namely, there is a consistent movement from the individual to the community. As discussed earlier, the older sanctification studies viewed progressive sanctification predominantly individualistically. Recent trends have consistently moved the discussion toward a community orientation. While this passage may originate with the individual, it is necessary contextually to place this orientation within the broader community of believers to understand the full import of the passage. Peter is not discussing the impact on the individual as much as he is the impact that the church is to have, *as a community*, on the world for God's glory. Viewing Peter's theology at the individual level apart from the community overlooks his predominant point. This principle will be evaluated more extensively in the Pauline corpus in chapter 3.

44 "The corporate identify of the epistle's readers is summed up in the phrase, 'a spiritual house'." Michaels notes that this term cannot be isolated from the verb οἰκοδομεῖσθε identifying the process and the phrase εἰς ἱεράτευμα ἅγιον identifying their function. The linkage of the corporate picture of the "house" with the concept of being built together and the related function of a holy priesthood deemphasizes the individual aspect and emphasizes the corporate nature of our position in Christ. In other words, the nature and function of our priesthood are located in community. This is consistent with Israel's priestly role (before the nations) discussed earlier.

45 Peter H. Davids, *The First Epistle of Peter*, NICNT, ed. Gordon D. Fee (Grand Rapids: Eerdmans, 1990), 18–19, argues that communal holiness is one of the major unifying themes of the epistle. Notwithstanding the individual aspect, Peter's emphasis on the tongue must be understood in the context of community and the effects on the community of the individual's proper or improper speech. This is also supported by his emphasis on "love, hospitality, service according to gifts, servant leadership, and humility." Davids concludes that "the reason for his stress on these virtues is obvious. They are all community-preserving virtues. This form of holiness will maintain communal solidarity." The concept of solidarity as it relates to the redeemed is discussed later in this chapter.

46 This is a consistent biblical pattern in which God asks his people to demonstrate faith, but always based on the reality of God's direct involvement with them. The concept of "blind faith" with no demonstration of power or relational foundation is not consistent with the biblical story and message.

47 Michaels, *1 Peter*, 111. "Conversion from paganism to Christianity was commonly viewed by the early Christians as a passage from darkness to light, so that believers in Christ viewed themselves in some instances as 'light' or at least as already living in the light."

CHAPTER 4

The God Who Initiates

One of the significant theological truths of the Bible relates to God's initiatives toward his creation. This study has already revealed one aspect related to God's initiatory nature. Every view analyzed in chapter 2 started with the assumption that it was God who moved toward people in order to redeem and sanctify them. This is seen in both the creative as well as the redemptive acts of God. But is this where God's initiative ceases? This section considers the relational acts of God to determine if there is a pattern that will later be used by Paul in his teachings concerning the role of the community in the process of growing in maturity.

Foundational to this evaluation is a basic understanding of the issues surrounding the image of God in people. The reason is, if people are made in the image of God, and that image can be defined, then people necessarily should replicate what they see in God. Part of image-bearing includes a divine design that is dynamic and relational in nature and forms the basis for Paul's later ethical teachings. In this regard, the view taken here is that image-bearing is teleologically oriented.[1]

The Image of God

As noted by Stanley Grenz, "With the possible exception of human sin, perhaps the single most debated topic of Christian anthropology is the meaning of the designation 'image of God.'"[2] He identifies the three basic positions that have emerged. First, the "structural view" understands the image of God "primarily as an anthropological concept."[3] It is something that is possessed by people and is qualitative in nature. It includes the various "properties" that characterize human personality. It is a natural gift which belongs to us by virtue of creation and is part of our essential nature.

Second, the "relational view" understands the image of God in terms of a "standing before God." This view emerged during the Reformation. The divine image is something that was lost at the fall, but is restored by Christ over time. It is rooted in the concept of "original righteousness" which was either lost or severely distorted at the fall. In this regard, it shifts the focus from the present to the past to understand the image concept. Since Christ is the restorer of the divine image, it is christological in nature. The divine image is restored only as "the Spirit works Christ-likeness in us."

Third, the "dynamic view" understands the image of God in eschatological terms. This view also has its roots in the Reformation. Rather than seeing the divine image as the restoration of something that was lost, it is seen as something toward which all believers are progressing which is higher than what was lost. It includes eternal life and conformity to Christ, neither of which was guaranteed as part of the garden experience. In this regard, to understand image-bearing it shifts the focus from the past and the present to the future and toward what the redeemed are becoming, rather than what they lost at the fall.

Divine image studies reflect a growing discussion and understanding of how believers reflect God's image. As defined by Grenz,

> At the heart of the divine image… is a reference to our human destiny as designed by God. We are the image of God insofar as we have received, are now fulfilling, and one day will fully actualize a divine design. And this design—God's intent for us—is that we mirror for the sake of creation the nature of the Creator.[4]

Without attempting to evaluate the strengths or weaknesses of various views, what is significant is the emergence of the dynamic aspect. Image-bearing is more than what was lost at the fall—it includes what believers are becoming.[5]

Earlier it was argued that one of the distinctive contributions of the New Testament regarding the holiness of the redeemed involves the finished work of Christ. Holiness is exclusively the work of God. It is only God who can declare one holy, and he has done so because of what his son accomplished on the cross. It is this definitive nature of holiness that has led Peterson to argue that the concept of "progressive sanctification" is misleading. While he agrees that there is a progressive aspect resulting from sanctification, he argues that believers do not grow in holiness. Their holiness is accomplished by the work of Christ.[6]

This raises the question regarding what is being accomplished in the progressive sanctification of the believer. The survey presented in chapter 2 suggests that the answer to this question varies with theological position. For example, the Wesleyan views orient the change around the restoration of the moral image with an emphasis on the restored ability to obey the love commands. In contrast, the Reformed views orient the change toward transition from all that is sinful to a total dedication to God and growing in Christ-likeness. The Pentecostal views, while rooted in Wesleyanism, tend to orient the change toward the capacity of living a dynamic and spirit-filled holy life. Lutheran theology emphasizes the definitive act of justification, with the progressive nature of sanctification being more related to becoming aware of ("used to") God's grace, rather than an actual change in holiness. Keswick theology orients the change around growing in the capacity to live and experience a fulfilled and abundant life. It was suggested in chapter 2 that one of the common patterns found in these views is the focus on the individual. In other words, the terminology used and the theological concepts explored reflect more of an individual emphasis in the process and the resulting changes in the individual.

It is at this point that Grenz's argument regarding the dynamic view of the image of God is pertinent. For Grenz, the proper and biblical focus in image-bearing studies relates to the ultimate goal of redeemed humanity as a community—an eschatological orientation. The image of God is redeemed humanity's "divinely given goal or destiny, which lies in the eschatological future and toward which humans are directed."[7] And for Grenz, both the process and the goal are community-oriented. However, the question raised earlier concerning the nature of progressive sanctification and how this relates to image-bearing remains.

Christ is the Image of God

Understanding the image of God begins with the concept of Christ as *the* image of God and the true human.[8] In the New Testament the image of God is explicitly linked to Christ (Col 1:15),[9] and Christ as the image of God is most clearly communicated and understood in the idea of Christ reflecting the glory of God. The concept of δόξα in the New Testament has the core idea of reflection in the sense of "divine and heavenly radiance."[10] It approaches more the idea of "image," "though with varying emphasis on the element of visibility."[11] This is seen in the Christmas story (Luke 2:9), the account of the transfiguration (Luke 9:31; 2 Pet 1:17), and Paul's Damascus road experience (Acts 22:11).

It is in applying this concept to Christ that the New Testament demonstrates progression. As noted by Gerhard Kittel, "The whole dynamism of the relationship of God and Christ is reflected in the use of the term [δόξα]."[12] And this glory will ultimately be fully revealed in the coming of the Son of Man (Matt 19:28; 24:30; 25:31; Mark 13:26; Luke 21:27). In contrast, John presents a "glory-christology" that is focused in the earthly ministry of Christ.[13] Jesus Christ is the glory of God incarnate (John 1:14), so that seeing the Son is the same as seeing the Father (John 14:9). Jesus' mission is fundamentally that of glorifying God the Father (John 7:18; 11:40; 12:28; 13:31–32; 14:13; 17:4–5).[14]

This "glory-christology" naturally leads to the idea that Christ is the image of God.[15] This direct connection is made in 2 Cor 4:4–6. In this passage, Paul is making the point that unbelievers are blinded to the gospel (2 Cor 4:3–4). In the context, the "god of this age" has blinded their minds so that they would not see "the light of the gospel that displays the glory of Christ (τοῦ εὐαγγελίου τῆς δόξης τοῦ Χριστοῦ), who is the image of God" (2 Cor 4:4 TNIV[16]). Here the glory of Christ is linked to the light of the gospel. Ralph Martin argues that τὸν φωτισμὸν here is functioning as an adjective describing τῆς δόξης. "It describes the δόξα, 'glory,' as 'revealed.'" He then relates δόξα to Christ,

> Paul goes on to describe the content of his kerygma in the following way: its 'glory' (a looking back to chap. 3 where Moses' δόξα and the Christian counterpart are set in opposition) is none other than Christ himself, 'who is the image of God.'[17]

Philip Hughes similarly argues, "For the gospel light is the glory of the Messiah, who Himself is God's image."[18]

Paul then goes on to declare that the glory of God is visible in the face of Christ when God gives believers "the light of the knowledge of God's glory (τῆς γνώσεως τῆς δόξης τοῦ θεοῦ) displayed in the face of Christ" (2 Cor 4:6 TNIV). Here, again, glory is emphasized when the phrases "the light of the gospel that displays the glory of Christ" (2 Cor 4:4) and "the light of the knowledge of God's glory" (2 Cor 4:6) are set in parallel. As Martin points out, "The knowledge of God's glory is what the Pauline Gospel is all about."[19] The light of the gospel of the glory of Christ (2 Cor 4:4) and the knowledge of the glory of God (2 Cor 4:6) are both anchored in the ministry of Christ. Not only is he the image of God (2 Cor 4:4), but it is in his face that the knowledge of God's glory is revealed. Martin argues that this is a reference to Moses' face and the fading glory (2 Cor 3:7) and the unveiled face of believers who behold the glory of the Lord (2 Cor 3:18). As such, "In the new age of eschatological fulfillment God's glory is found, not in the Old Testament or the Mosaic covenant, but in Christ who is the εἰκιών, 'image,' of God."[20]

Here, the reflection idea discussed above surfaces. Paul's argument that Christ reflects God's glory is at the center of understanding Christ as the image of God. Accordingly, Grenz concludes, "Paul's linking of God's glory and the divine image to Christ produces the strongest christological statement possible."[21]

The Redeemed are being Transformed into the Image of Christ

This theological concept of Jesus as the true image of God sets the stage for understanding the redeemed humanity as being transformed into the image of

Christ. "Not only is Jesus the divine image, but also he is the head of the new humanity destined to be formed according to that image in fulfillment of God's intent for humankind from the beginning" (p. 224).[22] This perspective surfaces in several Pauline texts.

Romans 8:28–29. In Rom 8:28–29, Paul reveals that those whom God foreknew "he also predestined to be conformed to the image of his Son, that his Son would be the firstborn among many brothers and sisters." In language reminiscent of Gen 1:26–27, Paul argues that it is God's intention that those in Christ participate in his destiny and conform to his image.[23] Here, Paul is providing a clear picture of the certainty of the future of the redeemed who are in Christ—the eschatological goal of the new humanity.[24]

And yet, while his emphasis is primarily eschatological in this passage, in the typical "already-not yet" Pauline scheme, the "already" remains in view as well.[25] The context of Rom 8 reveals an emphasis on the present life. Paul is discussing the present sufferings of the believer (Rom 8:18), the present struggles of the creation (Rom 8:22) and the believer (Rom 8:23), and the present weakness of the believer (Rom 8:26). It is in this context that Paul presents the believer with genuine hope when he links conformity with the image of Christ to God's ultimate purpose (Rom 8:28–29).[26]

Furthermore, the use of $\epsilon\grave{\iota}\varsigma$ $\tau\grave{o}$ $\epsilon\hat{\iota}\nu\alpha\iota$ to describe Christ's relationship to the redeemed humanity (Rom 8:29) reveals a more pervasive aspect of God's purpose than simply conformity to the image of Christ. This clause expresses the primary intent of God's foreordination. "Beyond its anthropological goal, therefore, foreordination serves a christological intent."[27]

And the use of $\dot{\alpha}\delta\epsilon\lambda\phi o\hat{\iota}\varsigma$ reveals a community orientation.[28] John Murray, who argues that this "fraternal relationship" is included in the ultimate end of God's purpose, states, "This means that the preeminence of Christ carries with it the eminence that belongs to the children of God."[29] And, the use of $\dot{\alpha}\delta\epsilon\lambda\phi o\hat{\iota}\varsigma$ reveals the context in which Jesus will be shown to be preeminent. In some respects, the preeminence of Jesus, as pictured by Paul, requires the community. The fact that it was foreordained by God informs Gen 1:26–27 such that the image-bearing aspect of humanity was eschatological in that it was God's intent from the beginning. As Grenz states, "God's purpose has never been that Christ will merely radiate this human fullness, but that as the Son he will be preeminent among a new humanity who together are stamped with the divine image."[30] This then reveals the ultimate goal of what God is working out in the redeemed community.

1 Corinthians 15:49. In a related passage, Paul exhorts believers in 1 Cor 15:49, "And just as we have borne the image of the man of dust, let us also bear[31] the image of the man of heaven." The eschatological orientation of the context is made clear with the emphasis on the resurrection of believers. Using a series of parallel descriptions beginning in 1 Cor 15:42, Paul develops the idea that there is a physical as well as a spiritual body (1 Cor 15:44). Gordon Fee argues that the primary concern at this point is not christological, but rather to demonstrate the reality of the coming spiritual body for every believer.[32] Then in 1 Cor 15:45–47, quoting from Genesis 2:7, Paul revisits the Adam-Christ analogy introduced earlier in 1 Cor 15:20–28.

In 1 Cor 15:20–28 Paul argues that Christ has, in fact, been raised from the dead. Fee notes that in this section Paul's primary concern is not the resurrection from the dead, but rather the resurrection together of all who are in Christ (p. 750). In this analogy, Christ stands at the beginning of the new humanity, or order, just as Adam stands at the beginning of the old humanity. Paul is arguing from a community perspective that those who are "in Christ"—those who have entered into the new humanity by grace—will assuredly "be raised from the dead into the *shared life* of the risen One" (p. 751).[33]

In the second use of the Adam-Christ analogy, Paul presents "the nature of the resurrected body that the new humanity will share through their connection to Christ (vv. 35–49)… Paul sets forth Jesus' resurrected body as the paradigm for all who will bear his image."[34] Thus Adam and Christ become archetypes that represent corporate life before Christ and corporate life in Christ.

At one level, Paul is arguing that believers will be raised with a spiritual body acquired through the resurrection "and adapted to the life of the Spirit in the coming age."[35] The linguistic connection between ψυχικός and πνευματικός (1 Cor 15:44) and ψυχή and πνεῦμα (1 Cor 15:45) reveals that the two kinds of bodies mentioned in 1 Cor 15:44 refer to Adam and Christ. Thus the imagery carries a double meaning. First, believers presently carry a physical body subject to decay. In the resurrection, they will inherit a spiritual body prepared for eternity. Second, as 1 Cor 15:46–48 reveals, association with Adam is fundamentally a human association with an old order which is mortal and decays and involves dishonor and weakness (1 Cor 15:42–43). In contrast, association with Christ fundamentally involves the giving of life and association with a new order and with it eternity, glory and power.[36]

In commenting on 1 Cor 15:46–48, Fee states,

> Paul insists that the latter comes 'first,' that is, that they must reckon with the physical side of their present life in the Spirit. 'Then,' meaning at the Eschaton, comes the *pneumatikos*; and they must reckon with the reality that since the *psychikos* comes first and has a body, so too the *pneumatikos* that comes after will have a body, a transformed body appropriate to eschatological spiritual life.[37]

It is within this context that Paul exhorts the Corinthian believers to "bear the image of the man of heaven" (1 Cor 15:49). As those who now share the character of Christ, he is urging these believers to conform to the life that this represents.[38] Here is another example of Paul's "already-not yet" eschatological thinking. Whereas final glorification comes with the resurrection, believers are called upon to bear the image of Christ—"to become what they are by grace."[39]

2 Corinthians 3:18. In 2 Cor 3:18 Paul states, "And we all, with unveiled faces reflecting the glory of the Lord, are being transformed into the same image from one degree of glory to another, which is from the Lord, who is the Spirit." This is perhaps the clearest passage in which the transformation into the image of Christ is presented as a present reality.[40] Regarding this passage, Grenz notes, "Insofar as they reflect the new corporate reality in Christ, believers are in the process of becoming the image of God and hence fulfilling their divinely given, human destiny."[41]

In the preceding context, Paul argues that his ministry possesses a glory which surpasses that of Moses (2 Cor 3:9). It is amazing that the glory produced by Moses' ministry was so bright that the Israelites could not look steadily at his face (2 Cor 3:7). Paul's argument here involves a series of contrasts all centering on the concept of glory.[42] The parallelism appears as follows:[43]

εἰ δε	θάνατος	πῶς οὐχὶ μᾶλλον	πνεῦμα (vv. 7–8)
But if	death	how much more	Spirit
εἰ γὰρ	κατάκρισις	πολλῷ μᾶλλον	δικαιοσύνη (v. 9)
For if	condemnation	how much more	righteousness
εἰ γὰρ	τὸ καταργούμενον	πολλῷ μᾶλλον	τὸ μένον (v. 11)
For if	fading away	how much more	remains

The central argument based on this structure is if the old covenant involved glory, how much more glorious is the new covenant? Grenz argues that δόξα "functions here as a kind of theological code word."[44]

In the next section Paul expands the concept of the greater ministry and glory even more. Once again, Martin has helpfully identified the parallel structure as follows:[45]

οὐ	καθάπερ Μωϋσῆς	ἀλλὰ	ἐπωρώθη τὰ νοήματα (vv. 13–14)
Not	like Moses	but	their minds were closed
μὴ	ἀνακαλυπτόμενον	ἀλλ'	κάλυμμα... κεῖται (vv. 14–15)
Not	been removed	but	a veil... lies over their minds

Not only is glory increased with the new ministry, Paul now identifies why this is true. Martin explains that the structure

> shows how the points of antithesis are not (a) the Christian's παρρησία ('boldness') over against Moses' veiled face (v 13), but (b) the Israelite's disability to gain direct access to God—because Moses wore a veil that concealed the divine glory—and the Christian's access through Christ (v 14), a thought that becomes central in vv 16–18. (p. 60)

This means that the primary contrasting sets in this passage are Israelites—Christians, Moses—Paul, law—Spirit, and letter—covenant. And Paul transfers the picture of the veil, with which Moses covered his face, to the Israelites to explain their spiritual condition. The veil symbolizes their hard hearts—the condition keeping them from understanding and responding to the old covenant (2 Cor 3:14–15).[46] It is only in Christ that the "veil" is removed (2 Cor 3:16).

This is the context for Paul's statement, "And we all, with unveiled faces reflecting the glory of the Lord, are being transformed into the same image from one degree of glory to another, which is from the Lord, who is the Spirit" (2 Cor 3:18). Here, Paul brings together the key elements in the preceding argument—veil, Spirit, face, glory, Lord.[47]

For the purposes of this study, there are several exegetical issues that need to be addressed in this verse. The first issue is the meaning of κατοπτρίζω. This word can mean either "to show in a mirror" or "to reflect."[48] The exegetical question relates to whether believers are "reflecting the glory of the Lord" or "beholding the glory as in a mirror?" Martin, Hughes and Grenz all note that either meaning is feasible and conclude that the best meaning is the one that fits the context.[49] The primary reason for interpreting it as "beholding in a mirror" is consistency with the imagery of the Israelites beholding the glory as they gazed into Moses' face. Martin argues that interpreting the meaning as some form of reflection removes the contrast and is, therefore, exegetically unacceptable.[50] N. T. Wright takes an opposing view when he says,

> At the climax of Paul's whole argument, he makes (if I am right) the astonishing claim that those who belong to the new covenant are, by the Spirit, being changed into the glory of the Lord: when they come face to face with one another they are beholding, as in a mirror, the glory itself… Unlike the Israelites, those in the new covenant can look at the glory as it is reflected in each other.[51]

The fact that this is the only occurrence of the word in the New Testament lends to the complexity. While the contrast is primarily between the Israelites and Christians, the fact that Moses veiled himself was to prevent the Israelites from gazing at him too long and, therefore, to shield the glory. The context reveals that both meanings are possible. If so, then the creation of a double-image with the use of this metaphor increases the richness in meaning. Not only do believers behold the glory of the Lord with the veil lifted, they also reflect the glory. This is consistent with the earlier discussion of Christ reflecting God's glory, and the reflection concept inherent in image-bearing.[52]

A second exegetical issue is the meaning of μεταμορφόω. It has as its root meaning the idea of change. Of interest here is whether the transformation referred to by Paul has an external dimension to it.[53] Outside of Paul, the only other occurrences of this word involve the transfiguration of Jesus which involved visible change (Mark 9:2; Matt 17:2). The only other use by Paul is in Rom 12:2, where it is clear that genuine transformation starts with internal change. Both Pauline contexts reveal that limiting the range of meaning to an internal and invisible change should be rejected.

In both passages, the immediate context reveals that Paul had external dimensions in mind. In the Corinthians passage, he continues the theme of his ministry and states, "But we have rejected shameful hidden deeds, not behaving with deceptiveness or distorting the word of God, but by open proclamation of the truth, we commend ourselves to everyone's conscience before God" (2 Cor 4:2). He then concludes the paragraph with, "For God, who said 'Let *light shine out of darkness,*' is the one who shined in our hearts to give us the light of the glorious knowledge of God in the face of Jesus Christ" (2 Cor 4:6). As discussed earlier, Christ is here presented as reflecting God's glory. In a similar way, believers reflect God's glory as they live their lives in conformity with his will. In the context faithful obedience—reflecting God's glory—becomes the basis for effective ministry (2 Cor 4:1).

Similarly, the context of Rom 12 begins with the exhortation for believers to present their bodies as living sacrifices (Rom 12:1). The command to be transformed is specifically for the purpose of testing and approving the perfect will of God (Rom 12:2). The following context expands and illustrates this presentation and transformation concept in highly behavioral language.[54]

Colossians 3:9–10. In a final related passage, Paul states,

> Do not lie to one another since you have put off the old man with its practices and have been clothed with the new man[55] that is being renewed in knowledge according to the image of the one who created it (Col 3:9–10).

In this passage, David Dockery notes that the current understanding of the old person and the new person is to see them as more related to the corporate whole, rather than the individual parts, or natures, of a person. In his estimation, these terms designate "the complete person viewed in relation to the corporate whole to which he or she belongs."[56] This is supported by Paul's use of καινὸς ἄνθρωπος (Eph 2:15) to describe the newly created community of re-deemed Jews and Gentiles. Similarly, J. Knox Chamblin argues, "To 'put on' the new humanity is to embrace Christ himself."[57]

Similarly, the use of the rare verb ἀπεκδύομαι (found only in Col 2:15 and 3:9) communicates a vivid picture of stripping away the old person, a metaphor of what life was like under the old order.[58] Grenz argues that the use of this verb forms a linguistic link with ἀπέκδυσις (Col 2:11).[59] In Col 2:11, the re-deemed community is pictured as being circumcised in and by Christ by the "stripping away," or removal, of the fleshly body through baptism. The context and linkage between these words reveals that for Paul, putting off the old per-son and putting on the new (Col. 3:9–10) is a metaphor for the conversion and baptism experience found in Christ. As such, the "putting off" and "putting on" imagery reflects an exchange of identities. "The old human and the new human are two frames of reference from which participants in each realm gain their identity, and out of which, on the basis of which, or in keeping with which they conduct their lives."[60] In other words, they represent a change in relation-ship.[61] What Christians have cast off is the old order and, therefore, the old way of living should likewise be abandoned. In contrast, what they have put on is the new order found in Christ and, therefore, the new way of living should be adopted. Paul draws these concepts together under the metaphor of the "old person" and the "new person."

Further, this new person is being renewed according to the image of the one who created it. Here Paul brings together the concept of the new person with the image of God. And since he had earlier clarified that Christ is the im-age of God (Col 1:15), he means that the renewal of the "new person" is in the image of Christ.[62] Locating this idea contextually within the imperatives to "put off" certain sinful attitudes and behaviors (Col 3:8) and to "clothe yourselves" with certain righteous attitudes and behaviors (Col 3:12–13) has ramifications for the present study. Peter O'Brien argues that this is "nothing other than… transformation into the image of Christ."[63]

Whereas the passages evaluated previously emphasized the certainty of transformation, this passage begins to address what this process entails. It seems that for Paul, it is in obedience that renewal into the image of Christ—transformation into Christ-likeness—occurs. The indicatives and the impera-tives are inextricably bound together. This is what Grenz refers to as the indica-tive being the source of the imperative.[64] Whereas inclusion in the new human-ity is a present reality, transformation into the image of Christ—the capacity for reflecting God's glory—is a product of obedience within the context of this new humanity.

The God Who Initiates

Old Testament

In the Garden of Eden account God initiates relationship with Adam and Eve in at least two ways. First, he instructs them in order to give them guidance. "God blessed them and said to them, 'Be fruitful and multiply! Fill the earth and subdue it! Rule over the fish of the sea and the birds of the air and every creature that moves on the ground" (Gen 1:28). This is also seen in the prohibition he gave the man. "You may freely eat fruit from every tree of the orchard, but you must not eat from the tree of the knowledge of good and evil, for when you eat from it you will surely die" (Gen 2:16–17).[65]

Even God's statements in the curse can be seen in this light. He not only pronounced a curse but he also provided for the man and woman and all later offspring information regarding the future. Woven throughout the curse is evidence of God's guidance and grace. The woman learned that she would have children and that one of her children would somehow reverse the tragedy that had occurred (Gen 3:15–16). Since God had earlier told the man that they would die, what a surprise it must have been to see God providing them insight and guidance in the aftermath.

Second, he provides for their care and well-being. This is seen in several examples. He provided for the physical needs by supplying food. He also provided for the man's relational needs by creating the woman.[66] It is interesting that after the fall God still initiated relationship with the man and woman by seeking them. This is set in contrast to the man and woman hiding from God (Gen 3:8–10). The skins that he provided for them also reflect his desire to care for their well-being, both physically and spiritually (Gen 3:21). Perhaps one of the greatest acts of God's mercy and provision occurs in his expelling the man and woman from the garden. The reason given is related to their ability to gain eternal life in a fallen state (Gen 3:22–24).

These actions in the Garden reveal two things. First, there is a desire in God to move toward people. His movement toward the man and the woman both before and after the fall reveals a consistency to initiate relationship with people regardless of their status before him. Second, there is a need in people to depend on God. At no point in the story do the man and woman know what is needed or have the ability to care for themselves.

In the giving of the law at Mt. Sinai, this aspect of God's nature is again seen clearly. After he had introduced himself to them (Exod 19), the story picks up again with the people standing at a distance (Exod 20:18). The context reveals that they were terrified and wanted Moses to mediate for them (Exod 20:19). In response Moses says, "Do not fear, for God has come to test you, that the fear of him may be before you so that you do not sin" (Exod 20:20). God's actions were partly designed to introduce himself to them as well as to demonstrate his power. Here the concept of reverential awe surfaces. There is a balance between a healthy respect for God's power and a deep need not to fear God. The balance between these two is what produces in his people a genuine desire to obey him.

The giving of the law itself ranks as one of the greatest examples of God's giving to his people what they needed to live in relationship with him and with each other. In addition, the "tutoring" aspect of the law spoken of by Paul reveals that God was moving eschatologically to demonstrate to his people their sinfulness and need for the Messiah (Gal 3:19–22).

Even God's "passive" responses are rooted in earlier action. When God says to Moses, "I have surely seen the affliction of my people who are in Egypt. I have heard their cry because of their taskmasters, for I know their sorrows" (Exod 3:7), he was the one who sent them to Egypt to begin with (Gen 45:5). God's initiatory acts during the Exodus and Passover event are well known and provide further examples of how God moves toward his people to give them guidance and care for their well-being.

The prophets reveal God consistently moving toward his people to call them back, even after they had sinned repeatedly and rejected him. For example, in Hosea he cries out, "But I am the LORD your God, who brought you out of Egypt. Therefore, you must not acknowledge any God except me; there is no Savior except me. I cared for you in the wilderness, in the dry desert which had no water" (Hos 13:4–5). Again, he cries out,

> Listen to me, O family of Jacob, all you who are left from the family of Israel, you who have been carried from birth, you who have been supported from the time you left the womb. Even when you are old, I will take care of you, even when you have gray hair, I will carry you. I made you and I will support you; I will carry you and rescue you (Isa 46:3–4).

In light of this short survey, it is clear that taking initiative toward humanity is part of God's nature. In the discussion on the attributes of God, there has been much analysis on how to classify his attributes. As noted by Grenz, the classification schemes have typically divided the attributes into two broad categories.[67] Grenz argues for two groups as well but orients them relationally. The first group speaks about God's "eternality." They describe God "in his noetic and purposeful relationship to creation." The second group speaks about God's "goodness." They describe God's "moral uprightness in all his dealings with creation."[68]

Unsurprisingly, Grenz argues that love has always been interrelationally present within the Trinity. However, because of his creative acts, love surfaces as the fundamental attribute of God.[69] Love describes the way God interacts with creation. It is essentially that element in his character that expresses his sharing of himself. In this regard, the initiatory acts of God reflect his character and, therefore, necessarily become part of image-bearing.

New Testament

By the time of the Gospels, God's initiatory acts toward humanity were more than a pattern that reflected his character. It was fulfillment of prophecy. Both birth accounts make this clear.

> 'Joseph, son of David, do not be afraid to take Mary as your wife, because the child conceived in her is from the Holy Spirit. She will give birth to a son and you will name him Jesus, because he will save his people from their sins.' This all happened so that what was spoken by the Lord through the prophet would be fulfilled: *'Look! The virgin will conceive and bear a son, and they will call him Emmanuel,'* which means *'God with us'* (Matt 1:20–23).

This is echoed to Mary as well when the angel tells her

> you have found favor with God. Listen: you will become pregnant and give birth to a son, and you will name him Jesus. He will be great, and will be called the Son of the Most High, and the Lord God will give him the throne of his father David. He will reign over the house of Jacob forever, and his kingdom will never end (Luke 1:30–33).

The presence of the angels as God's messengers and the specific content of the message using fulfillment terminology demonstrate God's direct involvement with humanity.

In Hebrews the author weaves throughout the argument a balanced presentation of initiation on both the part of God and Jesus. In Hebrews, there is constant interplay between the Father and the Son where the Father initiates and then the Son initiates. It is present right from the start with the Father when the readers are told, "After God spoke long ago in various portions and in various ways to our ancestors through the prophets, in these last days he has spoken to us in a son, whom he appointed heir of all things, and through whom he created the world" (Heb 1:1–2). Within the same sentence the author says of Jesus, "And so when he had accomplished cleansing for sins, *he sat down at the right hand of the Majesty on high*" (Heb 1:3). This blend is seen again in his atoning acts. "Therefore he had to be made like his brothers and sisters in every respect, so that he could become a merciful and faithful high priest in things relating to God, to make atonement for the sins of the people" (Heb 2:17).

In Hebrews, the role of the redeemed community is consistently modeled after God's initiatory acts. For example, the author argues from Psalm 95 with the following, "Therefore, as the Holy Spirit says, '*Oh, that today you would listen as he speaks! "Do not harden your hearts as in the rebellion, in the day of testing in the wilderness"*'" (Heb 3:7–8). This is the basis for the following community exhortation to "see to it, brothers and sisters, that none of you has an evil, unbelieving heart that forsakes the living God. But exhort one another each day, as long as it is called 'Today,' that none of you may become hardened by sin's deception" (Heb 3:12–13).

Again, in Hebrews 10 the community is exhorted to

> take thought of how to spur one another on to love and good works, not abandoning our own meetings, as some are in the habit of doing, but encouraging each other, and even more so because you see the day drawing near (Heb 10:24–25).

In the preceding context the author related the exhortation to Jesus' shed blood. Access to the sanctuary through the curtain was inaugurated by Jesus (Heb 10:19–20). The use of ἐπισυναγωγή certainly has conceptual, if not linguistic, linkage to the use of temple/tabernacle imagery in Hebrews where Christ is presented as the fulfillment of all that the temple/tabernacle represented as well as the reason believers are allowed to enter with him.[70] The initiatory acts of Jesus form the basis for community movement toward one another.

The New Testament authors consistently present God as one who takes initiative in relationship with the community. This pattern becomes the basis for how the community is to act toward one another. God's normal method of moving his people to righteous living is through the catalytic affect of believers in each other's lives. This is true of exposure and confrontation of sin as well as provoking one another to holy living. Since both of these are elements in the process of growing in maturity, the community plays an essential role in helping the individuals within the community grow.

Summary

In Pauline theology, the transformation of believers into the image of God is significant in understanding the role of the community in progressive sanctification. Paul makes it clear that Christ is the image of God and, as such, he reflects his glory to the creation. As the image of God, Christ represents what the community of believers is destined to become in eternity. In this regard, believers together represent the new humanity—the new person—brought about by the death of Christ. In the "already-not yet" Pauline eschatological scheme, this future aspect represents the "not yet" phase.

Paul also makes it clear that there is a present and progressive aspect to image-bearing. This is captured by the idea of transformation. In the present age believers are being transformed into the image of Christ. This transformation occurs as believers living within community obey the imperatives of the New Testament. In addition, this transformation results in the believing community reflecting the glory of God to each other and to the rest of creation. This concept is central to understanding the progressive aspect of sanctification. As believers are transformed, their capacity for reflecting God's glory is increased. As was concluded earlier one of the necessary aspects of sanctification is an outward focus. This dynamic aspect in image-bearing reflects this outward focus. It is in obedience that believers are transformed and reflect God's glory.

The predestining and transforming work of God in the redeemed community represents perhaps the primary initiatory act of God toward the redeemed in the present age. However, they are not the only ways that God moves toward his creation. He also moves to provide guidance and to care for the well-being of his creation. From the beginning of time to the eternal state, God consistently moves toward his people in love. The giving of the law and the establishment of relationship between him and the redeemed are evidence of this. Each of these initiatory acts is characterized by love. Love describes the way God interacts with creation. And since love is central to God's character, the initiatory acts of God are also a reflection of his character.

And yet, it is more than an attribute. It is the model given to the redeemed to illustrate how they are to live and function within community. As the community obeys the commands—moves toward one another in love—the community becomes one of the means for transformation.[71] The pattern of God's initiatory acts forms the basis for how the community is to live together in relationship. As believers imitate God in community for the purpose of obedience, transformation occurs. Later, the Pauline corpus will be evaluated to understand how the various situations addressed by Paul and the ensuing exhortations are necessary for transformation into the image of Christ.

NOTES

1 This is not to say that image-bearing does not include an ontological aspect. It is reasonable based on the biblical data that our ontology is necessarily made in God's image as well. However, it is outside the scope of this study to consider in detail this aspect of image-bearing studies. The teleological aspect, however, is very relevant since it forms the basis for the relational teachings throughout the Bible.

2 Stanley J. Grenz, *Theology for the Community of God* (Grand Rapids: Eerdmans, 1994), 168.

3 This short survey is taken largely from Grenz, *Theology*, 168–80. See also, Millard J. Erickson, *Christian Theology*, 2d ed. (Grand Rapids: Baker, 1998), 495–512, who categorizes the views under the terms "The Substantive View," "Relational Views," and "The Functional Views."

4   Grenz, *Theology*, 177.

5   Erickson, *Theology*, 512–15, disagrees and presents an opposing view. He views the relational and dynamic views as expressing "consequences" or "applications" of the divine image. "By contrast the focus of the relational and functional views is actually on consequences or applications of the image rather than on the image itself. Although very closely linked to the image of God, experiencing relationships and exercising dominion are not themselves that image" (p. 513). Also, "Man is most fully man when he is active in these relationships [with others] and performs this function [exercising dominion], for he is then fulfilling his *telos*, God's purpose for him" (p. 514).

    However, as noted in the NET Bible SN on Gen 1:26, "Following the cohortative ('let us make'), the prefixed verb form with *vav* conjunctive indicates purpose/result (see Gen 19:20; 34:23; 2 Sam 3:21). God's purpose in giving mankind his image is that they might rule the created order on behalf of the heavenly king and his royal court. So the divine image, however it is defined, gives humankind the capacity and/or authority to rule over creation." Similarly, D. J. A. Clines, "The Image of God in Man," *TynBul* 19 (1968): 101, concludes, "The image is to be understood not so much ontologically as existentially: it comes to expression not in the nature of man so much as in his activity and his function."

6   David Peterson, *Possessed by God: A New Testament Theology of Sanctification and Holiness*, NSBT, ed. D. A. Carson (Downers Grove, IL: InterVarsity, 1995), 13, states, "In systematic theology, sanctification has become the basket into which every theme related to Christian life and growth has been placed… [This] obscures the distinctive meaning and value of the terminology in the New Testament, confusing sanctification with renewal and transformation."

7   Stanley J. Grenz, *The Social God and the Relational Self: A Trinitarian Theology of the Imago Dei* In The Matrix of Christian Theology (Louisville, KY: Westminster John Knox, 2001), 177. Similarly, F. LeRon Shults, *Reforming Theological Anthropology: After the Philosophical Turn to Relationality* (Grand Rapids: Eerdmans, 2003), 237, concludes regarding the eschatological view of the divine image, "Whether or not we agree with the details of these particular proposals, the value of this eschatological hermeneutic is the way it opens up a trajectory that may help us in the task of reforming the doctrine of the image of God after the turn to relationality, in which the dynamics of temporality have played such an important role. An eschatological interpretation does not exclude the other interpretations but may incorporate and integrate them."

8   While it is outside the scope of this study to provide a thoroughgoing analysis of Grenz's argument, it is necessary to understand the central concept of image-bearing as it relates to progressive sanctification. Grenz's articulation of this view represents a growing trend in New Testament studies that relates the transformation of the believer to image-bearing and the "new humanity." See Grenz, *Social God*, 183–264; Peterson, *Possessed by God*, 115–37; James D. G. Dunn, *The Theology of Paul the Apostle* (Grand Rapids: Eerdmans, 1998), 266–93, 390–412, 466–72, 533–64; David J. A. Clines, "Image of God," in *DPL*, 428. In this regard, the current trend is community and eschatologically focused. In the "already-not yet" scheme, these studies focus on the "not yet" aspect of what the new humanity is becoming in Christ. This study agrees with this orientation, but is more focused on the "already" aspect and the role of the community in the transformation process.

9   Clines, "Image of God," in *DPL*, 427, states, "When Christ is spoken of as the 'image' of God, the idea is that he is the visible representation of God." Similarly, Grenz, *Social God*, 204–5, argues that linking the image of God explicitly to Christ is a key theological agenda of the New Testament authors.

10 Gerhard Kittel, "δοκέω, δόξα"in *TDNT*, 2:237. Kittel further argues that this is a progression of the meaning found in the Old Testament, and that the New Testament usage follows the LXX and has no corresponding Greek analogy (p. 247).

11 Ibid., 2:237, 248.

12 Ibid., 2:248. Grenz, *Social God*, 206, similarly concludes, "This uniquely New Testament concept of *doxa*... is crucial to New Testament Christology." See also Richard B. Gaffin, "Glory, Glorification," in *DPL*, 349, who states, "The new covenant *doxa* in Christ is the climactic revelation of God's glory; it is eschatological glory... Christ's glory-light answers to the light of the original creation; his is the splendor of a new and final creation."

13 Grenz, *Social God*, 206, uses the term "glory-christology" to connect the glory of Christ in the New Testament with the more prominent Old Testament theme of the glory of God. Gary M. Burge, "Glory," in *DJG*, 269, states, "This brings us to what is by all accounts a most unexpected development in the Fourth Gospel. Glory is never associated with any futurist Son of man saying. John vigorously advances the theme into the earthly ministry of Jesus."

14 Grenz, *Social God*, 208, states, "The hour of the Father's glorification of the Son or of the Son's full glory [in John] is none other than the crucifixion itself (7:39; 12:16, 23; 13:31). This event marks the 'hour' of the self-disclosure of the Father in the Son, as Jesus Christ completes his vocation in the divine work on behalf of sinful mankind." Raymond E. Brown, *The Gospel According to John (I–XII): Introduction, Translation, and Notes*, AB, ed. William Foxwell Albright and David Noel Freedman, vol. 29 (New York: Doubleday, 1970), 503–4,similarly states, "The whole NT agrees that the resurrected Jesus was the vehicle of *doxa* because the resurrection was the mighty act of God par excellence. Since John conceives of passion, death, and resurrection as the one 'hour,' John sees the theme of glory throughout the whole hour."

15 Grenz, *Social God*, 209.

16 Here, the TNIV is used rather than the NET which takes τῆς δόξης as an attributive genitive to τοῦ εὐαγγελίου, "glorious gospel" and τῆς δόξης as an attributive genitive to τῆς γνώσεως, "glorious knowledge" in 4:6.

17 Ralph P. Martin, *2 Corinthians*, WBC, ed. David A. Hubbard and Ralph P. Martin, vol. 40 (Dallas, TX: Word, 1986), 79.

18 Philip Edgcumbe Hughes, *The Second Epistle to the Corinthians*, NICNT, ed. F. F. Bruce (Grand Rapids: Eerdmans, 1962), 130. Both Martin and Hughes are correct in disagreeing with the NET Bible, which takes τῆς δόξης as an attributive genitive to τοῦ εὐαγγελίου, "glorious gospel."

19 Martin, *2 Corinthians*, 80; see also Hughes, *Second Corinthians*, 134. Again, Martin and Hughes correctly disagree with the NET Bible, which takes τῆς δόξης as an attributive genitive to τῆς γνώσεως, "glorious knowledge."

20 Martin, *2 Corinthians*, 81.

21 Grenz, *Social God*, 211. He goes on to argue that the New Testament authors unanimously approach the concept of the image of God christologically. "In [the NT authors'] perspective, the Genesis narrative points to Jesus Christ, who as the revelation of the nature and glory of God is the image of God" (p. 223).

22 Dunn, *Theology of Paul*, 293, similarly concludes, "In Christ God's original design for humanity finally takes concrete shape."

23 Grenz, *Social God*, 225.

24 Douglas J. Moo, *The Epistle to the Romans*, NICNT, ed. Gordon D. Fee (Grand Rapids: Eerdmans, 1996), 534–36. This is reinforced by the only other use of σύμμορφος (Phil 3:21). In this passage, the transformation of the Christian's earthly body into a glorious body is clearly future. Conformity with Christ ultimately includes both the material and the immaterial.

25 C. E. B. Cranfield, *The Epistle to the Romans*, vol. 1, ICC, ed. J. A. Emerton and C. E. B. Cranfield (Edinburgh: T&T Clark, 1975), 432, states, "It is probable… that Paul is here thinking not only of their final glorification but also of their growing conformity to Christ here and now in suffering and in obedience—that is, that συμμόρφους… is meant to embrace sanctification as well as final glory, the former being thought of as a progressive conformity to Christ, who is the εἰκών of God, and so as a progressive renewal of the believer into that likeness of God which is God's original purpose for man." See also, Leon Morris, *The Epistle to the Romans*, (Grand Rapids: Eerdmans, 1988), 333; Grenz, *Social God*, 232.

26 Moo, *Romans*, 531; F. F. Bruce, *Romans*, rev. ed. TNTC, ed. Leon Morris, vol. 6 (Leicester: InterVarsity, 1985), 167; Morris, *Romans*, 332–33; Grenz, *Social God*, 229.

27 Grenz, *Social God*, 230; John Murray, *The Epistle to the Romans*, The NICNT, ed. F. F. Bruce, vol. 1 (Grand Rapids: Eerdmans, 1965), 319, states, "This specifies the final aim of the conformity just spoken of. We might well ask: What can be more final than the complete conformity of the sons of God to the image of Christ? It is this question that brings to the forefront the significance of this concluding clause. There is a final end that is more ultimate than the glorification of the people of God; it is that which is concerned with the preeminence of Christ."

28 BDAG, "ἀδελφός," 18, states in reference to the use of ἀδελφοῖς here, "Hence used by Christians in their relations w. each other."

29 Murray, *Romans*, 1:320.

30 Grenz, *Social God*, 231.

31 The text critical problem is between φορέσομεν (B I 1881) and φορέσωμεν (𝔓⁴⁶ ℵ A C D F G Ψ 33 1739 *Byz*). As noted by the NET Bible SN on this verse, "If the original reading is the future tense, then 'we will bear' would be a guarantee that believers would be like Jesus (and unlike Adam) in the resurrection. If the aorist subjunctive is original, then 'let us bear' would be a command to show forth the image of Jesus, i.e., to live as citizens of the kingdom believers will one day inherit." The geographical distribution and genealogical solidarity favor the aorist subjunctive with the establishment of the Alexandrian, Western and Byzantine text-types. Regarding internal evidence, the context favors the future indicative in that the indicatives of 1 Cor 15:42–49 suggest a future indicative (note the possible parallel construction in verse 49 if both verbs are indicative). As such, the aorist subjunctive best accounts for the origin of the future indicative since the context is eschatologically oriented and it seems the tendency would be to change the verb to a future indicative, rather than the opposite. As questioned by Gordon D. Fee, *The First Epistle to the Corinthians*, NICNT, ed. F. F. Bruce (Grand Rapids: Eerdmans, 1987), 787, "If the reading of B *et al.* were original, given that it makes so much sense in context, how is one to account for such a nearly universal… change to the hortatory subjunctive?" Given this, it is probably best to regard the aorist subjunctive as original.

32 Fee, *First Corinthians*, 787.

33 Grenz, *Social God*, 235, similarly argues that the resurrection is an eschatological and corpo-

rate event and that forms the basis for Paul's thinking throughout this passage. "In this sense, Adam and Christ become the representatives of two corporate realities."

34 Grenz, *Social God*, 236.

35 Fee, *First Corinthians*, 788. Grenz, *Social God*, 236, concludes that "Paul's christological reading of this Old Testament text yields the conclusion that the advent of the spiritual body was in view at the creation, yet not as an aspect that was simply inherent within human nature from the beginning but as the eschatological destiny of the new humanity in Christ. Paul's Adam-Christ typology, therefore, indicates that the creation of Adam did not in and of itself mark the fulfillment of God's intention for humankind as the *imago dei*." Once again, this reveals the ultimate goal of what God is accomplishing in redeemed humanity through Christ.

36 Dunn, *Theology of Paul*, 289. Grenz, *Social God*, 236, agrees when he says, "The resurrected Christ is not only the pattern of the resurrected body that believers will share; he also is the spiritual vitality who will one day bring about the glorious transformation of the new humanity."

37 Fee, *First Corinthians*, 791, goes on to argue that this explains 1 Cor 15:47–48 as qualitative expressions of life in the flesh and life in the Spirit (pp. 792–93).

38 BDAG, "φορέω," 1064, "represent in one's own appearance." Konrad Weiss, "φορέω," in *TDNT*, 9:84, notes that this verb usually has the idea of "carrying for a longer time or continually" and in relation to 1 Cor 15:49, "in a transf. sense the bearing of the εἰκών." Grenz, *Social God*, 236, explains that "Paul sets forth Jesus' resurrected body as the paradigm for all who will bear his image."

39 Fee, *First Corinthians*, 795.

40 The present tense of μεταμορφόω is taken as a progressive present. Buist M. Fanning, *Verbal Aspect in New Testament Greek*, Oxford Theological Monographs, ed. J. Barton et al (Oxford: Clarendon, 1990), 199, argues that the progressive present "involves a *specific* situation (either action or state) viewed *as it is going on*... to denote close simultaneity with another situation." It describes a scene in progress. The emphasis is on what is occurring in the present. In this passage there are two simultaneous and ongoing actions occurring— reflecting (discussed later) and transforming. The use of the present tense with both of these words reinforces the progressive aspect and introduces a vividness to the transformation process. In addition, the prepositional phrase ἀπὸ δόξης εἰς δόξαν reflects a durative aspect to the transformation Paul has in mind. As argued by Martin, *2 Corinthians*, 72, "This process of 'transformation'... is gradual and progressive, ἀπὸ δόξης εἰς δόξαν, from one stage of glory to yet a higher stage." Similarly, Hughes, *Second Corinthians*, 118, states, "The effect of continuous beholding is that we are continuously being transformed 'into the same image', that is, into the likeness of Christ—and increasingly so: 'from glory to glory.'"

41 Grenz, *Social God*, 240.

42 Gaffin, "Glory," in *DPL*, 348, states, "The highest single concentration of glory vocabulary in Paul's letters (ten occurrences of the noun and verb) is in 2 Corinthians 3:7–11." This reinforces the emphasis of δόξα in this passage.

43 Martin, *2 Corinthians*, 59.

44 Grenz, *Social God*, 242.

45 Martin, *2 Corinthians*, 60.

46 Hughes, *Second Corinthians*, 112, suggests the interesting idea that Paul used this metaphor

because he found evidence of this problem in his own life before his encounter with Christ.

47   Grenz, *Social God*, 244.

48   Kittel, "κατοπτρίζομαι," in *TDNT*, 2:696; BDAG, "κατοπτρίζω," 535, defines it as, "prob. w. the mng. look at someth. as in a mirror."

49   Martin, *2 Corinthians*, 71; Hughes. *Second Corinthians*, 118; Grenz, *Social God*, 246.

50   Martin, *2 Corinthians*, 71.

51   N. T. Wright, *The Climax of the Covenant: Christ and the Law in Pauline Theology* (Minneapolis, MN: Fortress, 1992), 185. This is also the view taken in the NET Bible translation "with unveiled faces reflecting the glory of the Lord."

52   Kittel, "κατοπτρίζομαι," in *TDNT*, 2:696–97, approaches this idea when he notes that as believers are "changed into the likeness of what they see… they themselves acquire a share in the δόξα." He repeats a similar idea, "δόξα," in *TDNT*, 2:251, when he says in reference to the ἀπὸ δόξης εἰς δόξαν construction in 2 Cor 3:18, "We have the whole simultaneity of possession and expectation which is the basis of NT piety." The possession of glory implies the reflection of glory.

53   BDAG, "μεταμορφόω," 639, when applied to 2 Cor 3:18 defines it as, "to change inwardly in fundamental character or condition." Similarly, J. Behm, "μεταμορφόω" in *TDNT*, 4:758, says, "In Paul the idea of transformation, in the two passages in which it occurs (2 C. 3:18; R. 12:2), refers to an invisible process in Christians which takes place, or begins to take place, already during their life in this aeon." And yet Behm goes on to argue that "Paul obviously shares formally the ideas of Hellenistic mysticism in respect of transformation by vision, transformation into the seen image of God, and transformation as a process which is progressively worked out in the righteous" (p. 758). He further argues that both the Jewish apocalyptic and Hellenistic concepts of transformation (which Paul is borrowing from in his estimation) include the ideas of perceptible change (pp. 756–57). So whereas the process may be invisible, the effect is obvious. Margaret E. Thrall, *2 Corinthians 1–7*, ICC, ed. J. A. Emerton, C. E. B. Cranfield, and G. N. Stanton (London and New York: T&T Clark, 1994), 285, similarly states, "the thought must be that assimilation to Christ as the image of God produces a visibly Christ-like character, so that the divine image becomes visible in the believer's manner of life."

54   Moo, *Romans*, 756–57, brings balance to the discussion when he argues that, whereas the mind is inwardly focused and the means by which transformation takes place, "'Approving' the will of God means to understand and agree with what God wants of us with a view to putting it into practice" (p. 757).

55   The term used here is νέος, while the term used in the parallel passage (Eph 4:24) is καινὸς ἄνθρωπος. Conceptually they are referring to the same theological point being made by Paul. As noted by Peter T. O'Brien, *Colossians, Philemon*, WBC, ed. David A. Hubbard, Glenn W. Barker, and Ralph P. Martin, vol. 44 (Waco, TX: Word, 1982), 190, "The new man has been put on in place of the old. The Greek adjective νέος… stands in contrast to παλαιός ('old') and means the same as the synonym καινός." See also, BDAG, which defines νέος in this usage as, "pert. to being superior in quality or state to what when before, *new*," and J. Behm, "νέος, ἀνανεόω," in *TDNT*, 4:896, 899.

56   David S. Dockery, "New Nature and Old Nature," in *DPL*, 628. It is outside the scope of this study to review the history and debate regarding the understanding of these terms. However, it is important to understand the current thinking regarding the corporate aspect and how this concept relates to transformation. At issue is whether these terms refer to the

individual or the new community in Christ. It is conceivable, as argued by Peter T. O'Brien, *The Letter to the Ephesians*, Pillar New Testament Commentary, ed. D. A. Carson (Grand Rapids: Eerdmans and Apollos, 1999), 331, that both are in view by Paul. What is significant for the present study is the development of the concept of the new community in Christ and how these passages understand this community aspect as it relates to transformation.

57 J. Knox Chamblin, "Psychology," in *DPL*, 772. Both Dockery and Chamblin, in their respective articles, argue that this terminology is rooted in the contrast between Adam and Christ. Dockery, "New Nature," in *DPL*, 628, best explains this concept when he says, "The 'old person' is what believers were 'in Adam' (in the old era)... the 'new person' is what believers are 'in Christ' (in the new era)." Similarly, the NET Bible, SN on Col 3:10, argues, "it is nonetheless clear, on the basis of Paul's usage of the expression, that the *old man* refers to man as he is in Adam and dominated by sin (cf. Rom 6:6; Eph 4:22), while the *new man* refers to the Christian whose new sphere of existence is in Christ." See also Larry J. Kreitzer, "Adam and Christ," in *DPL*, 9–15, and Ronald Y. K. Fung, "Body of Christ," in *DPL*, 76–82. The use of the Adam-Christ analogy to illustrate association with the old order and the new order reinforces the community aspect of the new humanity in both of these passages.

58 See O'Brien, *Colossians, Philemon*, 188–90, for an analysis of the semantic range and usage of this word, especially as it relates to the metaphor of clothing.

59 Grenz, *Social God*, 254. See also F. F. Bruce, *The Epistles to the Colossians, to Philemon, and to the Ephesians*, NICNT, ed. F. F. Bruce (Grand Rapids: Eerdmans, 1984), 146.

60 Grenz, *Social God*, 255. Similarly, Dockery, "New Nature and Old Nature," in *DPL*, 629, states, "The metaphor of 'putting off' and 'putting on' clothes... does not simply mean promising to behave differently. Rather it is the gracious action of God's Spirit moving believers into a different sphere where the new rule of life obtains." See also, O'Brien, *Colossians, Philemon*, 189.

61 Dockery, "New Nature and Old Nature," in *DPL*, 628, argues, "'Old person' and 'new person' are not, then, ontological but relational in orientation. They speak not of a change in nature, but of a change in relationship."

62 O'Brien, *Colossians, Philemon*, 191.

63 Ibid. See also, Bruce, *Colossians, Philemon, Ephesians*, 146, and Grenz, *Social God*, 256, both of whom argue similarly. Orienting the renewal around knowledge (εἰς ἐπίγνωσιν) reflects the internal aspect of transformation. This is consistent with the discussion earlier on Rom 12:1, where it was argued that transformation has both internal and external dimensions, and the earlier discussion of 2 Cor 4:6, where the knowledge of the glory of God that is given to believers is found in Christ as he reflects God's glory. Dunn, *Theology of Paul*, 468, agrees and relates the putting on the new self directly to the language of "image" and "glory" of 2 Cor 3:18.

64 Grenz, *Social God*, 252.

65 While we are not told what the man understood by the concept of dying, the fact that it is placed in opposition to what could be eaten implies that it meant something negative. To eat from the tree of knowledge meant adverse relations with God.

66 Contextually, the creation of woman may be more related to the man's ability to carry out his God-given responsibility to "be fruitful," rather than his relational needs (see the NET Bible footnote on this verse). However, it seems that man's response at the first sight of the

woman reveals that he himself was grateful for having someone else like himself. It seems that latent in the term הָעֶזְמ was also the idea of relationship. Philip P. Roland, "עֶזְפ", in *NIDOTTE*, 3:651, interprets this term as, "this one at last." John H. Sailhamer, "Genesis," in *Expositor's Bible Commentary*, ed. Frank E. Gaebelein, vol. 2 (Grand Rapids: Zondervan, 1990), 47. He refers to man's "jubilant response."

67 Grenz, *Theology*, 90–91. "Theologians in the Protestant scholastic tradition tended to group the attributes of God into two or more basic categories. One widely used partition divides them into the 'incommunicable' and the 'communicable' attributes." See also Erickson, *Theology*, 266–67.

68 Grenz, *Theology*, 91; Erickson, *Theology*, 267. Erickson argues similarly. His two categories include attributes of "greatness" and attributes of "goodness."

69 Grenz, *Theology*, 71–74; Erickson, *Theology*, 292. In addressing this conclusion, Erickson states, "There is some scriptural basis for this. For example, in 1 John 4:8 and 16 we read: 'He who does not love does not know God; for God is love.'"

70 F. F. Bruce, *The Epistle to the Hebrews*, rev. ed., NICNT, ed. F. F. Bruce (Grand Rapids: Eerdmans, 1990), 257–58.

71 This is not to downplay the role that God and his Word play in the transformation process. All of the views evaluated in chapter 1 rightly reflect a strong commitment to these two means. As stated in chapter 1, this study assumes that both God and the Word are essential means for the transformation of believers. Therefore, the focus is on the role of the community.

CHAPTER 5

Solidarity of the Redeemed Community

A nother major theological consideration is the solidarity of God's redeemed people. Solidarity may be defined as "the way in which God has given humanity in general and his people in particular a common life with common concerns and responsibilities, so that the actions of one may deeply affect others for good or ill."[1] It involves a group identity or "corporate solidarity"[2] wherein individuals, while distinct from the group, locate and develop their identity within the community. As such, the individual's value, well being, and actions are evaluated and determined by the larger group identity. This characteristic of God's people permeates the Bible, starting with Israel and ending with the eschatological community of God.[3] Israel's solidarity was both a gift and responsibility and was to be used to invite the pagan nations into a life-changing relationship with God.[4] Israel's inappropriate use of this gift to exclude the pagan nations was severely condemned throughout the Old Testament.

In addition, it seems that one of Christ's purposes during his life was to expose the inappropriate and sinful way in which solidarity had been exploited to exclude the Gentiles. In this regard, he set about exposing the ways in which the Jewish leadership had twisted God's original plan to reach the entire world into a self-centered, self-protective scheme, thus rejecting God's plan to bless all the nations with the gift of salvation.

It is relevant to this study because Paul picks up this theme in his discussion of unity and applies it to the church. In this regard, if Jesus disrupted Israel's social scheme, the New Testament authors continued the progression by reorienting the concept of unity within the church in ways originally intended by God for his redeemed people.

Discussions regarding the maturing process have traditionally ignored this theme of corporate solidarity. This section surveys the issue of community within ancient Israel, especially as it relates to solidarity, both from the perspective of God's original design intent and the following historical corruption and disintegration, and how this theme is deployed within the New Testament specifically as it relates to the maturing of the believer. Paul's specific treatment is evaluated later.

Solidarity and Israel

Solidarity in the Old Testament begins with the concept of corporate solidarity.[5] Individuals are perceived as being "parts of some total relationship."[6] As part of this concept, individuals find themselves within a much larger unity that has significant impact on the way they view themselves and their value as defined by and their contribution to the whole. Israel itself was conceived of as a unity and individual Israelites formed their identity by being part of the nation. In other words, individuals were Israelite individuals precisely because they were part of the nation as a whole (p. 5).[7]

N. T. Wright, in *The New Testament and the People of God*, noted that one of the requirements for being a community with solidarity was the existence of a common world view. He identified "four things which worldviews characteristically do, in each of which the entire worldview can be glimpsed."[8] First, worldviews entail developed *stories* through which people view and understand reality. Second, worldviews adequately answer the basic *questions* that relate to human existence. Third, worldviews express the stories and answers to the questions in "cultural *symbols*," including both artifacts and events. Fourth, worldviews entail "praxis," a way of living, which necessarily involves *action*; in other words, the things that people habitually do. It is the third category which is of interest in this chapter.

In discussing symbols, he further notes that all cultures produce and maintain them (p. 123). Their primary purpose is to *express* the answers to the questions regarding identity, environment, evil and eschatology. As such, they function as "cultural *boundary-markers*," or markers to identify who is in the group and who is not. Their primary significance is found in their function of determining how members of the culture will view the world around them and the whole of reality (p. 124).

Similarly, Clifford Geertz has noted that symbols within a cultural system denote historically transmitted patterns of meaning to that culture. These symbols, then, become the means by which people "communicate, perpetuate, and develop their knowledge about and attitudes toward life."[9] Symbols, then, represent behaviors and beliefs that rise to a national level and serve as a vehicle for meaning within a culture. Within this construct, he sees symbols as synthesizing a people's worldview, or "the picture they have of the way things in sheer actuality are, their most comprehensive ideas of order."[10] Religious symbols, in particular, have the added function in society of merging a particular style of life with a particular metaphysical belief system.[11] These national symbols, at an individual level, establish powerful and long-lasting motivations in the people within the culture.

With this as a framework, it is necessary to identify the cultural symbols of ancient Israel, both from the perspective of God's design as well as Israel's corruption of those symbols. Whereas cultural anthropologists see cultures and symbols as purely representative of a certain people group's beliefs and behaviors, their insight into analyzing cultures in regard to these symbols has done much to identify the development of national values. Assuming a sovereign God, this insight grows as his original intent is compared with the people's understanding and application of the symbols he established. This is true for the whole issue of community and the resulting solidarity. While there were many factors that defined the Old Testament concept of solidarity for Israel, this study is concerned with the role played by God himself, the Mosaic Covenant, and the temple.[12]

Israel's God

The first and most important unifying factor for Israel was God himself. Israel is one people because they believe in one God. In other words, the "unity of the people corresponds to the unity of God."[13] This identity is established early on with Abraham. In Gen 12, God commanded Abraham to leave his country and go to a new one that he would show him. As part of this command, God promised to make him into a great nation, bless him and make his name great. This initial establishment of identity in God became a deeply imbedded cultural symbol that is found throughout the history of Israel. In other words, Israel was Israel because they belonged to a God who had called them in a unique way.[14]

God himself reinforced this national identity in the Exodus event. By leading Israel out of Egypt, God accomplished what had never been accomplished before and acted in a manner "never to be forgotten by the Israelites."[15] His demonstration of his power during the Exodus and later at Mt. Sinai revealed to Israel their chosen status before him from all of the other nations of the world. This created a corporate identity in which every individual Israelite found the location of their individual identity. And, as noted earlier, the Exodus event plays a significant role in understanding the concept of sanctification.

God not only reinforced this national identity; he became part of it. Israel's unity was centered in their relationship with God. "Actions by other nations which affect them are looked upon as directed against God."[16] When Israel is insulted, God is insulted (Ps 79:9–12). When Israel is attacked, God is attacked (Ezek 35). When Israel suffers at the hands of others, God is displeased.

Cry out that the sovereign LORD says, 'I am very much moved for Jerusalem and for Zion. But I am greatly displeased with the nations that take my grace for granted. I was a little displeased with them, but they have only made things worse for themselves' (Zech 1:14–15).

"He is thus a part of the corporate personality or racial solidarity which they form" (p. 204).

Israel's Law

The second unifying factor for Israel was the giving of the Mosaic Covenant. At the base of Mt. Sinai, God told Israel that if they would diligently obey him and keep his covenant, they would be his special possession out of all the nations, a kingdom of priests and a holy nation (Exod 19:5–6). While keeping the covenant required individual obedience, the context reveals that it was the nation who was partnering with God in the covenant, and to sever oneself from the community was to be cut off from the covenant and from God who made the covenant (p. 26). The covenant then becomes part of the basis for conceiving of Israel as an entity.[17]

No other nation had a god who had spoken so powerfully as to provide clear direction regarding his character and commands. "Their call to holiness was based on the fact that they had become God's possession by virtue of his separating them from the nations (Lev 20:26; Deut 7:6; 14:2; 26:19)."[18] The law unified the people. Every individual had the same interest in and obligations to the law. Since the law regulated so much of everyday life, it created a "certain conformity" among the people as a whole. Everyone was mutually responsible for seeing the law obeyed since they were blessed and punished as a group. In other words, all stood to gain or lose on how the nation, as a whole, kept the law.[19] So fundamental was the covenant to Israel's solidarity that the heart of their national unity was based on their religious beliefs.[20]

In addition, inherent within the law was the concept of justice and concern for social inequities. Justice included caring for everyone who belonged to the group. Throughout Israel's history, there was a tendency to overlook the poor. This violated the basic rules of solidarity and created a fragmented and competitive nation. As noted by Thomas Leclerc,

The task of maintaining social justice so that equity and freedom prevail is the particular responsibility of the king. Unfortunately, because it was so rarely achieved in Israel, it came to be expected as the defining quality of the eschatological king."[21]

This is consistent with Prov 29:14, "If a king judges the poor in truth, his throne will be established forever."

Isaiah strongly rebuked the leaders of Israel for overlooking the needs of the poor and oppressed (Isa 1:10–17). The hypocrisy described in this passage presents a clear contrast between religious practices and genuinely honoring the Lord and serving his people. The leaders seemed to be diligent in offering their prescribed sacrifices and observing all of the festivals and holidays (Isa 1:10–14). And yet, God was displeased with them. "When you spread out your hands in prayer, I look the other way; when you offer your many prayers, I do not listen, because your hands are covered with blood" (Isa 1:15). Why? Because they had not promoted justice. They had oppressed the poor. They had ignored the widows and orphans (Isa 1:16–17). As a result, God exhorted them to "Learn to do what is right!" (Isa 1:17).

The concept of justice carried with it a great emphasis on relationship and service.

> The one who lives uprightly and speaks honestly; the one who refuses to profit from oppressive measures and rejects a bribe; the one who does not plot violent crimes and does not seek to harm others—This is the person who will live in a secure place (Isa 33:15–16).

This included addressing social inequities and wrongs and caring for the poor and destitute. This is not something that could be accomplished by a court edict, but by personal involvement of the individuals within the nation (p. 12). And, failure of the individual meant failure of the nation as a whole.

Israel's Temple

The third unifying factor for Israel was the tabernacle, and later the temple and the ensuing cultic nature that the temple system created. As discussed earlier, the tabernacle represented the dwelling place of God, and it was significant that the tabernacle was placed in the center of Israel throughout their wanderings. This highlighted the solidarity of the people in relation to their holy God. In other words, their relationship with God was inextricably linked to the temple and to their unity such that their unity was incomplete without God.[22] How could there be an Israel without God dwelling in their midst?

Although overt in the New Testament, the concept that God's people would be a temple in which God would dwell was latent in the Old Testament.[23] Hebrews confirms that the temple was a picture of things to come; a relationship with an indwelling God. However, the idea is present in seed form in the Old Testament. The new covenant language indicates that God would put his Spirit within them (Ezek 36:27). This foreshadowing is seen a little later when God, speaking through Ezekiel, says, "My dwelling place will be with them; I will be their God, and they will be my people. Then, when my sanctuary is among them forever, the nations will know that I, the LORD, sanctify Israel" (Ezek 37:27–28).

In order to teach this basic principle, just before entering the land, God gave specific instructions concerning corporate worship. In Deut 12, God instituted a new practice wherein they were to worship God in the place he designated. They were not allowed to follow earlier customs and the customs of the surrounding nations and worship where they pleased. They were to worship in the area chosen by him.

> When you do go across the Jordan River and settle in the land that he is granting you as an inheritance, and you find respite from all your surrounding enemies and live in safety, then you must bring to the place the LORD your God will select as the place of residence for his name everything I am commanding you—your burnt offerings, sacrifices, tithes, the personal offerings you have prepared, and all your choice votive-offerings which you devote to him (Deut 12:10–11).

This introduced in Israel the concept of unified corporate worship at one location, and it became the center of the whole nation. It was in the temple that the people found God and it was from the temple that God ruled over Israel and established both national unity and religious unity. In virtually every way imaginable, the temple was the center of Israel, and thus became a predominant unifying factor for the nation.[24]

This foreshadows a later reality for the church. Accordingly, the temple was a picture designed to help the people anticipate a genuine eschatological reality and unity. It was in the temple that sin was dealt with. In addition, it was in the temple that God was worshipped and joy was expressed and experienced. Since God's throne was represented by the temple, it was seen as secure and the location from which God defeated all of Israel's enemies (Pss 46:1–7; 74:12–14; 89:6–15; 93:2–5). Finally it was in the temple that the nation experienced a corporate and relational unity not found when the nation was dispersed (p. 13–14).

Summary

In summary, the solidarity generated in Israel by God was related to God himself, the law, and the temple system. It was in the existence of all three that Israel discovered her uniqueness among the nations. It was here that the nation discovered her chosen status before God. These three seemed to define the quintessential nature of Israel as the prized possession of God. What distinguished them from the other nations was that these three were given and established by God himself. Without his direct and real involvement, the practices of the Israelites might have mimicked the other nations, that is, they would be empty and without genuine substance. With God's direct and personal involvement, the cultic center of Israel was to be life-generating and profound; a place where Israel could find God in relationship, encourage one another in relationship, and invite others into that relationship.

God's design for choosing Israel and creating this complex system and living environment also included reaching the world through Israel. This is intrinsic to his statements to Abraham in Gen 12 about blessing the entire world through him. It is reiterated by the Psalms. For example, the psalmist exclaims,

> None can compare to you among the gods, O sovereign Master! Your exploits are incomparable! All the nations, whom you created, will come and worship you, O sovereign Master. They will honor your name. For you are great and do amazing things. You alone are God (Ps 86:8–10).[25]

Again, "Sing to the LORD a new song! Sing to the LORD, all the earth! Sing to the LORD! Praise his name! Announce every day how he delivers! Tell the nations about his splendor! Tell all the nations about his amazing deeds!" (Ps 96:1–3). Finally, "The LORD reigns! Let the earth be happy! Let the many coastlands rejoice! Dark clouds surround him; equity and justice are the foundation of his throne" (Ps 97:1–2). Clearly it was God's design from the very beginning to reach the world. And, as was discussed earlier, an outward focus is a central concept in living a "sanctified" life.

In the next section, these three symbols are reviewed to see how they had developed at the time of Christ, in order to determine if corruption or misunderstanding of the symbols had occurred and if Israel was carrying out its divine design. It is evident that God designed the three symbols to unite Israel, to promote the growth of his people because they belonged to a community, and to reach the world around them as a community representing him.

Solidarity and Jesus

These three unifying factors become very important in the Gospels and in the ministry of Jesus. In assessing the worldview created through such powerful solidarity, Wright argues that Jesus intentionally attacked the specific symbols of the Second Temple Jewish worldview, both implicitly and explicitly.[26] In addition, Jesus not only attacked these symbols, but in attacking them, he redeveloped the "symbolic world" to communicate his intentions within the framework of eschatology. This is what Geertz refers to as cultural change, which requires a driving force, or some form of cultural tension. This tension usually occurs as discontinuities develop between culture ("an ordered system of meaning and of symbols, in terms of which social interaction takes place") and social structure ("the pattern of social interaction itself").[27] Thomas Overholt has further noted that cultural change involves a "local hero" standing at the key juncture where the tension is developing.[28]

This seems to be the scenario that Wright has in mind. Wright's conclusion is that Christ's redevelopment of the symbolic world was provocative and, because it laid out his announcement about the kingdom in clear terms, became the actual cause of the hostility against him. This is understandable in that any culture would rebel if their primary cultural symbols were attacked, undermined and shown to misrepresent truth.[29]

Jesus and Israel's God

Jesus redefined Israel's view of God himself. When he said to the paralytic, "Your sins are forgiven" (Matt 9:2), he was "undercutting the official system and claiming by implication to be establishing a new one in its place."[30] This is confirmed by the response of the Jewish leadership. Their charge that he was blaspheming (Matt 9:3) reveals that they understood that God alone could forgive the man's sins. Jesus' statement was a way of saying that something new was dawning in and through his work.

His command for forgiveness (Matt 18:21–22) represents a genuine view of how the law was supposed to be understood. In a related verse involving judging others, Jesus taught, "For by the standard you judge you will be judged, and the measure you use will be the measure you receive" (Matt 7:2). In addition, his consistent welcoming and feasting with "sinners" revealed his legitimate claim of deity and offer of forgiveness. Later in the section "Jesus and the Law" it will be argued that Jesus redefined the view of the law to ensure inequities were addressed and people were invited into relationship and free to experience grace.

By the time Jesus entered the scene, as discussed earlier, Israelite solidarity was rooted in the existence of God and his choosing Israel for himself. They believed in a specific God. He had made the world and was present and active within it. He was personal and not remote. Rather, he was "the maker of all that exists and remained powerful and involved within, though by no means reduced to terms of, the creation itself" (p. 101).

Wright goes on to argue that the status of being chosen prompted Israel to see God as a rescuer with a purpose in mind. Subsequent to the Exodus event, whenever they suffered at the hands of others, they looked back to the story of the Exodus to seek deliverance similar to what their forefathers had experienced (p. 102). And, as noted earlier, it was in the Exodus event that God began to ingrain the idea that he desired and would dwell in their midst, initially through the tabernacle and later through the temple.

And yet, when Jesus came onto the scene, there was no evidence that God dwelt in the temple. There was no cloud of glory evident. He had been "silent" for several hundred years. Israel was occupied by and under the control of the Roman army and Roman leadership. This led to the development of the twin ideas that God would someday return to Jerusalem and recapture the throne through the Messiah.

It is noteworthy that the extra-biblical literature, while predicting a future glory with a reigning king, did not present God as having returned in glory since the exile. In addition, the rebuilt temple under Herod was not viewed as the eschatological temple spoken of by Ezekiel. Israel's enemies had not been destroyed, nor had the eschatological kingdom been established. Israel was aware of a coming eschatological glory where God would rescue them once again and rule over them once and for all.

It was in this context that Jesus arrived. And, as noted by Wright, at the very center of his vocation, he "believed himself called to do and be in relation to Israel what, in scripture and Jewish belief, the Temple was and did" (p. 111). It was in Jesus, rather than the physical temple, that Israel's God had decided to dwell with his people. Jesus was the answer to the hope of Israel and the Old Testament promises. The problem is that they rejected him since he did not fit their eschatological profile of future events.

In this regard, the Gospels offer "new information about God's purposes, which are now advanced significantly and definitively in Jesus."[31] Jesus believed that God was in the process of judging Israel and redeeming his people. As Wright notes, "not just as one such incident among many but as the climax of Israel's history."[32] In this context, much of his judgment terminology was focused on the temple.

His presence in Jerusalem was in competition with the temple. It was at the temple that the people came to meet and worship God. Jesus' claims to be God directly interfered with the established view of God's dwelling place being in the temple. If Jesus was the perfect manifestation of God, and if he came in the true sense to live among the people as the true God, then the temple's usefulness was finished.[33]

Jesus' challenging and redeveloping their view of God ultimately involved the establishment of a "messianic community focused on Jesus himself that would replace the temple once and for all" (p. 66). In him was the offer of the New Covenant. What the Israelites were supposed to find and receive at the temple was now found in Jesus. Jesus represented the eschatological hope and fulfillment of what Israel had been longing and hoping for.

This aspect is supported by his teaching regarding the family. In a scene wherein Jesus was teaching, his mother and brothers came to find him. When Jesus was alerted that his family was outside, he looked around the room and responded with, "Here are my mother and my brothers! For whoever does the will of God is my brother and sister and mother" (Mark 3:34–35). In Israel, the basic level of solidarity involved family relationships. This statement was designed to redefine the concept of solidarity around Jesus himself. It was to be a new concept of community, one that involved family formed around Jesus. "But the way Jesus formed and celebrated this new family spoke of God's new world opening up, bringing healing and blessing wherever it went. A powerful combination in a world where power meant danger" (p. 69).

In addition, just as the Exodus event served to set Israel apart as unique, in a similar way the Christ-event set Christians apart as unique. Just as God came down and rescued and delivered his people, Jesus ushered in the New Covenant (Jer 31:31–34) and brought true redemption to his people. Just as God was moved to pass over the first-born children of Israel when they put the blood on the doorpost, so Jesus became the "Lamb of God, who takes away the sin of the world!" (John 1:29). Just as God provided the law at Mt. Sinai, so Jesus came as the Word of God (John 1:14). Just as God dwelt in their midst through the tabernacle, so Jesus becomes the incarnate representative of all that God is and represents.[34]

In redeveloping the symbolic aspects related to God himself, and ultimately dying because of it, Jesus also ushered in a new era. It is one in which the Gentiles are included. It is also one in which true solidarity is now attainable through the Spirit and the New Covenant between God and his people. It is one which at the very core involves true spiritual unity of all those who belong to the redeemed community.[35]

Although the people of God did not realize it until later, God was redeveloping their solidarity around Jesus. Whereas Israel was one precisely because they believed in one God, the church would come to realize that their oneness was based on the person and work of Christ. Just as Israel's identity was located in the uniqueness of Abraham's calling, the church's identity would be based on the uniqueness of Jesus' life and ministry. Just as the Exodus event helped create a corporate identity, so the Christ-event created a new identity in which every believer ultimately finds their individual identity. Finally, just as God himself became part of the solidarity of Israel, so Jesus would integrate himself into every fabric of Christianity.

Jesus and the Law

The law had become very important to Israel, especially during the exile when Israel did not have access to the temple system. During this time, the law and good works had replaced the sacrifices and worship found in the temple system.[36] This led to Israel valuing the law at a much deeper level than before. After the exile, the religion of Israel developed into much more of a legal system where keeping the law became the primary characteristic of belonging to the elect.[37]

It is within this context, as noted by Douglas Moo, that

> Jesus, living in the overlap between the old covenant and the new, is generally obedient to the Mosaic Law, but at the same time he makes clear that he has sovereign rights both to interpret and to set aside that Law.[38]

As such, he criticizes and denounces the Jewish leadership for their strict and unforgiving literalness in both their interpretation and application of the law to the people.

When approached by an expert in the law concerning which law was the greatest, Jesus responded with,

> The most important is: '*Listen, Israel, the Lord our God, the Lord is one. Love the Lord your God with all your heart, with all your soul, with all your mind, and with all your strength.*' The second is: '*Love your neighbor as yourself.*' There is no other commandment greater than these (Mark 12:29–31).

It was in these two commands that Jesus located the heart of the law. In addition, he "used these basic demands to interpret and apply the law in accordance with its author's intention" (p. 450).

In dealing with that aspect of the law regarding justice earlier, it was noted that a core part of the law was to promote just and right behavior. The law required that disadvantaged people be treated fairly and that everyone be granted access to God. This aspect is reinforced by Jesus' use of Lev 19:18 to show that the heart of the law included loving one's neighbor. As discussed later under the section entitled "Jesus and the Temple" it will be argued that failure in these two areas is what prompted Jesus to "cleanse" the temple.

Failure on the part of the Jewish leadership to interpret and apply the law appropriately is what led to an unhealthy corporate solidarity. While the leadership taught that the law was of central importance in life, they brought with it a legalistic dimension. "Fueling this development were two central postulates: that the Jew must obey God, and that the complete guide for that obedience is to be found in the Torah" (p. 451). It was this very commitment to the law that separated the Jews from the Gentiles and led to relational confusion and a bifurcation that was growing in intensity. By the time of Jesus, the posture toward foreigners pertaining to religious practices was more related to hostility and rejection than openness and invitation. The resulting mentality was of keeping the Gentiles out in order to remain pure and clean.[39]

Jesus also attacked the Jewish leadership regarding their handling of social inequities. As discussed earlier, maintaining solidarity through justice was a major purpose of the law. It is significant that Jesus, after reading from Isa 61 said, "Today this scripture has been fulfilled even as you heard it being read" (Luke 4:21). It is clear from his choice of Old Testament prophecies that he saw part of his ministry as setting free "those who are oppressed" (Luke 4:18). His treatment of the oppressed, widows and orphans as recorded in the Gospels reflects that he consistently acted on this understanding.

For example, speaking of the experts in the law Jesus declares that they "devour widows' property and as a show make long prayers. These men will receive a more severe punishment" (Mark 12:40; Luke 20:45–47). Immediately after that, he exalts a poor widow for her sacrificial giving (Mark 12:41–44). In another instance, upon entering a town and seeing that a widow's son had died, "he had compassion for her and said to her, 'Do not weep'" (Luke 7:13). He then healed her son. In addition, Jesus consistently had compassion on the sick and healed them. When approached by a man with leprosy who begged him to heal him he said, "'I am willing. Be clean!' And immediately the leprosy left him" (Luke 5:13).

These are representative examples of how Jesus consistently rebuked the leadership for their mishandling of the law. Since the law was highly revered in the eyes of the people, the misuse of it led people away from God's original intentions. Jesus' summing up the law in the two love commands revealed that the law was meant to be interpreted with those commands in mind. Here are clear examples of how Jesus redefined the symbol represented by the law.

In addition, the misuse of the law destroyed solidarity within Israel since there were divisions between the different classes. Allowing the existence and growth of social inequities in Israel was in clear contradiction to the law. It is no wonder that such estrangement developed between the Jews and the Gentiles (Eph 2). If the leadership had developed and employed their solidarity appropriately, it would have been enticing to the outside world. As it was, it represented corruption and, since it was being done in God's name, it ultimately tarnished his name among the nations.

Jesus' authority to challenge the Jewish leadership and clarify the intent of the law reveals part of his true purpose for coming. As noted by John he was the Word of God become flesh (John 1:14). His authority to restate and reinterpret the law reveals that he really was the perfect revelation of God in the midst of his people. He was not simply another prophet in a long line of prophets; he was The Prophet *par excellence* and, as such, represented a new dimension of how God would live in the midst of his people.[40]

Jesus and the Temple

Regarding the temple, it is almost impossible to overstate the significance of the temple system during the time of Jesus. As noted by Wright,

> The Temple was, in Jesus' day, the central symbol of Judaism, the location of Israel's most characteristic praxis, the topic of some of her most vital stories, the answer to her deepest questions, the subject of some of her most beautiful songs. And it was the place Jesus chose for his most dramatic public action.[41]

This is supported by the fact that the story of the cleansing of the temple occurs in all four Gospels.

In addition, by the time of Jesus the temple had gained enormous political as well as religious significance. The religious significance was discussed earlier and had much to do with the priesthood, sacrificial system and central location of worship for all of Israel. During the Second Temple period, this religious significance only grew as the Jews returned from deportation.

The political significance was rooted in the value that the temple system had in the eyes of the people. As noted by Wright, "If the one true and living god has deigned to dwell in this particular building, the people responsible for the building acquire great prestige" (p. 411). Control of the temple meant, in some regard, control of the people. This partly accounts for the various historical attempts to control the temple throughout the history of Israel. Protecting the temple meant gaining the favor of the people (p. 411).[42] Thus the temple served to remind the people that God promised to dwell in their midst and "legitimize" the people who ran it.

This serves as the background for Jesus' actions to cleanse the temple.[43] Jesus' actions in the temple were not primarily interested in reshaping the institution.[44] Rather, his actions were oriented toward an eschatological view of the purpose of the temple. In other words, "The time had come for God to judge the entire institution" (p. 64). The temple in the time of Jesus had come to symbolize the injustice that characterized Israel as God's people.

This is supported by his use of Isa 56:7 and Jer 7:11. The Isaiah context reveals that the temple was to be "a source of access to Yahweh for all peoples and denounces the perversion of that purpose by those who have made it 'a cave of social bandits.'"[45] The beginning of the section in Isaiah reveals that God was indicting Israel for injustice. "This is what the LORD says, 'Promote justice! Do what is right! For I am ready to deliver you; I am ready to vindicate you in public'" (Isa 56:1). In this context, Isaiah proclaims, "No foreigner who becomes a follower of the LORD should say, 'The LORD will certainly exclude me from his people'" (Isa 56:3).

The Jeremiah context reveals a similar denunciation. "You must change the way you have been living and do what is right. You must treat one another fairly" (Jer 7:5). This is the context for the following statement against Israel, "Stop oppressing foreigners who live in your land, children who have lost their fathers, and women who have lost their husbands. Stop killing innocent people in this land" (Jer 7:6). It is interesting that the Jeremiah context includes a strong judgmental aspect.

> So I will destroy this house which I have claimed as my own, this temple that you are trusting to protect you. I will destroy this place that I gave to you and your ancestors just like I destroyed Shiloh. And I will drive you out of my sight just like I drove out your relatives, the people of Israel (Jer 7:14–15).

In keeping with the prophetic warnings of the Old Testament, God would not allow the practice to continue, namely, that of treating the common people unjustly and prohibiting foreigners from having access to him. In this context, Jesus' actions in the temple were designed to bring judgment and begin the renewal process predicted in the New Covenant texts. This action by Jesus, then, represents a redefinition of the symbol of the temple and all of its related systems and purposes. It was to be a place where people had unhindered access to God. In addition, it was to be a place where people were to be treated fairly and where God would make them "happy" as they prayed to him (Isa 56:7).

Jesus' authority to challenge the Jewish leadership and cleanse the temple revealed part of the reason he had come. As noted earlier, if he came as the perfect manifestation of God, and if he came in the true sense to live among the people as the true God, then the temple's usefulness was finished. The temple no longer served as God's dwelling place.[46] He now came to dwell among his people in the person of his Son.[47]

Summary

In summary, Jesus' life on the earth was significant in redemptive history in that he attacked and redefined the specific symbols of the Second Temple Jewish worldview. The symbols considered in this study included God himself, the law and the temple. These three symbols all revolved around the actions of God earlier in Israel's history. In addition, these three symbols were given by God and represented the solidarity that was initiated by God and distorted over time. As noted earlier, Jesus redefined them in such a way so as to communicate his intentions within the framework of eschatology.

These three symbols were critical to the corporate solidarity of Israel because they were all God-given and interrelated. It was God himself who had chosen and delivered Israel through the Exodus event. It was God himself who entered into human history to form a people of his own with whom to have a relationship. It was God himself who led Israel through her various stages of life beginning as a young nation all the way to the Messiah. Finally, it was God himself who gave Israel the law and the temple.

Jesus' life and ministry significantly altered these cultural symbols. In addition, his ushering in the New Covenant provided a new spiritual basis for understanding how these symbols contribute to true solidarity. In effect, Jesus' life and teachings redefined true solidarity around himself. Regarding the first symbol—God himself—Jesus exercised authority in a variety of areas to demonstrate that he was God and that he had come to provide ultimate deliverance and dwell in the midst of his people.

Similarly, it was in the second symbol—the law—that God's desires regarding holiness and relationship were found. In a world where all of the other gods were silent, it was Israel's law that told them how to be in communion with God and with each other. It was the law that provided the framework for true solidarity through true relationship with one another oriented around a living God. Finally, it was the law that communicated how the nation was to live in harmony, moving to ensure all peoples were treated fairly and justly, and that everyone grew together in their relationship with God.

Israel's distorted view of the law is what prompted Jesus to clarify and redefine the purpose of the law. In so doing, he revealed that he himself was the perfect revelation of God—he was the very word of God—and that he had the authority to correctly interpret the law. It was in this capacity that he reoriented the law around the love commands and reemphasized the community aspect of the law.

The third symbol—the temple—represented the location where God dwelt among his people and where his people could experience relationship with him. It was in the temple that the people consistently heard the law taught. It was in the temple that the people came to meet God. It was in the temple that people celebrated their relationships with him and with each other. Finally, it was in the temple that Israel offered up their sacrifices and found forgiveness. The temple represented God living among them, thus bringing a corporate solidarity that was designed to invite the unredeemed into relationship with God. Since Jesus had come and ushered in the New Covenant, God's law was now to be written on the hearts of his people, and his Spirit was now to indwell his people personally, thus eliminating the need for the physical temple.

There are two factors regarding the solidarity of Israel and Jesus' redefinition that are significant for this study. First, the solidarity of Israel was a gift from God that carried with it the responsibility to impact the world for his glory. Solidarity establishes the environment out of which the nation was to reach the surrounding nations. The nation, by God's grace, was to accomplish together what they could not accomplish as individuals. This is evident in the language used which reveals that part of the purpose of sanctification involves an outward focus. It is also evident in Jesus' cleansing of the temple, since the temple was to be a place where people had unhindered access to God and where they were to enjoy relationship with him and each other.

Second, the solidarity of Israel was the environment in which Israel was to establish and develop their identity. Personal identity was established and individuals cared for because they were part of the nation. This was evident in the law and its role in creating conformity and structure in relationship. It was in the law that social equity was addressed. It was also in community that sin was addressed. Solidarity meant that the nation was blessed and cursed as a group.

However, Jesus' ministry on the earth surfaced another aspect of solidarity that was rooted more in personal impact. His reorienting the law around love revealed that under the New Covenant God had in view relationships that had righteous impact with one another as love was demonstrated. What was present in the law becomes clearer with Jesus' teachings and ministry. This becomes a defining characteristic that was to distinguish his people from the rest of the world.

Solidarity is a gift from God and is centered in Christ. Christ came to provide ultimate deliverance from sin and to dwell in the midst of his people. The uniqueness of Christ and belief in him is what distinguishes the redeemed from the rest of creation. Within this context, solidarity serves two distinct purposes related to progressive sanctification. First, solidarity provides the primary means by which to impact each other and the world for God's glory. The impact with each other involves growth to maturity and the impact with the world involves evangelism. It is not only the environment from which outreach occurs; it is a means as well. In other words, believers living in unity are to reflect God's glory to the world in ways not possible as individuals. The sanctification of believers is to include an outreach focus, and solidarity provides the means. Second, solidarity creates a group identity wherein individuals, while distinct from the group, develop and understand their personal identity. As discussed earlier, it is within community that progressive sanctification occurs as believers reflect God's glory to each other and help each other grow in Christ-likeness.

All three symbols come together in the person and work of Jesus. It was this redefining of these core symbols that led to his death and reshaped the way the church would come to view these three symbols. In the following chapters, the Pauline Epistles will be evaluated to understand how these redeveloped symbols become part of the basis for unity within the church and the progressive sanctification of believers.

NOTES

1 G. W. Grogan, "The Old Testament Concept of Solidarity in Hebrews," *TynBul* 49 (May 1998): 159–60. He adds the concept of inter-relatedness wherein dependency is established within relationship. This is seen in such relationships as kinship, marriage, family, clan, tribe, and ultimately nation.

2 The term "corporate personality" was coined by H. Wheeler Robinson, *Corporate Personality in Ancient Israel*, rev. ed. (Philadelphia: Fortress, 1980). His overly strong emphasis on the group at the expense of the individual has been criticized and revised. See for example, J. W. Rogerson, *Anthropology and the Old Testament* (Atlanta, GA: John Knox, 1979). Nevertheless, this field of study has revealed that the concept of solidarity was very powerful in Old Testament Israel.

3 Russell Philip Shedd, *Man in Community: A Study of St. Paul's Application of Old Testament and Early Jewish Conceptions of Human Solidarity* (Grand Rapids: Eerdmans, 1964), 3. "The derivative implications of group solidarity were important elements in Israelite life in the period of Old Testament history. There are few pages in the Chronicle of Sacred History which do not multiply the evidence of a conception of a very strong group unity."

4 C. Lattey, "Vicarious Solidarity in the Old Testament," *VT* 1 (October 1951): 269. "Solidarity itself is founded deep in human nature, so that it is dangerous to disregard it." This is evident throughout the scriptures. For example, "Judah can mean either the patriarch himself, or the tribe descended from him, or his territory." It is also evident throughout society in general. "It is in virtue of this principle that we have elective assemblies and ambassadors, and many such institutions" (p. 270).

5 Stig Hanson, *The Unity of the Church in the New Testament: Colossians and Ephesians*, ASNU, ed. A. Fridrichsen, vol. 14 (Uppsala: Almquist & Wiksells Boktryckeri, 1946; reprint, Lexington, KY: American Theological Library Association, 1963), 11.

6 Shedd, *Man*, 4. Shedd goes on to define a second major aspect of solidarity, that of continuity. "The application of the term to a group means that a nation or family, including its past, present, and future members, might function as a single individual through any one of those members conceived as a representative of it. The community was therefore conceived as an interminable continuity." This aspect is later applied by Paul to the first Adam – second Adam concept in Rom 5. From a theological and redemptive perspective, the concept is of profound significance. However, from the perspective of the role of the community in the maturing process, its significance is minimized. Therefore, no further treatment is given of the continuous aspect of solidarity.

7 "It might be declared with slight modification that the group is a mass individual living through its constituent members."

8 N. T. Wright, *Christian Origins and the Question of God*, vol. 1, *The New Testament and the People of God* (Minneapolis, MN: Fortress, 1992), 123.

9 Clifford Geertz, *The Interpretation of Cultures* (New York: Basic Books, 1973), 89.

10 Ibid. Daniel A. Helminiak, "Human Solidarity and Collective Union in Christ," *AThR* 70 (January 1988): 46. Similarly, Helminiak notes that "two humans are solidary insofar as they both embody the same meanings and values. To the extent that they have embraced the selfsame meanings and values, their concrete being, identical with those meanings and values, has become one and the same. To that extent, what they are is one."

11   Geertz, *Interpretation*, 89.

12   Other factors included their language, ancestry, worship, families, clans, and conception of humanity. The factors selected have a bearing on the discussion of the role of community in the maturing process, especially as they are developed later within the Pauline corpus.

13   Hanson, *Unity of the Church*, 11; Jeffrey H. Tigay, "Sharing Weal and Woe: Expressions of Solidarity," in *Emanuel: Studies in Hebrew Bible, Septuagint, and Dead Sea Scrolls in Honor of Emanuel Tov*, ed. Shalom M. Paul et al. (Lieden: Brill, 2003), 812–13. Tigay argues that solidarity is a dynamic concept that conceptually starts with the individual and ends with community in solidarity with God. As an example he refers to the solidarity language expressed between Ruth and Naomi where Ruth tells Naomi, "Stop urging me to abandon you and to leave you! For wherever you go, I will go. Wherever you stay, I will stay. Your people will be my people, and your God will be my God. Wherever you die, I will die and I will be buried there. The LORD will punish me severely if I do not keep my promise! Nothing but death will separate you and me" (Ruth 1:16–17). This formula is repeated in God's declarations including, "I will bless those who bless you, but the one who treats you lightly I must curse" (Gen 12:3) and "I will be an enemy to your enemies, and I will be an adversary to your adversaries" (Exod 23:22). This is what he refers to as sharing weal and woe together. This binding relationship establishes solidarity.

14   Grogan, "Solidarity in Hebrews," 162. He notes, "Israel's relation to Yahweh was not based on natural kinship as in some ancient ethnic mythologies, but on a covenant he initiated. Israel's consciousness of national solidarity became firmly based on its corporate covenant with Yahweh."

15   Hanson, *Unity of the Church*, 11.

16   Ernest Best, *One Body in Christ: A Study in the Relationship of the Church to Christ in the Epistles of the Apostle Paul* (London: SPCK, 1955), 204.

17   This lesson was learned severely with the sin of Achan. "But the Israelites disobeyed the command about the city's riches. Achan son of Carmi, son of Zabdi, son of Zerah, from the tribe of Judah, stole some of the riches. The LORD was furious with the Israelites" (Josh 7:1). Here, while one man committed the infraction, the Lord held it against the entire nation. After their initial defeat at Ai, Joshua and the leaders humbled themselves before the Lord to understand the cause for the defeat. God explained that it was because *Israel* had sinned; it was *Israel* who had violated the covenant with God (Josh 7:11). See also J. R. Porter, "Legal Aspects of Corporate Personality," *VT* 15 (July 1965): 366–67, who argues that there is a distinction between God's punitive actions to the individual and to the community. The individual is responsible for his own actions as they fall within "the regular operation of the law." In contrast, the group becomes responsible when they fail to take action for an individual who either breaks some ancient religious prohibition, or commits a sin with a "high hand" (Num 15:30).

18   Thomas E. McComiskey, "קָדַשׁ," in *TWOT*, 2:788.

19   Hanson, *Unity of the Church*, 15; Tigay, "Weal and Woe," 816. Tigay demonstrates that the Jewish conversion ceremony requires the Jewish proselyte to be warned about "present-day Jewish suffering." As part of this ceremony, the proselyte is instructed in the rewards and punishments that come from keeping the law and if conversion still is desired, the proselyte would share in the sufferings as well as the "future good fortune" of Israel. He uses Moses' invitation to Hobab as an example of this idea (pp. 822–23). As they were journeying to the Promised Land, Moses invites Hobab to join them. As part of the invitation, he promises, "Come with us and we will treat you well, for the LORD has promised good things for Israel" (Num 10:29). After Hobab refuses to go with them, Moses further states, "If you

come with us, it is certain that with whatever good things the LORD will favor us, we will treat you well" (Num 10:32).

20   Hanson, *Unity of the Church*, 22.

21   Thomas L. Leclerc, *Yahweh Is Exalted in Justice: Solidarity and Conflict in Isaiah* (Minneapolis: Fortress, 2001), 12–13.

22   "Temple," in *DBI*, 849. "No doubt the songs, fragrances, prayers and rituals surrounding a visit to the temple, the biggest structure of its kind in the ancient Near East, left an indelible impression on the senses and served as a fountainhead of religious imagery. After all, the temple was not only the worship center of Hebrew culture but also the art gallery, concert plaza and poetry library." This reiterates how strong a role the temple played in the cultural and religious center of Israel.

23   Best, *One Body*, 204.

24   Hanson, *Unity of the Church*, 12. He argues that for Israel the temple was the very center of the world. There was a strong horizontal aspect in which community occurred and people were united in worship and in the cultic rituals. It was in the temple where groups brought thank offerings to honor God for his generosity and blessing. It was in the temple that the Word of God was presented and taught. Hanson argues further that, "At the same time as the Temple is the centre on the horizontal plane, it is also the uniting bond in a vertical direction. It is the connection between heaven and earth, and is the gate to heaven."

Psalm 42 vividly portrays this idea. Here, the psalmist laments that he is unable to go up with his people to worship in the temple. This psalm reflects the solidarity felt, and missed, by the psalmist. Even though the psalmist engaged in individual worship, it was not complete without the community. The closing verse reflects that ultimate worship was found and expressed in community.

25   N. T. Wright, *What Saint Paul Really Said: Was Paul the Real Founder of Christianity?* (Grand Rapids: Eerdmans, 1997), 58. He argues that at the heart of "the 'gospel' of Paul the apostle was also a message about God, the one God of Israel, the creator of the world. It, too, was a summons to reject pagan idolatry and to turn to the true God, the source of life and all good things." This idea is present in this verse.

26   N. T. Wright, *Christian Origins and the Question of God*, vol. 2, *Jesus and the Victory of God* (Minneapolis, MN: Fortress, 1996), 369.

27   Geertz, *Interpretation*, 144.

28   Thomas Overholt, *Cultural Anthropology and the Old Testament*, GBS: Old Testament, ed. Gene M. Tucker (Minneapolis, MN: Fortress, 1996), 54.

29   Wright used the American flag as an example. In addition, one wonders how American identity would be undermined if someone seriously challenged their right to freedom of speech since it is a constitutional right and therefore has evolved into a symbol for many.

30   N. T. Wright, *The Challenge of Jesus: Rediscovering Who Jesus Was and Is* (Downers Grove, IL: InterVarsity, 1999), 65.

31   Larry W. Hurtado, "God," in *DJG*, 270.

32   Wright, *Challenge of Jesus*, 65.

33   As will be discussed later, he also fulfilled the sacrificial aspect thus eliminating the need for the physical temple.

34   While it outside the scope of this study to defend these statements, Wright is correct in drawing such tight parallels between the Exodus event and the life and ministry of Christ. Wright, *Challenge of Jesus*, 113–16.

35   This topic is examined in more detail later.

36   Paul R. Trebilco and Craig A. Evans, "Diaspora Judaism," in *DNTB*, 292. They argue that the law formed a key element in developing Jewish identity during this period of time and is one of the key factors that helped maintain Jewish solidarity as a nation.

37   Hanson, *Unity of the Church*, 14.

38   Douglas J. Moo, "Law," in *DJG*, 450.

39   Scot McKnight, "Gentiles," in *DJG*, 259. McKnight has clearly articulated the relationship between the Jews and the Gentiles in this article. He notes two basic dynamics at work in the relationship. There is evidence of resistance to Gentile ways, especially regarding religious practices and beliefs. The Jews were intent on separation, exclusion from temple worship, avoidance of intermarriage, violent reactions when Gentile reforms were imposed on them, and a strong belief that God would one day judge and punish the Gentiles.

   In contrast, he also notes friendliness toward the Gentiles, especially regarding social customs. There is evidence that they integrated themselves into Gentile ways as long as the above conditions were not present. The Jews allowed the Gentile to participate in basic levels of synagogue worship, participated in Hellenistic education and practiced intermarriage, even though they taught against it. His conclusion, however, is that "it is not the case, as much of recent scholarship has demonstrated, that Judaism as a whole can be categorized as a missionary movement."

40   Wright, *Challenge of Jesus*, 114.

41   Wright, *Jesus and the Victory of God*, 406.

42   Wright notes as an example Herod's rebuilding of the temple as part of his claim to be king of the Jews.

43   William R. Herzog, "Temple Cleansing," in *DJG*, 820. Much analysis has been done regarding the interpretation behind Jesus' actions. As noted by Herzog, the interpretations fall within four general categories. First, it was a religious event in which Jesus was attempting to cleanse the temple of commercial business. Second, it was a messianic event in which Jesus was attempting to include the Gentiles in temple life and ministry. Third, it was a prophetic event in which Jesus was announcing the "destruction of the Temple and its eschatological restoration." Fourth, it was a political event in which Jesus was attempting to disrupt commercial business activities.

44   Wright, *Challenge of Jesus*, 62–64 The idea of reshaping the institution was a common thought throughout this period of history. Wright uses as examples, Judas Maccabeus, Herod, Menahem, Simon bar-Giora, Bar-Kochba, the Essenes each of whom was somehow dissatisfied with the operation of the temple, which included the responsible parties.

45   Herzog, "Temple Cleansing," in *DJG*, 818.

46   The concept of centralized worship in Deut 12 has interesting parallels in Jesus' ministry as well. In the story of Jesus with the Samaritan woman (John 4), near the end of their conversation she says, "You people say that the place where people must worship is in Jerusalem" (John 4:20). Jesus' response directly relates to the redevelopment of the temple symbol as it impacts corporate worship. "Believe me, woman, a time is coming when you will worship the Father neither on this mountain nor in Jerusalem. You people worship what you do not

know. We worship what we know, because salvation is from the Jews. But a time is coming—and now is here—when the true worshipers will worship the Father in spirit and truth, for the Father seeks such people to be his worshipers. God is spirit, and the people who worship him must worship in spirit and truth" (John 4:21–24). Here is a foreshadowing of what was to occur under the New Covenant.

47 G. K. Beale, *The Temple and the Church's Mission: A Biblical Theology of the Dwelling Place of God*, NSBT, ed. D. A. Carson (Downers Grove, IL: InterVarsity and Apollos, 2004), 192–93. He argues that Jesus' statements about destroying the temple in John 2:14–22 "may well be a reference to his own person that had begun to replace the temple and that would be destroyed by death and then rebuilt again by resurrection. If so, his resurrection would be an escalated form of the new temple that had begun to exist in Jesus during his pre-crucifixion ministry."

CHAPTER 6

Solidarity and Progressive Sanctification in Paul

In this chapter, the Pauline corpus will be examined in order to determine the role of the community in the progressive sanctification of the individual believer. Specifically, community texts within the Pauline corpus are evaluated first against the theological considerations developed in chapters 3–5 to determine if Paul further develops the concept of solidarity as oriented in Christ and, if so, the impact it has on the relationship between the individual and the community.

Definitional Considerations

Community

For the purposes of this study, the term "community" refers to the visible church. In chapter 5, it was argued that one of the fundamental characteristics of a group is the presence of solidarity, or group identity. James Dunn notes that group identity is formed by "distinctive features" which distinguish the group from other groups.[1] Similar to Israel and the Exodus event, the Christ-event sets the church apart today. This is the fundamental event that distinguishes the church from the rest of the world.

When Jesus completed his mission on the earth he had redefined Israel's view of God, the law and the temple, thus reorienting the solidarity of the redeemed around himself and the work that he had accomplished. He was God dwelling in the midst of his people. He was also the perfect revelation of God and the one through whom the redeemed could have a personal relationship with God. What were cultural symbols for Israel—God, the law, and the temple—became a spiritual reality under the New Covenant for the church in the person and work of Christ. It is this spiritual reality which gives the church its solidarity. And it is within this spiritual reality that Christians develop their identity in Christ.[2]

When referring to the community, this study does not limit the concept to the local church. While much of what occurs regarding progressive sanctification occurs within the local church environment, it is not necessary to conclude that all aspects of progressive sanctification occur within this setting. Therefore, the community is being viewed as the broader context of Christianity.[3]

Community Text

Given the breadth of the Pauline corpus it is necessary to establish criteria by which to identify and analyze texts for impact on the present study. In chapter 5 it was argued that solidarity within the community had two resultant characteristics relevant to this study. It is these two characteristics which establish the criteria by which Pauline texts are identified as "community texts."[4]

Criterion #1. Texts are considered community texts when the context reveals that growing in Christ-likeness could only be accomplished by living and obeying the New Testament commands within community. In chapter 5 it was argued that one of the purposes of solidarity was that it creates a group identity wherein individuals, while distinct from the group, develop and understand their personal identity. It was also argued that progressive sanctification occurs within community as believers reflect God's glory to each other. As such, community is a means of progressive sanctification. Therefore, this criterion considers those texts where progressive sanctification—transformation—is accomplished within community.

Criterion #2. Texts are considered community texts when the context reveals that the outreach in view could only be accomplished by the community functioning together. In chapter 5 it was argued that one of the purposes of solidarity is to provide the primary means by which to cause growth to maturity in each other and evangelism in the world for God's glory. It is not only the environment from which outreach occurs; it is a means as well. In other words, believers are to accomplish together what they are unable to accomplish alone. The language of sanctification includes an outreach focus, and community solidarity provides the means. Since community is a means of impacting the world for God's glory, this criterion considers those texts where outreach is accomplished via community.

Solidarity and Unity

In chapter 5, solidarity was defined as "the way in which God has given human-ity in general and his people in particular a common life with common concerns and responsibilities, so that the actions of one may deeply affect others for good or ill."[5] It involves a group identity wherein the individual, while distinct from the group, locates their individual identity within the community. By indi-vidual identity, this means that the individual's value, well being, and actions are evaluated and determined by the larger group identity. The use of the term "unity" in this study implies a similar meaning, but with regard to the church living under the New Covenant.

The concept of unity begins with the union of the believer with Christ. This is the foundational position of all the redeemed. Robert P. Meye defines "union with Christ" as referring to "the extensive Pauline teaching regarding Christ dwelling in and with the believer, and the believer being in and with Christ."[6] It is union with Christ in his suffering and death and risen life, and a union with all believers who profess faith in Christ (p. 909). And true union with Christ is only possible because of his faithfulness. Just as "the destiny of the race was once decided once and for all in Adam... similarly in the Christ event the des-tiny of the new humanity is determined."[7]

However, the theological significance of believers' union with Christ is not limited to their forensic placement in or association with Christ. Conversely, it is more than relational harmony. It is perhaps helpful to see these two points— union and relational harmony—as two points on a continuum of unity. The concept of unity is more broad and multi-dimensional in nature. While it is true that unity is founded in the faithfulness of Christ and results in relational har-mony, there is another aspect needing consideration. Movement along the con-tinuum from union with Christ to relational harmony requires that the commu-nity continue to grow together into the new humanity. As such, unity in this study is as much concerned with that dimension wherein relationship is a means of progressive sanctification; a catalyst for transformation and outreach.

This dimension is best captured by Paul's use of ἑνότης in Eph 4:3.[8] In this passage, the concept of preserving unity is fundamentally at the center of living a worthy life (Eph 4:1).[9] Although discussed in greater detail later, here is an example of a text that meets criterion 1. Obeying the command in Eph 4:1 can only be accomplished in community. From a definitional perspective, the foren-sic aspect of union with Christ is represented by the series of "ones" in Eph 4:4–6. However, the concept of unity is more complex than this. The catalytic affect is seen in the examples throughout the remainder of Ephesians. Regard-ing this aspect, Ethelbert Stauffer argues, "Since, however, the Church is to

bring unity to men, its own unity is a paramount consideration."[10] The maintenance of unity is directly related to how we impact each other in relationship.

This dimension of unity captures the essence of solidarity as defined earlier.
This is especially made clear in Ephesians. God's giving his people a common
life is at the center of the theology of Ephesians. This life is founded upon the
work of Christ and is lived out in the life of the Spirit who creates unity. As another example, having common concerns and responsibilities is captured by the
discussion of the gifts (Eph 4:7–16) with the conclusion, "As each one does its
part, the body grows in love" (Eph 4:16). As a final example, an individual
deeply affecting others within the group for good or ill is illustrated by Paul's
reference to those who steal and those who destroy unity with improper speech
(Eph 4:28–29). These examples are all discussed in detail later.

Therefore, the concept of unity used in this study is closely related to solidarity and refers to the catalytic effect of Christians working together and caus-
ing growth to maturity in each other, including both transformation and outreach. It is assumed that union Christ is accomplished based on the work of
Christ and relational harmony is the result of this impact within community.

Solidarity and Progressive Sanctification

In this section, the concept of solidarity discussed in chapter 5 will be analyzed
in the Pauline Epistles to identify what role it plays in the progressive sanctification of believers. In chapter 5 it was proposed that the solidarity of Israel as
originally defined by the cultural symbols of God himself, the law, and the temple system was redefined by Christ as part of the inauguration of the New
Covenant to create a true spiritual unity of all the redeemed. And just as the
individual Israelite experienced solidarity with the larger group oriented around
these symbols, Christ revealed that true spiritual unity was also to be found in
the larger group of the redeemed. However, in order for this to occur it was
necessary for the cultural boundary markers to be understood in their truest
sense, namely, as a spiritual reality centered in Christ to which these tangible
markers of the Mosaic Covenant pointed.

What originated with Israel, and was redefined through the life and ministry
of Christ, comes to fruition in Paul. Although the people of God did not realize
it at the time of Jesus, God was redefining their solidarity around Jesus. But it
was a solidarity that generated true spiritual unity anchored in Christ. In other
words, just as God himself became part of the solidarity of Israel, so Jesus
would integrate himself into the very fabric of Christianity. The following discussion reveals that there are several aspects of that unity in Paul that are in
continuity with and expand the Old Testament concepts.

The Messiah

Whereas Israel was one precisely because they believed in one God, the church would come to realize that their oneness was based on the uniqueness of the person and work of Christ. This is emphasized throughout the Pauline corpus and is one of the central truths in Paul's theology.[11] And, as was argued in chapter 4, Christ is the image of God. He represents in all respects what believers are becoming in the transformation process. He is the perfect human that is in the process of creating the new humanity to which all believers belong. In addition to the passages considered in chapter 4, the following are examples that express the uniqueness of Christ as it relates to the unity of believers and the new humanity.

Christ is the true Passover (1 Cor 10). Here, the uniqueness of Christ and solidarity of the new corporate identity is seen in Paul's use of the Exodus terminology. The repeated use of πᾶς throughout this section reveals that Paul has the community in mind. This is further supported by his distinguishing those who had disobeyed from the larger whole (1 Cor 10:5).[12] Within this context, Paul identifies the rock from which the Israelites drank as Christ (1 Cor 10:4). He is presented as the one foreshadowed by the Exodus event. In this way, Paul emphasizes the work of Christ and the communion meal and how it relates to the Passover (1 Cor 10:14–22).[13] Paul concludes his Exodus-Passover imagery by relating the uniqueness of Christ to the establishment of the community with "Because there is one bread, we who are many are one body, for we all share the one bread" (1 Cor 10:17).

In the middle of this context Paul illustrates the significance of the solidarity of the church with pictures of disobedience from the Exodus wanderings (1 Cor 10:5–10).[14] He looks back on the golden bull sin (Exod 32), the immorality with the Moabite women (Num 25), the impatience of Israel as they traveled around Edom (Num 21), and the rebellion led by Korah (Num 16). In each of these examples the community was punished because they failed to take action and live holy lives.

Similarly, in each case the sin was stopped by the actions of others in the community. In the case of the golden bull, it was Moses' intervention that led the Lord not to destroy the entire nation (Exod 32:11–32). In the case of the unfaithfulness with the Moabite women, it was Phinehas who executed the Israelite man and the Moabite woman and stopped the plague (Num 25:6–8). In the case of the grumbling Israelites, it was Moses who made the bronze snake and intervened on behalf of the people so that they did not die (Num 21:9). In the case of the rebellion led by Korah, it was Moses' and Aaron's intervention that led the Lord not to destroy the nation (Num 16:20–35). In each case, those who intervened were joined by other faithful Israelites in their stance against the sin. The consistent pattern is that the nation was affected both by the actions of those few who sinned and those few who stood against the sin.

Paul applies this to the Corinthian problem when he says, "These things happened to them as examples and were written for our instruction, on whom the ends of the ages have come" (1 Cor 10:11). Paul's warning seems to be that the sin of a few in the Corinthian church and the failure of the community to deal with the sin would have consequences for the community at-large.[15]

He reinforces his point with his exhortation, "So let the one who thinks he is standing be careful that he does not fall" (ὥστε ὁ δοκῶν ἑστάναι βλεπέτω μὴ πέσῃ) (1 Cor 10:12). Here the singular substantival participle and verb reveal that Paul has individuals, versus the community, in view. In the very next verse he returns to a plural object—a community view—when he says,

> No trial has overtaken you (ὑμᾶς) that is not faced by others. And God is faithful: he will not let you (ὑμᾶς) be tried too much, but with the trial will also provide a way through it so that you may be able to endure (1 Cor 10:13).

The point he seems to be making corresponds with his use of the Exodus examples, namely, one person's sin is a community trial with community ramifications. And the community can be assured that God is faithful to help them work through the trial. This reinforces his warning that failure of the community to deal with the sin of a few would have consequences for the entire community. Here Paul makes it clear that the maintenance of unity is a community function.[16]

The emphasis on Christ appears again in the communion text involving the sharing in the blood and body of Christ (1 Cor 11:23–26). It was the broken body of Christ that established the spiritual body and it was the blood of Christ that instituted the New Covenant with that spiritual body. This is why Paul says with some incredulity, "For in the first place, when you come together as a church I hear there are divisions among you, and in part I believe it" (1 Cor 11:18). The uniqueness surrounding the death of Christ is what enables Paul to present the communion experience as an exercise in unity with Christ and with each other.[17] It symbolizes the partnership that believers have with Christ and one another. It also symbolizes sanctification which clearly has ongoing aspects within the community. That is why communion is shared in community on an ongoing basis.[18]

Christ is the true Adam (Rom 5). The uniqueness of Christ as it relates to solidarity is addressed in Rom 5:12–21 (1 Cor 15:20–22). Here, the Adam-Christ comparison sets the stage for emphasizing the uniqueness of Christ as well as the corporate solidarity that resulted from his person and work. Paul argues that solidarity was established with Adam regarding humanity, sin and death.[19] And in this context, Israel's experience with the law, sin and death in some way becomes a paradigm for humanity as a whole.[20] What was experienced in Adam becomes a reality with Israel and, thus, with humanity as a whole.

In contrast, using the argument from the lesser to the greater, Paul emphasizes the uniqueness of Christ over Adam,

> But the gracious gift is not like the transgression. For if the many died through the transgression of the one man, how much more did the grace of God and the gift by the grace of the one man Jesus Christ multiply to the many! (Rom 5:15).

Again, "For if, by the transgression of the one man, death reigned through the one, how much more will those who receive the abundance of grace and of the gift of righteousness reign in life through the one, Jesus Christ!" (Rom 5:17). Just as God established and became part of the solidarity of Israel, so Jesus established and became part of the unity of the redeemed.

In chapter 4 it was argued from 1 Cor 15 that Adam and Christ become archetypes which represent corporate life before Christ and corporate life in Christ. Here, Paul develops in greater detail this fundamental truth. Whereas Adam denotes the old humanity, Christ denotes the new humanity. While Paul is attesting to the historical existence and actions of Adam and Christ, his main theological point seems more related to their typological function within God's redemptive plan.[21] Adam and Christ represent the two orders of sin and death, and life and righteousness, to which all people belong. And the "one" and the "many" imagery reinforces this sense of association—solidarity with one of the two figures and the associated community.

For Paul, the conclusion is that Christ accomplished for the redeemed what they could not accomplish on their own.[22] It was through the obedience of Christ that righteousness came and life was made possible for humanity (Rom 5:18–19). And in so doing, he established a new corporate order to which all believers belong. Set in the context of the totality of sin, Paul uses this line of argument to demonstrate the uniqueness of Christ, and for those who believe in Christ, the reality of corporate solidarity.[23]

Christ is the true sacrificial servant (Phil 2). One of the clearest passages in the New Testament relating the uniqueness of Christ to unity is Phil 2:5–11. It is the unique example of Christ which reveals that genuine unity begins with the sacrifice of Christ for humanity through his death and exaltation. For Paul, this becomes the *par excellence* example of how unity is maintained in the church—by serving one another and putting one another first (Phil 2:1–4). In Philippians, the reverse is also true; unity is not possible without serving one another and putting one another first. And yet, even though this passage is oriented toward unity in relationships, the centrality of Christ shines forth. While there is much debate as to the background and source of this passage, the exalted person and work of Christ is central to its significance in the argument.[24]

N. T. Wright has argued persuasively that Paul's christology in Philippians emphasis community life in the present. He bases this on the combination of the christological hymn and the emphasis on heavenly citizenship (Phil 3:20). Earlier commentators saw the concept of citizenship as primarily oriented in heaven. As such, the emphasis was on a future destiny, even though they saw a present aspect.[25] In contrast, Wright orients the passage around Paul's and the Philippian Christians' understanding of the role of Caesar and their relationship with him. Citizens of Rome were not living in anticipation of an ultimate trip to Rome. Rather, what they expected was "the emperor to come *from* Rome to deliver them from any local difficulties they might be having."[26]

In this context, Paul's strong exaltation language (Phil 2:9–11) was designed to help the Philippian Christians understand that it was Jesus who was Lord and not Caesar, and it was Jesus who was exalted and therefore currently in power. As such, this passage "positively shouts that it is Jesus, not Caesar, who holds power over all things" (p. 232). If Wright is correct, then Paul is teaching that the Philippians—and by extension, all believers—as citizens of heaven (Phil 3:20), could rightfully expect Christ to be powerful and present among them in the present age. While this does not eliminate the "not yet" aspect of Paul's "already-not yet" eschatological thinking, it orients the emphasis of the christological hymn to the present life in Christ.

This forms the basis for Paul's statement that "our citizenship is in heaven" (Phil 3:20). Since believers are citizens of heaven currently, it is the ministry and example of Christ which serves as the primary example by which all believers are to live in the present life. This example is to be incarnated in the lives of the individuals within community as a tangible expression of what it means to live worthily (Phil 1:27).[27] Wright argues further that

> the aim had been, all along, as in Genesis 1, that this [present community life under the reigning Messiah] should be put into operation through the agency of the image-bearing human race. Paul sees this plan fulfilled in Jesus, and now to be completed through Jesus' people sharing his glory, reflecting God's image in the same way.[28]

Therefore, in a tangible way, it is within this community expression, oriented around the death and exaltation of Christ that believers find their present as well as their eschatological identity, and it is the maintenance of unity and righteous living that form the basis for this expression.

Christ is the true image of God (Col 1). Another great christological passage that relates the uniqueness of Christ to the new humanity is Col 1:15–20.

Dunn argues for a series of parallels in this passage that express Paul's theology as follows:[29]

Col 1:15–17	Col 1:18–20
ὅς ἐστιν εἰκὼν τοῦ θοῦ	ὅς ἐστιν ἀρχή
He is the image of God	He is the head
πρωτότοκος πάσης κτίσεως	πρωτότοκος ἐκ τῶν νεκρῶν
the firstborn…all creation	the firstborn… among the dead
ἐν αὐτῷ ἐκτίσθη τὰ πάντα	ἐν αὐτῷ εὐδόκησεν πᾶν τὸ πλήρωμα κατοικῆσαι
all things… created by him	God was pleased… to have all his fullness dwell in the Son
τὰ πάντα δι' αὐτοῦ καὶ εἰς αὐτὸν ἔκτισται τὰ πάντα ἐν αὐτῷ συνέστηκεν	δι' αὐτοῦ ἀποκαταλλάξαι τὰ πάντα εἰς αὐτόν
all things… created through him… held together in him	to reconcile all things to himself

For Dunn, this construction is parallel with 1 Cor 15:45 and, therefore, represents an example of Adam christology—a balance between the old creation and the new creation. It reveals that through Christ, God brought into existence the "eschatological form of humankind equivalent to the original humankind" (p. 275).[30] As the true image of God, he represents what the new humanity is becoming. Wright agrees and notes that the form of the poem reflects a fulfillment of the original creation in anticipation of the creation of the new humanity. Jesus' death and resurrection function as the "moment of the new exodus, of the 'return' from the long exile of sin and death, of the overthrow of all the powers that enslaved the world, and those who now belong to the Messiah share the benefits of all this."[31] This forms the background for Paul's conclusion that all things are reconciled in Christ (Col 1:20).

Then Paul immediately presents a picture of the new humanity in Christ when he says, "But now he has reconciled you by his physical body through death to present you holy, without blemish, and blameless before him—if indeed you remain firm in the faith, without shifting from the hope of the gospel that you heard" (Col 1:22–23). In this passage, the tension between the "already" and the "not yet" regarding the new humanity surfaces in the combination of the aorist indicative ἀποκατήλλαξεν[32] with the conditional εἴ γε. The use of the aorist here is best classified as a constative aorist. Paul is emphasizing the *fact* of their reconciliation as accomplished without regard to the process.[33] Peter O'Brien explains, "Like the dying and rising with Christ motif, the verb in the indicative is used to denote the decisive transfer of the believers from the old aeon to the new which has taken place in the death of Christ."[34] Paul here is presenting the "already" aspect. And the purpose of this reconciliation relates to believers' future standing before Christ.[35]

The use of the purpose infinitive παραστῆσαι is significant in that it shifts the focus of the passage to the current process—what the new humanity is becoming in Christ. "The purpose of God's work of reconciling the readers through Christ's death was that they should be irreproachable when they finally stand before him."[36] In this regard, the successful conclusion to the process is envisioned with the use of the first class conditional sentence in verse 23. In other words, the presentation at the end entails remaining firm in the faith in the present. Although the statement is conditional, the use of the first class condition reveals that Paul has in mind their successful completion of the process and heightens the responsibility of the community[37] to remain faithful.[38] The progressive aspect of sanctification is strong in this passage, and it is directly related to the centrality of Christ and his reconciling work in the community.[39] In summary, as argued earlier, not only did Christ generate solidarity in himself, he essentially became part of it through his work.

Summary

In the four passages reviewed in this section the uniqueness of Christ is highlighted, albeit each from a different aspect. In 1 Cor 10 Christ is presented from an Exodus-Passover perspective in the communion meal. In this passage Christ, the true Passover and leader of the Exodus, is the one who created the new body. In Rom 5 Christ is presented using the Adam-Christ analogy. In this passage he is presented as the head of a new order to which all believers belong— one to which they have been transferred based on the faithfulness of Christ. In Phil 2 Christ is presented as a sacrificial servant who generates true unity within the community as the community engages in service to one another. In Col 2 Christ, the true image of God, is presented as the one in whom the new creation is established. As such, his reconciling work leads to the progressive sanctification of the new humanity and eventual presentation of the community as blameless before him.

In light of these passages, the solidarity of the community is based on the uniqueness of the person and work of Christ. He is the true human and the one who has created the new humanity. Not only did he generate true solidarity; he became part of it through his work. And his dynamic involvement with the community generates true spiritual unity wherein believers are engaged with each other in the transformation process.

The Word

In Israel the giving of the law was a key part of the history of creating solidarity since it separated them from the other nations. In addition, it revealed God's love for his people in that he provided instruction on how to live in relationship with him and each other. As such, it generated a "commonness" among the people in their lives and relationships including social equity. In chapter 5 it was argued that Israel's distorted view of the law is what prompted Jesus to clarify and redefine the purpose of the law. In so doing, he revealed that he himself was the perfect revelation of God and the fulfillment of the law. As such he had the authority to interpret the law correctly. It was in this capacity that he reoriented the law around the love commands and reemphasized that solidarity is now found in the church. In addition to the passages considered in chapter 5, the following passages reveal that Paul further argues for the fulfillment of the law in Christ and the corresponding redevelopment of the law around the love commands and the resulting new solidarity.

The law is fulfilled in Christ (Rom 10). In order to understand the Word of God symbol in Romans as it relates to Christ, it is necessary to begin with Paul's treatment of the law. The emphasis on the law is very extensive in Romans.[40] For Paul the law plays a predominant role in understanding salvation history and has several facets that relate to the current study.[41] To begin, the law plays a significant role in exposing and identifying sin. As such, it provides the measure of divine judgment. This is evident in the following passages: "For *no one is declared righteous before him* by the works of the law, for through the law comes the knowledge of sin" (Rom 3:20); and, "For the law brings wrath, because where there is no law there is no transgression either" (Rom 4:15).

Implicit in this idea is the fact that the law was a universal standard for judgment. This is seen in such passages as,

> For whenever the Gentiles, who do not have the law, do by nature the things required by the law, these who do not have the law are a law to themselves. They show that the work of the law is written in their hearts (Rom 2:14–15).

And yet, while the law may have had universal application, even for Paul the law was first and foremost the Mosaic Law.[42] It was the Jews who had the privilege of receiving the law (Rom 3:2). And it was the Jews whose unbelief resulted in the abuse of the law (Rom 3:3). It was in this context that Christ came and re-developed an accurate view of the law as fulfilled in himself.

The emphases on Christ and the law come together when Paul states, "For Christ is the end of the law, with the result that there is righteousness for every-one who believes" (Rom 10:4). As was concluded in chapter 5, Jesus located the heart of the law in the dual commands to love God and love people. For Paul, the concept of the law is expanded and goes beyond love. It finds its ultimate consummation in Christ. In Rom 10:5 he states, "For Moses writes about the righteousness that is by the law: *'The one who does these things will live by them.'*" In this section, Paul explains that Israel's rejection, in contrast to the Gentiles' sal-vation, was the result of both misunderstanding and misapplication of the law as well as their transgression of the law.[43] They deceived themselves into think-ing that the righteousness of God was to be pursued by works, rather than through faith (Rom 9:30–32). Had they correctly understood their privileged position as due to God's sovereign choice (Rom 9:1–29), they might not have pursued righteousness through their works (Rom 10:3). This seems to be the reason that Christ became a stumbling block.[44] As a result, their faith was placed in their works, rather than in God! This is, perhaps, the reason Paul cites Deut 9:4 in Rom 10:6; he was reminding them of God's previous warning on the plains of Moab *not* to say that they had achieved victory because of their own righteousness.

Having just explained that the Israelites had stumbled over the stumbling stone (Rom 9:32–33), and their misunderstanding of the law had led them to seek their own righteousness, Paul now comes to the startling conclusion that "they did not submit to God's righteousness" (Rom 10:3b). He is, in effect, say-ing that they did not submit to the person and work of Christ! This conclusion is a pivotal point in the argument. Throughout the entire letter he has been de-veloping the idea that Christ is the revealed righteousness of God. He further supports this conclusion by showing that Christ is the "end of the law" (Rom 10:4).[45] Israel had failed to recognize the true significance of Christ and his rela-tionship to the law, namely, everything about the law pointed to him and his work. If Christ, in this sense, is the goal of the law, it then follows that right-eousness is available to everyone who believes.[46]

As was concluded earlier, the law served to explain how Israel was to live in a covenant relationship with God and each other. In this regard, the law had a strong community justice aspect.[47] Keeping the law enhanced community life. Conversely, disobedience brought punishment or death. Paul's reorienting Deut 30:11–14 from the law to Christ (Rom 10:5–8) reveals that in Christ is found the true meaning and fulfillment of the law.

In addition, the New Covenant aspect comes into view when Paul concludes with quotations from Isa 28:16 (Rom 10: 11) and Joel 2:32 (Rom 10:13). He has just argued that the true meaning of the law is found in Christ. He then concludes that in Christ is found salvation (Rom 10:9–10). It is as this point that he returns to Isa 28:16. Earlier he referred to Isa 8:14 and 28:16 to argue the point that Israel's misunderstanding of their position led them to stumble over Christ (Rom 9:33). Now he uses this same reference from Isa 28:16 to demonstrate that those who look to Christ, rather than the law, find salvation.

Similarly, his use of Joel 2:32 closes out this portion of his argument by stating two related points. First, the context of Joel 2:32 reveals a New Covenant orientation, and it is within this theological framework that Paul is emphasizing the universal availability of salvation.[48] His use of the Old Testament passage reveals that it was God's intention all along to reach the world, and it would ultimately be accomplished in Christ. Second, in the Old Testament, the one on whom people called for salvation was Yahweh. Paul's use of Joel 2:32 identifies Christ with Yahweh, since the divine name occurs in the Joel citation. This informs Rom 10:9 in that the confession in view is "Jesus is Yahweh."[49] Redefining the law under the New Covenant in terms of Christ forms the basis for the identity of the redeemed community. In other words, just as the law formed part of the basis for corporate solidarity under the Old Covenant, Christ, as the fulfillment of the law, forms the basis for corporate identity under the New Covenant in Romans.

The law is obeyed by loving others (Rom 4, 8, and 13). In spite of the Jews' unbelief and abuse of the law, the giving of the law was a cause of rejoicing for Israel since, in a world where the gods were silent, the law was a blessing that was designed to have far-reaching impact in Israel and the rest of the world. As was argued earlier, Jesus' reinterpretation of the law around the love commands reveals that part of God's plan was for his people to be known as those who love one another. This logic seems to lie behind Paul's argument in Rom 4 (and Gal 3). In both passages Paul brings Abraham into the discussion to demonstrate that God's plan from the beginning was to bless the entire world. "And the scripture, foreseeing that God would justify the Gentiles by faith, proclaimed the gospel to Abraham ahead of time, saying, '*All the nations will be blessed in you.*'" (Gal 3:8; cf. Rom 4:13).[50] The Jews' failure to believe and act on this principle seems to be a major point of contention in Paul.

If the law was designed to "watch over," or be a "guardian" over Israel, perhaps it was in the sense of protectiveness and oversight (Gal 3:23–25).[51] If so, then the law was given as a benefit to Israel. As discussed in chapter 5 this benefit was related partly to the establishment of solidarity and relationship with a living God and each other. And yet, Gal 3:23–24 makes it clear that the role of the law was valid only until the coming of faith and the Messiah. In other words, it was temporary. With the coming of Christ, a new era dawned in eschatological and redemptive history. The law should have prepared the Israelites for this transition. "Instead they were concentrating too much on the law" and continued to assume that they "enjoyed a favoured nation status before God."[52] As such, the Jewish leadership abused the law concerning their own people and the rest of the world. When Christ came, they refused to embrace him and, instead, clung to the law.

It was in this context that Jesus located the heart of the law in the dual commands to love God and love people. For Paul, the concept of the law is expanded and goes beyond love. It finds its ultimate consummation in Christ and obedience reveals a redeemed relationship with Christ. This linkage surfaces when Paul says,

> For God achieved what the law could not do because it was weakened through the flesh. By sending his own Son in the likeness of sinful flesh and concerning sin, he condemned sin in the flesh, so that the righteous requirement of the law may be fulfilled in us, who do not walk according to the flesh but according to the Spirit (Rom 8:3–4).

The "righteous requirement" may very well be related to Jesus' emphasis on love as the heart of the law.[53] Colin Kruse argues that "what the law cannot do, Paul implies, is to bring to fulfillment its own just requirement in the lives of those who lived under the law."[54] C. E. B. Cranfield further argues that "the fault was not in the law but in men's fallen nature."[55] Douglas Moo links these concepts together and notes that what the law demanded was perfect obedience and, since Christ is the only one who perfectly obeyed the law, he is the one who fulfilled the demand of the law. As a result, the demand of the law is fulfilled in believers, "not through their own acts of obedience but through their incorporation into Christ."[56]

This sets the stage for Paul's later statement,

> The one who loves his neighbor has fulfilled the law. For the commandments, '*do not commit adultery, do not murder, do not steal, do not covet,*' (and if there is any other commandment) are summed up in this, '*Love your neighbor as yourself.*' Love does no wrong to a neighbor. Therefore love is the fulfillment of the law" (Rom 13:8–10).

Romans 8 and 13 come together in that fulfillment of the law is found in loving one another. And yet, the fulfillment is not achieved by obedience, as Rom 8:3–4 make clear. On the contrary, it is the work of Christ that makes possible what God had intended all along, that redeemed people love one another and reach out to the world around them for his glory.

Solidarity is redefined in Christ (1 Cor 5). Kruse argues that the law in the Corinthian Epistles is being used analogically. It serves as a "paradigm for

Christian behavior" demonstrating ways in which Christians are to relate to God and to each other.[57] For example, the law is used to demonstrate how the community is to live in purity (1 Cor 5:6–13). In this passage, Paul exhorts the Corinthian believers to deal with a man within the church who is involved in an incestuous relationship (1 Cor 5:1). And, rather than generating sorrow, which should lead to discipline, it has instead generated pride within the community (1 Cor 5:2–3). In this situation, Paul has two primary concerns in view. First, the community is to take action against the man as a catalyst for his own good. In 1 Cor 5:4–5, he says,

> When you gather together in the name of our Lord Jesus, and I am with you in spirit, along with the power of our Lord Jesus, turn this man over to Satan for the destruction of the flesh, so that his spirit may be saved in the day of the Lord.

Here is an example of how the community is to move catalytically in the life of one of its members.[58]

Second, Paul argues that since Christ is the true Passover Lamb who has been sacrificed, the community is to celebrate the festival with the new bread without yeast, which he refers to as "the bread of sincerity and truth" (1 Cor 5:8). It seems that Paul's primary concern here, as illustrated by the analogy of the bread and the yeast, is the maintenance of unity. Here is a New Testament example of how unhealthy solidarity can promote injustice and toleration of sin and how active involvement by the community is necessary to maintain spiritual unity.

Within this context he uses the law as an example to demonstrate that true unity entails maintaining purity within the group. And, maintaining purity involves dealing with sin and ultimately removing the sinning person from the group (1 Cor 5:13; Deut 17:7; 19:19; 22:21, 24; 24:7).[59] In the case of immorality, the community was to judge those inside the church and remove them.[60] This use of the law redefined the concept of solidarity. True solidarity is now found with those in the church, rather than with those of one's race.[61] It is spiritually based, rather than genealogically based. And judgment is to occur within the community to ensure solidarity is maintained.

Summary

In the passages reviewed in this section the redefinition of the law as it relates to solidarity was reviewed. In Rom 10:6–8, Paul, using Deut 30:11–14, reoriented the law to Christ to illustrate that Christ is the fulfillment of the law. As such, just as God used the law to create a corporate solidarity within Israel under the Old Covenant, Christ's fulfilling the law forms the basis for the new corporate solidarity under the New Covenant—a solidarity centered in himself. In Rom 4, 8 and 13, Paul argues that the law was to be obeyed and that the expression of that obedience involves love—to those within the community as well as outside of the community. This was God's intent all along, as confirmed by Christ's reorienting the law around the love commands. In this regard, love is the fulfillment of the law. However, the obedience required of the law is not possible because of sin. It was only in the death of Christ that the requirement for perfect obedience was accomplished. The result is that it is now possible to love others and thus reflect God's glory—the true meaning behind the law. In 1 Cor 5 the law is used to explain how to maintain unity. As such true solidarity is found in the believing community, rather than in one's race or genealogy, and true unity is maintained by maintaining purity within the group.

In light of these passages, the solidarity of the community is established on the fulfillment of the law in and by Christ. Because of Christ's work, the community is now enabled to carry out the true intent of the law—love that moves others toward salvation or progressive sanctification. The law thus captures the catalytic effect wherein the community, through obedience, maintains true spiritual unity.

The Spiritual Temple

In the history of Israel, the temple played a major role in establishing and maintaining the identity of the nation and the individuals within the nation. It was significant primarily because it represented God's dwelling place among his people—it was the place where the nation came to meet God in order to learn, worship, offer sacrifices and receive forgiveness. Unlike any other nation, God lived among his people and they were to make this known to the nations so that those who did not know God could come and meet him.

Jesus' incarnation effectively ended the role of the physical temple since he came as God who dwells among his people. In addition, his cleansing of the temple effectively judged the temple system and what it had become. This had the effect of replacing one of the key cultural symbols defining the solidarity of Israel with himself. And with his death and inauguration of the New Covenant, this important symbol took on even greater spiritual significance. In addition to the passages considered in chapter 5, the following are examples of how this symbol developed in the teaching of Paul and its relationship to progressive sanctification.

The Holy Spirit dwells in the spiritual temple—the community of God (1 Cor 3 and 6). The emphasis on the spiritual temple is clear in 1 Cor 3:16 where Paul states, "Do you not know that you are God's temple and that God's Spirit lives in you?"[62] In a context dealing with divisions in the Corinthian church, Paul begins by exhorting them because he could not speak to them as believers who are mature. The reason is because there was jealousy and dissension within the church (1 Cor 3:3). He goes on to discuss the importance of building the church in a unified manner with believers involved and depending on God "who causes the growth" (1 Cor 3:7). His concern is that believers together build carefully by laying a solid and lasting foundation. The reason is that the work done will be tested in the end and, therefore, it should be built with lasting quality.[63] It is in this context that he reminds them that they are God's temple and God's Spirit lives within them. This statement communicates several points in Paul's argument related to the present study.

First, building unity starts with the individual. Using temple imagery, Paul reveals an aspect of unity in which each member is involved.[64] While the emphasis is on the Spirit dwelling in the whole congregation, the sturdiness of the building is the responsibility of each individual.[65] This is clear from the emphasis on the individual in the surrounding contexts. Individuals are charged with building correctly (1 Cor 3:12–15) and individuals are warned against destroying the temple (1 Cor 3:17).

And yet, Paul's point is that they are individuals within community, having impact within community. This is evident by his arguing for individual responsibility within the community context. There is jealousy and dissension within the community (1 Cor 3:3). It is the community that is God's field and building (1 Cor 3:9). It is at this point that Paul shifts the imagery to a building, which he later identifies as the spiritual temple.[66]

Second, building the spiritual temple involves generating and maintaining unity. The introduction of the building metaphor leads to the second point, namely, it is a community responsibility to build the spiritual temple. He begins by arguing that, while he laid the foundation, each member is building upon the foundation.[67] His exhortation is to build properly, knowing that their work will be tested (1 Cor 3:10–15). The metaphors used to emphasize the quality of the building reveal the basic contrast that he has been making all along (gold, silver, precious stones, wood, hay, or straw). Once he identifies that these will be tested with fire, it becomes immediately obvious that these metaphors are divided into two groups: those that will withstand the fire (gold, silver, precious metals) and those that will be burned up (wood, hay, straw). "Thus the argument continues to be a frontal attack against the division and those primarily responsible for it" (p. 136). His point seems to be that each member contributes to building the temple and any member can create destruction (1 Cor 3:17). This is reminiscent of the language in 1 Pet 2:4–5 where Peter presents the image of a spiritual house that is in the process of being constructed.[68]

At the center of this building process is development and maintenance of unity. Earlier he had said, "The one who plants and the one who waters are united" (1 Cor 3:8). And yet, he seems to be saying that the divisions are present because of the immaturity with which they were relating with one another. Here, unity is pictured as based in the work of the Holy Spirit as well as interrelationships within the church.

Later in 1 Corinthians Paul states, "Or do you not know that your body is the temple of the Holy Spirit in you, whom you have from God, and you are not your own?" (1 Cor 6:19). In this passage, Paul is still dealing with the issue of unity. However, here he approaches it from the individual aspect and demonstrates that what happens at the individual level impacts relationships and, therefore, community.[69] It is clear that he is referring to the individual since he references each one's individual body. He takes the concept of union and applies it at the most personal level—a sexual encounter between two people. In this context he asks, "Do you not know that your bodies are members of Christ? Should I take the members of Christ and make them members of a prostitute? Never!" (1 Cor 6:15). In a similar way, the one who is immoral with a prostitute establishes union with the prostitute, rather than Christ (1 Cor 6:16–17).[70] This forms the basis for his command to "flee sexual immorality!" (1 Cor 6:18). Why? Because this destroys the unity of the church.

In both of these passages, the continuum of unity discussed earlier is apparent. At one level, Paul is arguing that they have basic union with either Christ or a prostitute. And yet, he is saying much more. The movement from union to relational harmony requires relational involvement with each other for good rather than evil. His point is that divisions and prostitution both have the opposite impact—they destroy true unity.

In both passages there is necessary movement from the individual to the community. Failure to take this to the community level misses the main point. Paul is expecting the individual believers to take his exhortation to heart and respond faithfully in obedience since the growth of the spiritual temple and corresponding unity within the group depends on it. His point is that individual relationships, whether inside or outside of the church, affect the unity of the community. He is more concerned with how relationships and faithfulness impact the community rather than the individual. And the context of these series of examples reveals that the community plays a vital role in helping the individuals live lives that reinforce this unity.

Third, the purpose of the spiritual temple is to reflect God's glory. His final point is that the Holy Spirit lives within the community which is the temple of God (1 Cor 3:16). God had earlier promised as part of the New Covenant to put his Spirit within his people (Ezek 36:26). With Paul's statement that the

Holy Spirit lives within God's people, he is affirming the fulfillment of that promise. And just as God's presence among the Israelites set them apart as a holy people, so God's Spirit dwelling among the Christian community sets them apart as holy. As noted by Gordon Fee, "The Spirit is the key, the crucial reality, for life in the new age. The presence of the Spirit, and that *alone*, marks them off as God's new people, his temple, in Corinth."[71]

In both passages above, it is clear that Paul has ownership in view. In chapter 3 it was argued that holiness implies ownership since God is the only one who can declare something holy. As Fee notes,

> Even though the body is 'one's own,' it is more properly God's since it is a temple of the Spirit and has been purchased through redemption. Thus the unique nature of sexual sin is not so much that one sins against one's own self, but against one's own body as *viewed in terms of its place in redemptive history.* (p. 263)

This is evidenced through the indwelling Spirit and the redemptive work of Christ and leads to Paul's question, "Or do you not know that your body is the temple of the Holy Spirit in you, whom you have from God, and you are not your own?" (1 Cor 6:19). The ownership aspect of holiness discussed in chapter 3 surfaces here. Since God has declared the believer holy, this infers ownership. And as with Israel, it is God's presence in the temple—the church—that is the central feature that establishes separateness and, therefore, solidarity.

Paul's final command in 1 Cor 6:20 is, "Therefore glorify God with your body." Concerning this verse, G. K. Beale argues that

> just as the Old Testament temple was to be kept clean from defilement, how much more so are they to keep their bodies clean and separate from immorality (6:18). In line with the purpose of the Old Testament temple, which was to house and show forth God's glory, Paul commands them to 'glorify God in your body' (6:20). Just as God's glory uniquely dwelt in Israel's old temple, so the glorious attributes of God are to be manifested in the Corinthians both individually and corporately, since they are the new temple.[72]

The connection between God's declaring one holy and the responsibility to reflect that glory has previously been established. This is at the center of progressive sanctification and Paul here reveals that it is the necessary conclusion to the declaration of holiness and the indwelling of God in community. What is explicit in 1 Cor 6:20 is implicit in 1 Cor 3:17 when Paul says, "For God's temple is holy, which is what you are." The implication is, because God has declared the temple holy, the community is responsible to build the temple in such a way as to reflect that holiness.

The community—the spiritual temple—is growing together in the Lord (Eph 2). In Ephesians, immediately after introducing the uniqueness of

Christ and how his work forms the basis for the new redeemed people of God (Eph 2:11–19), Paul introduces the redefined symbol of the temple when he says,

> You have been built on the foundation of the apostles and prophets, with Christ Jesus himself as the cornerstone. In him the whole building, being joined together, grows into a holy temple in the Lord, in whom you also are being built together into a dwelling place of God in the Spirit (Eph 2:20–22).

There are several principles in this passage related to the community and progressive sanctification.

First, the spiritual temple reveals the redeemed as the people of God. The emphasis in the temple imagery is on the people of God as a community rather than as individuals.[73] This is argued contextually as well as intrinsically. The primary point Paul has been arguing is the creation of the new humanity. Whereas the Gentiles formerly were without God and separated from the promises related to Israel, they have been "brought near" by the work of Christ (Eph 2:11–13).

The work that Christ did to accomplish this was to remove the barrier that separated the Jews and the Gentiles. He did this by rendering inoperative the commandments contained in the decrees (Eph 2:14–15). The barrier that separated the Jews and the Gentiles is important in this passage. At issue is the meaning of τὸ μεσότοιχον τοῦ φραγμοῦ. Following O'Brien, the barrier refers to "the outward expression of the Mosaic commandments."[74] Harold W. Hoehner argues similarly and notes that the context gives an example of the law creating hostility between the two groups, namely, the issue of the law of circumcision (Eph 2:11).[75] Paul is arguing that the barrier, of which circumcision is an example, has been removed in Christ.

Another important issue is the meaning of καταργέω, and how the barrier was removed. He removed this barrier by nullifying "the law of commandments in decrees" (Eph 2:15). Gerhard Delling argues that it means "to make completely inoperative."[76] This is consistent with the redefinition by Christ and expansion by Paul of the symbol of the law discussed earlier. Christ's fulfillment of the law brought the law to an end (Rom 10:4). And since this formed the basis for the barrier and hostility, making it inoperative allowed for reconciliation between the two groups.

Paul then argues that Christ accomplished this reconciliation by way of the cross, "He did this to create in himself one new man out of two, thus making peace, and to reconcile them both in one body to God through the cross, by which the hostility has been killed" (Eph 2:15–16). By fulfilling the law, he removed the barrier and hostility. By dying on the cross, he effected reconciliation. The result is peace between the two groups and the establishment of the new humanity—the church.

This establishes the context for Paul's statement, "In him the whole building, being joined together, grows into a holy temple in the Lord, in whom you also are being built together into a dwelling place of God in the Spirit" (Eph 2:21). Paul carries the community idea into this passage with the use of the temple imagery and the plural verbs and pronouns. The emphasis here is on the people of God as community rather than as individuals. Here is an example of a community text that meets criterion 1—it can only be fulfilled in community.

Second, the spiritual temple is the new dwelling place of God. This is consistent with the earlier discussion of 1 Cor 3:16 and 6:19. What was true of Israel has now become true of the new humanity—God lives in the midst of his people, thus distinguishing them from the rest of the world. Of particular interest is Paul's use of the term κατοικητήριον to describe the new spiritual temple as God's "dwelling place." This is the only occurrence in Paul.[77]

However, it is used in the LXX to refer to God's heavenly dwelling place. In Exod 15:17, in the Song of Moses, God is pictured as having a particular dwelling place, a sanctuary which he has made with his own hands. It is to this dwelling place that he will lead his redeemed. In 2 Chr 6:30; 30:27 and 1 Kgs 8:39, God is pictured as hearing the prayers of Israel and responding to them from his dwelling place in heaven. Psalm 32:13–14 declares, "The LORD watches from heaven; he sees all people. From the place where he lives he looks carefully at all the earth's inhabitants."

In the Eph 2 passage the dwelling place of God is pictured as the new spiritual temple. And yet the heavenly aspect is strong in Ephesians as well. In Eph 1:3, Paul says, "Blessed is the God and Father of our Lord Jesus Christ, who has blessed us with every spiritual blessing in the heavenly realms in Christ." His repeated usage of ἐπουρανίοις communicates the heavenly aspect that he has in mind.[78] In Eph 1:3, the spiritual blessings are linked with the heavenly realms. O'Brien argues that this is to be understood "within a Pauline eschatological perspective."[79] In the "already-not yet" Pauline scheme, it is not simply a future event, but a present reality for the church which is inextricably bound up with salvation history.

In Eph 1:20, Paul reveals that it is God's power which has instituted the blessings, including the resurrection of Jesus. Here, Paul reveals that Jesus has been exalted to God's dwelling place. The allusions to Ps 110 are striking and reveal a continued eschatological focus.[80] Christ's claims regarding Ps 110 as future (Matt 26:64; Mark 12:36; Luke 20:41–44) are regarded by Paul here as a present reality. In other words, "The Son's being seated by the Father points to the completion of his God-given task; his earthly mission was accomplished."[81]

In Eph 2:6, Paul pictures believers *already seated* with Christ in the heavenly realms. Continuing the eschatological scheme, this is remarkable since it links the entire community together—those who have come before, those who are now living, and those yet to live. This sets the contextual stage for Paul's statements about the creation of the new humanity, and reveals that the new humanity is the redeemed community in Christ.

In Eph 3:10, Paul reveals that the purpose of the disclosure of the mystery—Gentiles as fellow-members with the Jews in the new humanity (Eph 3:6)—is to display the wisdom of God to the rulers and authorities in the heavenly realms.[82] Paul's argument here demonstrates that the church's role is significant in displaying God's wisdom and that the true scene is being carried out in the heavenly realms.[83] The community's purpose in God's eschatological scheme is a present reality.

In Eph 6:12, Paul reveals that the true spiritual battle is against the rulers and authorities in the heavenly realms. With this verse the linkage in Ephesians is completed. The blessings of God are generated by his power—the same power that raised Christ and exalted him. Believers presently share in that resurrection and exaltation for the purpose of glorifying God by displaying his wisdom. Finally, because believers "have been identified with Christ in his resurrection and exaltation, they, too, have a position of superiority and authority over the evil powers."[84]

In the context of this heavenly eschatological theme, Eph 2:22 represents a climax in the flow of Paul's argument. Not only is the community being built into the dwelling place of God, but the community includes the Gentiles—a previously unrevealed "divine secret" (Eph 3:6). What was pictured in the Old Testament—a future outlook wherein God's people would join him—has become a present reality in Paul's eschatology. God has created and indwelt the new humanity.

Third, the spiritual temple is being built progressively. Even though the creation of the new humanity is a present reality, there is still a progressive aspect. This is revealed by the present tense verb αὔξει (Eph 2:21), indicating that "the building is still under construction" (p. 219). The present tense is best classified as a progressive present which, in this case, is emphasizing the action as it is occurring.[85] Paul is highlighting the aspect of growth, and this growth takes at least two forms. First, the temple itself is growing in size and quantity as believers are added.

Second, the temple is growing into a *holy* temple. Hoehner argues that the present passive participle συναρμολογουμένη is functioning as a participle of means, explaining how the growth of the community grows into a holy temple. "Specifically, as recipients of God's grace, [believers] grow by being carefully fitted together rather than growing apart individually from another."[86] Lexically, this is supported by the basic definition of the word. Christian Maurer argues that the basic meaning in Ephesians is related to the "inner relationship of the community and also the relationship between the community and Christ."[87]

O'Brien notes that this is "another way of saying that the new community of God is growing and progressing to its ultimate goal of holiness, an objective that is not simply personal or individual but in the present context must be corporate as well."[88] Here the progressive aspect of sanctification surfaces. Earlier it was argued that holiness is a definitive declaration by God and that progressive sanctification entails transformation into the image of Christ wherein believers grow in their capacity for reflecting God's glory. This is consistent with the context here and in the only other passage that συναρμολογέω occurs (Eph 4:16).

In Eph 4:16, Paul says, "From him the whole body grows, fitted and held together through every supporting ligament. As each one does its part, the body grows in love." The combination of αὔξανω and συναρμολογέω reveal that Paul is expanding on the process of the growth of the spiritual temple in Eph 2:21. The progressive aspect is strong in this passage. It is evident in the use of the terminology from Eph 2:21. It is also evident in the metaphors used to describe the result—"a mature person, attaining to the measure of Christ's full stature" (Eph 4:13). In chapter 4 it was argued that Christ is the image of God and, as such, reflects his glory to the creation. The "full stature" (ἡλικία) of Christ includes the concept of image and glory. At its core meaning is the idea of "mature age or full physical maturity"[89] which fits well with the concept of the community growing into maturity (Eph 4:13). As Hoehner states, "As the church is filled by Christ, so is the stature of the church filled by him."[90] Similarly, F. F. Bruce concludes, "The glorified Christ provides the standard at which his people are to aim."[91]

The process of the church "growing up" to maturity will continue until the community attains to the unity of the faith and of the knowledge of the Son of God—the definition of maturity. This is what it means to grow into a holy temple, the dwelling place of God (Eph 2:21–22). And this explains Paul's benediction where he praises God who works abundantly in the church. It is in the church and in Christ that God is glorified (Eph 3:20–21). As the community grows together into the holy temple, they reflect God's glory.

Fourth, the spiritual temple provides the identity for believers. The identity aspect is captured by Paul when he says, "So then you are no longer foreigners and non-citizens, but you are fellow citizens with the saints and members of God's household" (Eph 2:19). Identity, as defined earlier, relates to the individual's value, well being, and actions, which are evaluated and determined by the larger group identity. When an individual enters into the church, their value, well being, and actions all change. This causes a change in identity. The individual ceases to be an individual in a godless society. Rather, Paul's point is that they now belong to a community where they have significance—they are part of a "building project" wherein each one is has an important role to play for the success of the project.

Here the solidarity aspects discussed earlier surface. Just as Israel located her solidarity partly in the temple system, so the church finds its solidarity similarly based in the spiritual temple. And, "as the body matures unity results."[92] Individuals find a new identity in Christ which is discovered in community as believers function together as the holy temple and God's dwelling place.[93]

Summary

In the three passages discussed in this section (1 Cor 3, 6; Eph 2) the redefinition of the spiritual temple as it relates to solidarity was reviewed and several principles identified. Just as the temple played a dominant role in establishing the solidarity of Israel, it also plays a dominant role in establishing solidarity within the new humanity. At the center of understanding the significance of the spiritual temple is the fact that God dwells among his people. This indicates that the redeemed are indeed the people of God and are presently enjoying relationship with him and each other. The eschatological promises surrounding God's people being with him are already realized in the form of the spiritual temple.

As such, there are several facets which relate to progressive sanctification. First, the spiritual temple provides identity for believers. When they enter the spiritual temple, their values, well being, and actions are changed and redefined to conform to a community life of holiness. Second, it is the community's responsibility to build the spiritual temple. This is a process which involves growing in holiness and living in community in such a way as to generate and maintain unity. Every individual within the community has a role to play in this process. Finally, the spiritual temple is to reflect God's glory. Since God has declared the redeemed holy, this implies ownership and carries the necessary responsibility to live holy lives. It is in the living of holy lives within community that God's glory is reflected to creation.

In light of these passages, the solidarity of the community is established in the presence of the spiritual temple and the community's involvement in building this temple. Because of the Spirit's indwelling the temple, the community can experience true spiritual unity with God and each other, and they can live holy lives so as to impact the world and each other for God's glory.

Paul develops the Old Testament concept of solidarity further in the form of unity. What is significant for Paul is that the individual is unable to experience this unity in isolation. Rather, the individual can only genuinely understand and experience this unity as they live and obey the biblical commands within community. Further, for Paul, the concept of the individual's identity in Christ can only be properly understood within the context of community.

The expression of this idea is captured by the uniquely Pauline ἐν Χριστῷ terminology. A review of recent Pauline works reveals that this phrase has engendered much discussion in Pauline studies.[94] While it is outside the scope of the present study to articulate precisely the various nuances behind this language, it is significant that it plays a dominant role in many of the passages presented herein. Of particular interest is its application to the body life concept. Mark Seifrid has argued that "it is not derived from or limited to a 'corporate' idea" and that there are legitimate reasons to "argue against supposing that the idea of an organic reality lies behind his usage." However, he readily admits that the variety of uses in the Pauline corpus suggests that it is a "flexible idiom" in Paul's thought.[95]

While there is no question of its objective use to describe the believer's position as being "in Christ" and Christ's work to accomplish this, there is also an ethical implication in the use of the phrase. In this regard it is often tied to behavior and character (p. 436).[96] While Seifrid may be correct in stating that the phrase itself does not intrinsically require a corporate idea, its consistent use in the context of corporate ideas creates an image that is pertinent to this study. Its richness is found in the concept of locating the identity of the believer in the person and work of Christ. When this concept is used in the community texts it reveals a commonality—a spiritual reality—that all believers share. It is participation in Christ *together as community* that is strongly emphasized in Pauline theology.[97] And these concepts are inseparable. It is in community that identity in Christ becomes a reality. And, without community, many of these same texts are impossible to obey. It is within this construct that the essentiality of the community surfaces.

Further, in Pauline theology the role of the Messiah, the law, and the temple are integrated into the larger concept of unity and participation in Christ. And the participation presented by Paul has much more in view than simple individual participation. There is a very strong community element wherein true unity, although initiated with the individual, finds its necessary immediate consummation within community and its ultimate consummation within the new person—the new humanity.

Paul's development of the solidarity argument is found in the combining of the ἐν Χριστῷ concepts with the role of the Messiah, the temple system, and the law (p. 396).[98] This solidarity forms the basis for the identity of the individual believer. Dunn rightly states, "Paul's perception of his whole life as a Christian, its source, its identity, and its responsibilities, could be summed up in these [ἐν Χριστῷ] phrases."[99] However, he goes on to say that the church would be remiss if they failed to speak of the "community which understood itself not only from the gospel which had called it into existence, but also from the shared experience of Christ, which bonded them as one" (p. 401).

In summary, all three symbols—the Messiah, the law, and the temple—come together in the person and ministry of Jesus. Paul understood this as he viewed these symbols from a christological perspective. It is these three symbols, operating together, that form the basis for unity within the church. It is the work of the Spirit in the community that makes possible the growth to maturity and impact in the world as the community together represents the Lord. This forms the basis for the remainder of Paul's teaching involving the community.

NOTES

1   James D. G. Dunn, *The Theology of Paul the Apostle* (Grand Rapids: Eerdmans, 1998), 536.

2   See Ibid., 533–64, for a thorough development of these ideas.

3   See Stanley J. Grenz, *Theology for the Community of God* (Grand Rapids: Eerdmans, 1994), 603–631, for an introduction to this discussion.

4   The use of the term "community text" is not meant to imply that Paul has developed a theology of community. Since the Pauline Epistles were written to churches, they are all in a sense "community" oriented. Rather, the term is being used to differentiate which texts meet the identified criteria and were reviewed in the present study.

5   G. W. Grogan, "The Old Testament Concept of Solidarity in Hebrews," *TynBul* 49 (May 1998): 159–60.

6   Robert P. Meye, "Spirituality," in *DPL*, 908.

7   Ethelbert Stauffer, "εἷς," in *TDNT*, 2:439.

8   BDAG, "ἑνότης," 338, defines it as, "a state of oneness or of being in harmony and accord, *unity.*"

9   D. Martyn Lloyd-Jones, *Christian Unity: An Exposition of Ephesians 4:1–16* (Grand Rapids: Baker, 1980), 35, argues that this is the first "particular" that Paul deals with because this is the central theme in Eph 1–3.

10   Stauffer, "εἷς," in *TDNT*, 2:440. Stauffer has rightly captured the concept of unity on the continuum of union to relational harmony. Along the continuum, between the forensic aspect of union and the resultant relational harmony, there is necessarily impact in each other's lives and in the world. He argues further, "Like every divine reality, however, [unity] is attained in the Church only to the degree that the Church takes this reality seriously in faith, thought *and action*" (p. 440; italics mine). Harold W. Hoehner, *Ephesians: An Exegetical Commentary* (Grand Rapids: Baker, 2002), 512; Peter T. O'Brien, *The Letter to the Ephesians,*

Pillar New Testament Commentary, ed. D. A. Carson (Grand Rapids: Eerdmans and Apollos, 1999), 279–80. Both Hoehner and O'Brien point out that the unity in view has already been established by the Spirit. As a result, the nature of the imperative is to maintain this previously established unity. O'Brien goes on to argue, "To *keep* this unity must mean to maintain it *visibly*. If the unity is real, it must be transparently evident, and believers have a responsibility before God to make sure that this is so" (p. 280). See also, Andrew T. Lincoln, *Ephesians*, WBC, ed. David A. Hubbard and Glenn W. Barker, vol. 42 (Dallas, TX: Word, 1990), 235, who argues similarly.

11   Ben Witherington III, "Christ," in *DPL*, 99; Ralph P. Martin, "Center of Paul's Theology," in *DPL*, 93.

12   Note the use of πολύς (1 Cor 10:5) to separate the disobedient.

13   Note the linguistic and conceptual linkage with 1 Cor 5:6–8 where Christ is clearly called our Passover.

14   C. K. Barrett, *A Commentary on the First Epistle to the Corinthians*, BNTC, ed. Henry Chadwick (London: Adam & Charles Black, 1968; reprint, Peabody, MA: Hendrickson, 1987), 219–20. Just as Israel failed to take God seriously during the Exodus, so the Corinthian church failed to take God seriously as well. Their security was perhaps in the rites of baptism and the communion meal. Thus Paul can make a direct connection between the Israelite experience of disobedience and unbelief and the similar experience of the Corinthians.

15   Note the result of the abuse of the communion meal in 1 Corinthians 11:30. Ben Witherington III, *Conflict and Community*, 448, ties these examples to 1 Cor 10:4 and the reference to Christ and argues that "the Israelites had the same sort of benefit as Christians do, even benefits from Christ himself, and even this did not secure them against perishing… and losing out." See also, Anthony C. Thiselton, *The First Epistle to the Corinthians*, NIGTC, ed. I. Howard Marshall and Donald A. Hagner (Grand Rapids and Cambridge: Eerdmans, 2000), 727–30.

16   Hans Conzelmann, *1 Corinthians: A Commentary on the First Epistle to the Corinthians*, trans. James W. Leitch, Hermeneia, ed. George W. MacRae (Philadelphia: Fortress, 1975), 168–69. It is interesting that, while Conzelmann argues that the context of the passage is more significant than "individual improprieties" and includes the whole community, he fails to carry this thought to verse 13. See a similar pattern in F. W. Grosheide, *Commentary on the First Epistle to the Corinthians: The English Text with Introduction, Exposition and Notes*, NICNT, ed. Ned B. Stonehouse (Grand Rapids: Eerdmans, 1953), 226–28. In contrast, Marion Soards retains the community aspect when he says that the church needs "to know, and to act on the one ultimate assurance that is their real security: God is faithful." Marion L. Soards, *1 Corinthians*, New International Biblical Commentary, ed. W. Ward Gasque (Peabody, MA: Hendrickson, 1999), 205.

17   Stig Hanson, *The Unity of the Church in the New Testament: Colossians and Ephesians*, ASNU, ed. A. Fridrichsen, vol. 14 (Uppsala: Almquist & Wiskells Boktryckeri, 1946; reprint, Lexington, KY: American Theological Library Association, 1963), 90–91; Dunn, *Theology of Paul*, 537–43. Dunn argues that the term ἐκκλησίας τοῦ θεοῦ (1 Cor 11:22; cf. 1 Cor 1:1; 10:32; 15:9; 2 Cor 1:1) is drawn "directly from Israel's self-identity" (p. 537). As such this term is technical and depicts "the little assemblies of Christian believers as equally manifestations of and in direct continuity with 'the assembly of Yahweh,' 'the assembly of Israel'" (p. 538). For Dunn, this represents a redefinition of the corporate identity of the church as the "people of God." And, it is within this redefinition that the individual believers locate their identity; their "distinctive features which both identify them and mark them out from others" (p. 536). Thus he can conclude, "It was not as isolated individuals that believers func-

tioned as 'the church of God' for Paul. Rather, it was only as a gathering, for worship and for mutual support, that they could function as 'the assembly of God'" (p. 542).

18   While communion emphasizes more of the community aspect, baptism is more individually oriented in its actual practice and is done only once. In this regard, it is representative of the justification of the believer which results in entrance into the redeemed community. Thus it is a public action witnessed by others symbolizing initiation into the new humanity.

19   This brief analysis is in no way meant to diminish the theological significance of this complex passage. Rather, it is necessary to establish that corporate solidarity has been accomplished between Christ and the believing community with the follow-up question as to how that impacts the community and the process of sanctification. For further discussion of the Adam-Christ imagery and all that is involved, see Dunn, *Theology of Paul*, 79–101; Douglas J. Moo, *The Epistle to the Romans*, NICNT, ed. Gordon D. Fee (Grand Rapids: Eerdmans, 1996), 314–50; John Murray, *The Epistle to the Romans*, vol. 1, NICNT, ed. F. F. Bruce (Grand Rapids: Eerdmans, 1965), 178–210; Herman Ridderbos, *Paul: An Outline of His Theology*, trans. John Richard de Witt (Kampen, The Netherlands: JH Kok, 1966; reprint, Grand Rapids: Eerdmans, 1975), 93–100.

20   Dunn, *Theology of Paul*, 94–97; Moo, *Romans*, 329–34.

21   Larry J. Kreitzer, "Adam and Christ," in *DPL*, 11.

22   C. K. Barrett, *On Paul: Aspects of His Life, Work and Influence in the Early Church* (London: T&T Clark, 2003), 59. He refers to this as the "paradoxical answer" to the "paradoxical question" of how God could be righteous and yet "fail to inflict suffering on the whole of universally guilty humanity."

23   Dunn, *Theology of Paul*, 101. In addressing the totality of sin, he states, "Humankind in the world is not just weak and corruptible. There is an inescapable dimension of sin, of failure and transgression, also involved. Humans were created for relationship with God, a relationship which is the essence of human life, a relationship which gives humankind fulfillment of being, as creature (in relation to God) and as human (in relation to the rest of the world)."

24   For a discussion of the various views, see Peter T. O'Brien, *The Epistle to the Philippians: A Commentary on the Greek Text*, NIGTC, ed. I. Howard Marshall and W. Ward Gasque (Grand Rapids: Eerdmans, 1991), 186–98.

25   N. T. Wright, *Christian Origins and the Question of God*, vol. 3, *The Resurrection of the Son of God* (Minneapolis, MN: Fortress, 2003), 229, notes, "Countless readers have assumed that what Paul means in 3.20 is that, being 'citizens of heaven', Christians look forward to the time when they will return and live there for ever." Note, for example, Marvin R. Vincent, *A Critical and Exegetical Commentary on the Epistles to the Philippians and to Philemon*, ICC, ed. Charles Augustus Briggs, Samuel Rolles Driver, and Alfred Plummer (New York: Charles Scribner's Sons, 1906), 119, who, even though he argues for a present reality with the use of the present tense ὑπάρχει, concludes, "The consummation of this citizenship, however, is yet to come. As members of the heavenly commonwealth they are still pressing on in obedience to the upward call (vs. 14). Hence they are in an attitude of expectation." For Vincent, the "expectation" to which he is referring is the ultimate resurrection of the believer and deliverance to heaven.

26   Wright, *Resurrection*, 230. He further argues that this concept is especially true for Philippi, which was a Roman colony. "Indeed, the colonists of Philippi a century before Paul's day had been placed there precisely because nobody wanted them back in Rome, or even Italy" (p. 230).

27 Compare the use of ἡμῶν γὰρ τὸ πολίτευμα ἐν οὐρανοῖς (Phil 3:20) with μόνον ἀξίως
    τοῦ εὐαγγελίου τοῦ Χριστοῦ πολιτεύεσθε (Phil 1:27). O'Brien, *Philippians*, 458–63, ar-
    gues that the heavenly aspect "is a present reality and determines their ongoing existence as
    they live in the world." This already-not yet aspect allows the community orientation to sur-
    face in clear imagery. The redeemed belong to an eschatological community. In this passage
    this is captured by the use of πολίτευμα, which emphasizes the commonwealth, or com-
    munity aspect. See Dunn, *Theology of Paul*, 328, who argues that this is a metaphor which
    communicates "enjoying citizenship, or community membership." Andrew T. Lincoln,
    Paradise Now and Not Yet: Studies in the Role of the Heavenly Dimension in Paul's Thought with Spe-
    cial Reference to His Eschatology, SNTSMS, ed. R. McL. Wilson and M. E. Thrall, vol. 43
    (Cambridge: Cambridge University Press, 1981), 99, argues that this term carries a dynamic
    force emphasizing "the state as a constitutive force regulating its citizens." As such, it ori-
    ents the believer's existence to a heavenly community that is a present reality with future
    consummation. This is further supported by his use of πολιτεύεσθε (Phil 1:27), which cer-
    tainly carries a behavioral nuance. For Lincoln, this allows for a "dual allegiance" in which
    the heavenly community is the determinative orientation that regulates present life within
    community. According to Hermann Strathmann, "πόλις," in *TDNT*, 6:535, it describes
    membership in the heavenly kingdom and includes the responsibilities of that status. In-
    deed, the catalytic effect discussed earlier is present here as well since the ministry of Christ,
    which is the primary example, was catalytic in that it effected redemption and community.

28 Wright, *Resurrection*, 232. The concept of Christ as the image of God in this passage and,
    therefore, an example of what the redeemed are becoming is assumed by Wright. In con-
    trast, both Dunn, *Theology of Paul*, 284, and O'Brien, *Philippians*, 263 argue this point explic-
    itly. In the references cited, they both note that μορφή and εἰχών are synonymous terms.
    Dunn further argues that it was probably literary considerations that moved Paul to use the
    former since it "made the appropriate parallel and contrast with 'form of a slave'" (p. 284).
    Christ as the image of God in this passage reveals what the new humanity are becoming as
    they are transformed.

29 Dunn, *Theology of Paul*, 275.

30 He further argues that this represents a "new movement both for Christ and for the new
    humanity he both represented and brought about" (p. 276).

31 Wright, *Resurrection*, 239.

32 This is true no matter which reading is taken on the text critical issue with this word. As
    noted by Peter T. O'Brien, *Colossians, Philemon*, WBC, ed. David A. Hubbard, Glenn W.
    Barker, and Ralph P. Martin, vol. 44 (Waco, TX: Word, 1982), 67, "The general sense is
    clear and on either reading it is plain."

33 Buist M. Fanning, *Verbal Aspect in New Testament Greek*, Oxford Theological Monographs,
    ed. J. Barton et al (Oxford: Clarendon, 1990), 256.

34 O'Brien, *Colossians, Philemon*, 67.

35 Although the point in time in view is not specifically identified here, it is made clear in 1
    Cor 1:8 where the Corinthian believers will be found blameless "on the day of our Lord Je-
    sus Christ."

36 O'Brien, *Colossians, Philemon*, 68.

37 The emphasis on the community is captured by the use of the plural verbs and pronouns
    throughout this section. In one sense this is common in Paul's letters since he is writing to
    various churches. And yet, this supports the primary thesis of this study. As will be argued

later, the use of plural verbs and nouns are frequently found in texts that meet one of the two criteria established earlier. This implies that Paul consistently had the community in mind in a functional sense rather than just a literary device because he was addressing groups of people. In addition, in this letter, the emphasis on community is also supported by the purpose of the letter. Responding effectively to heresy is a community exercise.

38 Daniel B. Wallace, *Greek Grammar Beyond the Basics* (Grand Rapids: Zondervan, 1996), 682–90. The best classification for this is probably cause-effect, although it would be interesting to explore the possible ramifications of inference-evidence classification—if believers are standing firm, this serves as evidence that they will be presented as blameless. However, this is outside the scope of this study. See also, O'Brien, *Colossians, Philemon*, 69, who states, "So the words in this sentence may be paraphrased: 'At any rate if you stand firm in the faith—and I am sure that you will.'"

39 This sets the stage for Paul's statement in Col 1:28, "We proclaim him by instructing and teaching all people with all wisdom so that we may present [ἵνα παραστήσωμεν] every person mature in Christ."

40 Of the 121 uses of νόμος in the Pauline epistles, 74 occur in Romans.

41 Dunn, *Theology of Paul*, 128–50. The following distinctions are taken from Dunn's argument in order to set the stage for understanding Christ's relationship with the law in Pauline thought.

42 Moo, *Romans*, 145, states, "For Paul, the converted Jew, the 'law' refers, unless other qualifications are present, to this specific, historical body of commandments that functioned, more than anything else, to give Israel its particular identity as a 'people apart.'"

43 Note the progression οὐ κατ᾽ ἐπίγνωσιν (vs. 2b), followed by ἀγνοοῦντες (vs. 3). This failure to understand the law correctly naturally led to misapplication of the law (καὶ τὴν ἰδίαν δικαιοσύνην ζητοῦντες – vs. 3).

44 Note his citation of Isa 8:14 in 9:33. Moo, *Romans*, 628, argues, "On the one hand, Paul argues that Israel missed Christ, the culmination of the plan of God, because she has focused too narrowly on the law… On the other hand, Israel's failure to perceive in Christ the end and goal of the path she has been walking leads her to continue on that path after it had served its purpose."

N. T. Wright, *What Saint Paul Really Said: Was Paul of Tarsus the Real Founder of Christianity?* (Grand Rapids: Eerdmans, 1997), 108. Similarly, Wright argues that "Israel… is ignorant of what God has righteously and faithfully been doing in her history. In seeking to establish a status of righteousness, of covenant membership, which will be for Jews and Jews only, she has not submitted to God's righteousness. The covenant always envisaged a worldwide family; Israel, clinging to her own special status as the covenant-bearer, has betrayed the purpose for which that covenant was made."

The point is that, in some sense, Israel's misunderstanding of their privileged position led them to overlook Christ and the climax of salvation history such that he became an obstacle.

45 BDAG, "τέλος," 998–99. Much discussion has gone into the meaning of τέλος. It can carry the sense of termination, cessation, end, goal, conclusion, or outcome. By seeing it as "termination," many have come to the conclusion that the end of the law has been effected by the coming of Christ. See James M. Stifler, *The Epistle to the Romans: A Commentary Logical and Historical* (New York: Fleming H. Revell, 1897; reprint, Chicago: Moody, 1960), 174; Murray, *Romans*, 2:49–51.

However, earlier Paul made the case that the law ceased to have binding force, not because of the death of Christ, but because of the death of the person *in Christ* (Rom 7:1–6). The death of the person in Christ freed the believer from the restraint of the law. Therefore, it seems awkward, here, to link the misunderstanding of the Jews with Christ terminating the law. This seems to be antithetical to the contrast being drawn between faith in Christ and confidence in one's own righteousness as expressed by works. For excellent discussions and summaries, see Mark A. Seifrid, "Paul's Approach to the Old Testament in Rom 10:6–8," *TJ* 6 (spring 1985): 6–10.

Therefore, it seems best to see this as Christ is "the goal, the aim, the intention, the real meaning and substance of the law—apart from Him it cannot be properly understood at all." C. E. B. Cranfield, *The Epistle to the Romans*, vol. 2, ICC, ed. J. A. Emerton and C. E. B. Cranfield (Edinburgh: T&T Clark, 1979), 519.

46 Wallace, *Greek Grammar*, 369–71. This argument sees εἰς as functioning in a resultative sense (i.e., with the result that), rather than in a referential sense (i.e., with respect to). In this construction, εἰς is attached to the assertion as a whole and is introducing a result clause; "Christ is the end of the law *with the result* that righteousness is available to every one who believes." See also, Moo, *Romans*, 637–38, who argues similarly.

47 Dunn, *Theology of Paul*, 150–55. He has argued persuasively that this is one of the primary functions of the law in Pauline theology.

48 Moo, *Romans*, 660.

49 Wallace, *Greek Grammar*, 188, argues, "Thus, the confession would be that Jesus is *the* Lord, that is, *Yahweh*." Similarly, Wright, *What Saint Paul Really Said*, 71, states, "Paul is not stupid. Again and again he is making the point… from the Jewish race comes the Messiah according to the flesh – who is also God over all, blessed for ever."

50 Nancy Calvert-Koyzis, *Paul, Monotheism and the People of God: The Significance of Abraham Traditions for Early Judaism and Christianity*. JSNT, ed. Mark Goodacre, vol. 273 (London: T&T Clark, 2004), 123–25. She argues that Abraham is the consummate Gentile and represents God's ultimate desire to reach the entire world.

51 BDAG, "παιδαγωγὸς," 748, defines it as, "One who has responsibility for someone who needs guidance." From Galatians 3:23, note a similar idea with "φρουρέω," 2, "to hold in custody," or 3, "to provide security."

52 Dunn, *Theology of Paul*, 144–45.

53 Moo, *Romans*, 482. He argues that ἐν ἡμῖν is an unusual way to indicate that loving was what Paul immediately had in view. Rather, he believes the requirement being discussed by Paul is related to walking by the Spirit, which ultimately has love in view. See also C. E. B. Cranfield, *The Epistle to the Romans*, vol. 1, ICC on the Holy Scriptures of the Old and New Testaments, ed. J. A. Emerton and C. E. B. Cranfield (Edinburgh: T&T Clark, 1975), 384, who argues that the requirement has more to do with obedience in faith. In other words, the singular use emphasizes the "recognizable and intelligible whole" which the believer is enabled to live out. James D. G. Dunn, *Romans 1–8*, WBC, ed. David A. Hubbard, Glenn W. Barker, and Ralph P. Martin, vol. 38A (Dallas, TX: Word, 1988), 423–4, argues that the requirement is related to "life in accordance with God's intention in the law." See also Dunn, *Theology of Paul*, 656. Here he expands this concept with the statement, "The whole law is fulfilled by loving the neighbor."

54 Colin G. Kruse, *Paul, the Law, and Justification* (Peabody, MA: Hendrickson, 1996), 218.

55 Cranfield, *Romans*, 1:379. See also, Moo, *Romans*, 478, and Leon Morris, *The Epistle to the*

Romans (Grand Rapids: Eerdmans, 1988), 302, both of whom argue similarly.

56 Moo, *Romans*, 484.

57 Kruse, *Paul*, 144–48, 158–61.

58 There is a question as to whether the man in view is a believer or not. Gordon D. Fee, *The First Epistle to the Corinthians*, NICNT, ed. F. F. Bruce (Grand Rapids: Eerdmans, 1987), 208–14, has argued that what is in view in this passage is the man's actual salvation. "What Paul was desiring by having this man put outside the believing community was the destruction of what was 'carnal' in him, so that he might be 'saved' eschatologically. In this case, as is most often in Paul, 'flesh' and 'spirit' designate 'the whole person as viewed from different angles… The intent of this action, therefore, is the man's salvation" (pp. 212–13). For the purpose of this study it is not significant whether the man is saved. What is significant is that the community is commanded by Paul to discipline the man, thus having a catalytic effect on his future. If he is unsaved, it is for his salvation. If he is saved, it is for his progressive sanctification. It was argued earlier that the catalytic effect was for either transformation or outreach.

59 Kruse, *Paul*, 118–19, further argues that the reference to the celebration of the Passover and the cleaning out of the old yeast (1 Cor 5:6–8) represents a second use of the law by Paul in this situation to illustrate his point.

60 Brian S. Rosner, *Paul, Scripture and Ethics: A Study of 1 Corinthians 5–7* (Leiden: Brill, 1994), 70–71, notes "A striking feature of the instructions of 1 Corinthians 5 is that they are not directed to the sinner himself but exclusively to the believers in Corinth as a group. Paul addresses the church as a body throughout… He wants the discipline to be carried out when they are assembled." Craig S. Keener, *1–2 Corinthians*, New Cambridge Bible Commentary, ed. Ben Witherington, III (Cambridge: Cambridge University Press, 2005), 50–51, argues that perhaps the leaven "functions here simply as a symbol of what spreads unchecked if not stopped. Everyone understood that it was better to amputate a member of the corporate than to let his behavior infect others."

61 Fee, *First Corinthians*, 218, notes, "They are to remove the incestuous man, which is like cleansing the house of leaven, in order that they might become what they are, God's 'new loaf' in Corinth. What makes them God's new people is the sacrifice of 'our Passover Lamb, Christ himself.'" The point is that, just as the Exodus event (and Passover) were used by God to establish solidarity within Israel, so the true Exodus event (and true Passover Lamb) establish true solidarity among the redeemed.

62 Wichmann von Meding, "Temple," in *NIDNTT*, 3:782. He notes that of the eight Pauline uses of ναός five of them are used metaphorically to describe the church as the temple of God (1 Cor 3:16; 6:19; 2 Cor 6:16; Eph 2:19–22). He argues that ναός in the New Testament is the preferred word to refer to the sanctuary, both physically and metaphorically, while ἱερόν is the preferred word to refer to the physical temple complex. After analyzing the uses in the LXX, his conclusion is that the 61 uses of ναός are carefully utilized to refer exclusively to the true temple of God. It is never used to describe any of the Gentile temples or places of worship, thus it is used to distinguish true worship from false. In addition, while both Paul and John (in Revelation) use ναός, neither of them use ἱερόν. The implication is that they are following the careful use of the term to refer to the true sanctuary, rather than the temple complex.

63 Fee, *First Corinthians*, 146, argues that one of Paul's purposes in using this imagery is to help the Corinthians understand that they are God's temple *in Corinth*. This is an interesting proposition and, if true, it reflects the outward focus of sanctification.

64 Dunn, *Theology of Paul*, 545.

65 Grosheide, *First Corinthians*, 88, notes that this is true of the individual church as well as the universal church. Referring to the church he says, "Her glory it is to be a temple of the Holy Spirit."

66 G. K. Beale, *The Temple and the Church's Mission: A Biblical Theology of the Dwelling Place of God*, NSBT, ed. D. A. Carson (Downers Grove, IL: InterVarsity and Apollos, 2004), 245–52. Beale suggests, interestingly, that Paul here is conceptually linking the spiritual temple with the "primeval sanctuary of the Garden of Eden." After noting the movement from agricultural metaphors in 1 Cor 3:5–9 to temple imagery in 1 Cor 3:10–17, he then compares this pattern with the imagery of Eden and Israel's temple. He concludes, "We have seen that the purpose of the garden descriptions was to reflect the primeval sanctuary of the Garden of Eden. This combination of precious metals with botanical depictions in Israel's temple would have been sufficient itself to facilitate a swift move on Paul's part from a 'cultivated field/vineyard' image to that of a temple" (p. 248). This linkage may reveal community implications within the Garden imagery.

67 Fee, *First Corinthians*, 136, points out that Paul had the various members of the Corinthian church in immediate view by the repetition of the various indefinite pronouns ἄλλος (v. 10), οὐδείς (v. 11), ἕκαστος (vv. 10, 13), and τις (vv. 12, 14, 15).

68 It is also reminiscent of Eph 2:20–22 which is discussed later.

69 Fee, *First Corinthians*, 264, sees a development of the temple idea. In the 1 Cor 3 passage, the emphasis is on the community as the temple and its corresponding contrast with the Corinthian culture. In the 1 Cor 6 passage, the emphasis is on the individual as the temple and the necessity to live holy lives. Paul relates the two to ensure that believers understand the individual role they play in maintaining corporate unity and reflecting God's glory to the culture as a community. Thiselton, *First Corinthians*, 475, further adds, "If believers are consecrated by the Holy Spirit, to sin either against a fellow Christian (6:1–8) or against one's own body (6:9–19, esp. 18) is sacrilege and desecration."

70 Rosner, *Paul*, 126–28, raises the interesting possibility that the immorality in view is based on cult prostitution. He further argues that since this form of prostitution was consistently condemned throughout the Old Testament because it led Israel astray from a spiritual perspective, perhaps Paul has in mind the effect that sexual immorality has on the group as a whole. This is supported by the link between idolatry and immorality (1 Cor 10:7–8) and the connection with temple imagery (1 Cor 6:19–20). If so, the community emphasis is very strong.

71 Fee, *First Corinthians*, 147.

72 Beale, *The Temple*, 252.

73 Markus Barth, *Ephesians 1–3*, AB, ed. William Foxwell, and David Noel Freedman, vol. 34 (Garden City, NY: Doubleday, 1974), 323, states, "Instead of the individual growth of initiates, the growth of the community is declared decisive." Here he is contrasting individual growth with the growth of the community.

74 O'Brien, *Ephesians*, 195. F. F. Bruce, *The Epistles to the Colossians, to Philemon, and to the Ephesians*, NICNT, ed. F. F. Bruce (Grand Rapids: Eerdmans, 1984), 296, argues similarly when he says, "The traditional barrier was both religious and sociological: as the following words make plain, it consisted of the Jewish law, more particularly of those features of it which marked Jews off from Gentiles—circumcision and the food restrictions, for example." See also, Lincoln, *Ephesians*, 141.

75 Hoehner, *Ephesians*, 370.

76 Gerhard Delling, "καταργέω," in *TDNT*, 1:453. He is followed by BDAG, "καταργέω," 525; Bruce, *Colossians, Philemon, Ephesians*, 298–99; Hoehner, *Ephesians*, 375; Lincoln, *Ephesians*, 142–43; O'Brien, *Ephesians*, 197; James I. Packer, "Abolish, Nullify, Reject," in *NIDNTT*, 1:73–74.

77 The only other New Testament occurrence is found in Rev 18:2 where it refers to fallen Babylon as the dwelling place of demons. Regarding this use, Hoehner, *Ephesians*, 413, notes, "Imagery of the dwelling place of demons is fitting in contradistinction with heaven as the dwelling place of God."

78 Of the 19 uses of this term in the New Testament, 12 occur in Paul (1 Cor 15:40, 48, 49; 5 in Ephesians; Phil 2:10; 2 Tim 4:18). The remainder are in John and Hebrews (John 3:12; Heb 3:1; 6:4; 8:5; 9:23; 11:16; 12:22). The phrase ἐν τοῖς ἐπουρανίοις occurs only in Ephesians, although the sense is captured in the other passages. The high percentage in Ephesians (26%) reveals its significance to the argument. See Helmut Traub, "οὐράνιος, ἐπουράνιος," in *TDNT*, 5:539.

79 O'Brien, *Ephesians*, 97.

80 Note καθίσας ἐν δεξιᾷ αὐτοῦ (Eph 1:20) and κάθου ἐκ δεξιῶν μου (Ps 109:1 LXX) and καὶ πάντα ὑπέταξεν ὑπο τοὺς πόδας αὐτοῦ (Eph 1:22) and ἕως ἂν θῶ τοὺς ἐχθρούς σου ὑποδόδιον τῶν ποδῶν σου (Ps 109:1 LXX).

81 O'Brien, *Ephesians*, 141.

82 Hoehner, *Ephesians*, 459–60; O'Brien, *Ephesians*, 246–47. The reference to the rulers and authorities probably includes both good and bad. The point is that this reveals a divine cosmic plan in which the church plays a dominant role in the display of God's wisdom.

83 The language here is similar to the language discussed in chapter 4 where the community is responsible for displaying the glory of God. Additionally, at the end of this section Paul concludes his benediction with "to [God] be the glory in the church and in Christ Jesus throughout all generations" (Eph 3:21). This further supports the role of the community in displaying the glory of God and, therefore, the dynamic view of image-bearing.

84 O'Brien, *Ephesians*, 171.

85 Fanning, *Verbal Aspect*, 199–200, argues that this classification most often utilizes a durative type verb "since the actional constraints of viewing a situation 'as it goes on' require an appreciable temporal extension. Of the three durative types he identifies—states, activities, and accomplishments—he labels αὐξάνω as an 'activity' verb; a "gradable transition (transitive or intransitive): verbs which lexically denote a change in the subject or object, but with a *relative* terminal point—there is no definite end at which the action must cease" (p. 144). BDF, § 101, "αὐξάνειν," 50, identifies this verb as intransitive in this passage. BDAG, "αὐξάνω/αὔξω," 151, as an intransitive is defined as, "to become greater, grow, increase." The criteria established by Fanning are met; therefore, the present tense here is best seen as progressive.

86 Hoehner, *Ephesians*, 409.

87 Christian Maurer, "συναρμολογέω," in *TDNT*, 7:856. Hoehner, *Ephesians*, 409, further argues that the imagery is drawn from the craft of masonry wherein an elaborate process of cutting and smoothing the stones was used to ensure an exact fit. This is consistent with the building metaphor in the context.

88 O'Brien, *Ephesians*, 219.

89   Johannes Schneider, "ἡλικία," in *TDNT*, 2:942–43.

90   Hoehner, *Ephesians*, 557.

91   Bruce, *Colossians, Philemon, Ephesians*, 350.

92   Hoehner, *Ephesians*, 556.

93   This is not to say that individuals lose their ethnic identity. Rev 7:9–10 and 21:24–25 seem to indicate that ethnicity remains intact in the eschaton. Lincoln, *Ephesians*, 156, correctly places the emphasis in this passage on the Gentiles being included in the temple imagery. Accordingly, the redefined symbol of the temple includes the idea of Gentiles and the notion that the original temple was designed to be a place where all the peoples of the world could come on an equal basis and worship the true God. This metaphorical linkage provides continuity with the idea that it was God's intention from the beginning to reach the entire world.

94   C. K. Barrett, *Paul: An Introduction to His Thought* (Louisville, KY: Westminster John Knox, 1994); Ernest Best, *One Body in Christ: A Study in the Relationship of the Church to Christ in the Epistles of the Apostle Paul* (London: SPCK, 1955); James L. Breed, "The Church as the 'Body of Christ': A Pauline Analogy" *Theological Reviews* 6, no. 2 (1985): 9–32; Charles E. B. Cranfield, "Paul's Teaching on Sanctification" *RefR* 48 (spring 1995): 217–29; Dunn, *Theology of Paul*; Grenz, *Social God*; Idem, *Theology*; Robert H. Gundry, *Sōma in Biblical Theology: With Emphasis on Pauline Anthropology* (Cambridge: Cambridge University Press, 1976); Anthony Hoekema, *Created in God's Image* (Grand Rapids: Eerdmans, 1988); David Peterson, *Possessed by God: A New Testament Theology of Sanctification and Holiness*, New Studies in Biblical Theology, ed. D. A. Carson   (Downers Grove, IL: InterVarsity, 1995); J. Paul Sampley, *Pauline Partnership in Christ: Christian Community and Commitment in Light of Roman Law* (Philadelphia: Fortress, 1980); Mark A. Seifrid, "In Christ," in *DPL*, 433–36; Louis B. Smedes, *Union with Christ: A Biblical View of the New Life in Jesus Christ*, rev. ed. (Grand Rapids: Eerdmans, 1983).

95   Seifrid, "In Christ," in *DPL*, 433–34.

96   See also the related discussions in Ridderbos, *Paul*, 232–33, and Dunn, *Theology of Paul*, 390–412.

97   Ridderbos, *Paul*, 398, refers to this as the "subjective" use. This is clearly seen in passages such as Gal 1:22; 3:28; 1 Cor 1:2, 30; Rom 12:5; 16:3.

98   Seifrid, "In Christ," in *DPL*, 433. Its uniqueness is emphasized in that this language is nearly absent from the other New Testament authors. In contrast, Dunn notes that the phrase ἐν Χριστῷ occurs 83 times in the Pauline literature. This does not take into account the uses of ἐν κυρίῳ and the pronominal uses and other related references to the believer's standing in Christ. The point being made here is that this is a distinctly Pauline expression.

99   Dunn, *Theology of Paul*, 399.

CHAPTER 7

Community in the Pauline Epistles

In the previous chapter, it was argued that Paul, interpreting the original cultural symbols of Israel spiritually (Messiah, the law, and the temple), develops the concept of solidarity further in the form of unity. As individuals participate in the new humanity, they are incorporated into a community that is being transformed into the image of Christ for the purpose of reflecting God's glory. As such, the individual can only experience this unity and transformation as they live and obey the biblical commands within community. Transformation—progressive sanctification—is a community function.

In this section, the remainder of the Pauline corpus will be surveyed to identify how the community is related to progressive sanctification.[1] Specifically, community texts that meet the criteria established in the last chapter will be reviewed to determine what role the community plays in the transformation process or what role the individual plays in growing the community. Since the criteria involve life within community and outreach, both of these aspects will be considered. Once a community text has been identified, the text will be studied to identify principles pertinent to this investigation. Since the purpose of this survey is to identify specific principles related to the community and the individual, principles are only stated once and not repeated.

Galatians

No matter how one distills the purpose of Galatians, it must include the concept of true liberty as found only in Christ. Throughout the epistle, Paul is addressing the tensions generated by the misunderstanding and misuse of the law.[2] And in this context, the community emphasis in Galatians becomes obvious right from the beginning when Paul says, "I am astonished that you are so quickly deserting the one who called you by the grace of Christ and following a different gospel" (Gal 1:6). Paul had the "churches of Galatia" in view at this point.[3] His concern was that they were being persuaded by a false gospel which threatened to remove the liberty and destroy the unity experienced by living by the Spirit. In this context a significant community principle arises.

Expressing Spiritual Fruit Requires Walking by the Spirit in Community (Gal 5)

This section begins with the exhortation to love one's neighbor (Gal 5:14) and is part of a larger pericope addressing the impact one has in community when walking by the flesh or by the Spirit (Gal 5:13–26).[4] After his discussion concerning circumcision and the associated bondage that results from attempting to keep the law (Gal 5:1–12), it is significant that he moves to love as the expression of the law. The parallel idea is that Christ has set believers free from the demands of the law (Gal 5:1). As argued earlier, it is this freedom that allows the believer to carry out the original intent of the law—loving others. Paul's summing up the law with the love command is significant here. It reveals that the expressions, the lusts of the flesh and the fruit of the Spirit, while rooted in walking by the flesh or the Spirit, respectively, are partly an issue of motivation.

Accordingly, in this passage, Paul's argument assumes that the community is necessary to walk by the Spirit. This principle is demonstrated in several ways. First, the basic command to love is carried out in the context of community.[5] Second, of Paul's "one another" passages five occur in this context (Gal 5:13, 15, 26), all of which require community for the commands to be obeyed or the conditions to be avoided.

Third, the language employed by Paul to describe the specific lusts and fruit demonstrates active involvement within relationships. The desires of the flesh are described by terms that destroy unity if expressed. Conversely, the fruit of the Spirit is described by terms that generate unity if expressed. Each of the terms used to describe the fruit have verbal cognates and, therefore, have an active nuance associated with them.[6] This indicates that

> the qualities enumerated are not the results of observing a legal code, but are to be attributed to the power of the Holy Spirit… The ethical characteristics produced by the Spirit are in sharp contrast to the natural activities and attitudes of the self-centered life.[7]

Finally, the following context reveals that the primary purpose of the fruit is oriented toward building up and edifying the community and, as argued earlier, reflecting God's glory to one another. The behavior of verse 25 is expressed in community terms in verse 26.[8] In addition, some of the terms and concepts are used in the remainder of Galatians to illustrate and provide instruction on how the fruit impacts community. In chapter 6 Paul applies the concept of walking by the Spirit (Gal 5:16) to practical examples experienced in life. The restoration of the sinning brother involves community action (Gal 6:1). Here gentleness is required. This is consistent with the role of the community presented earlier in Hebrews. This also fits a pattern consistently found in the history of God's people, namely, helping a believer come to the realization of sin in their life and restoration usually requires an outside catalyst in the form of another person.[9] Rarely is God presented as the one who directly exposes the sin. He consistently acts through others.

The carrying of one another's burdens (Gal 6:2–5) involves several of the fruit of the Spirit. In addition, Paul presents this exhortation as fulfilling the "law of Christ." Moisés Silva argues that the "law of Christ" is a reference to Christ's locating the heart of the law in the love commands—here expressed in Gal 5:13–14 as the summing up of the law.[10] A comparison of Gal 5:6 and 6:15 reveals a strong parallelism that communicates that the new creation is a community demonstrating faith through their love for one another. In between these two passages are the commands and examples to love. Here, both the redefinition of the law by Christ and the outward focus of the law are present. How can one carry out this reciprocal command without another person present? Inherent in the command is the necessity of community. And since living a holy life and growing in maturity involves obeying the commands, community necessarily is involved in the process.[11]

The doing good to others (Gal 6:6–10) is also community oriented. This pericope begins with sharing good things and ends with doing good things. In both cases, the recipients are others, with a special emphasis on believers (Gal 6:10). The agrarian imagery found between these two commands presents a hermeneutical challenge. The corruption in the flesh and eternal life from the Spirit may be relational in orientation as well. The earlier context reveals that walking in the flesh produces quarrels, conceitedness and jealousy (Gal 5:15, 26). In contrast, walking in the Spirit produces the fruit of the Spirit which builds up the community (Gal 5:22–23).[12] However it is interpreted, the inclusio points these truths toward community.

For Paul, the fruit of the Spirit is for the purpose of and is to be expressed in community. In other words, the desires are more oriented toward the impact they have in community than in the individual. Here is an example of the movement from the individual to the community. Both the desires of the flesh and the fruit of the Spirit begin with action at an individual level. However, their expression is necessarily in community. Failure to walk by the Spirit and thus indulge the desires of the flesh at the individual level severely affects the community by destroying unity. Similarly, walking by the Spirit and expressing the fruit of the Spirit *necessarily* benefits the community by building up believers and reflecting the glory of God. Failure to interpret the passage with a community emphasis misses this key point in Paul's argument.[13]

Here is the first clear example in Paul's teaching of the role of the community. Implicit in the command is the need for the community. This community text meets the first criterion, since it is neither possible to carry out the command to love nor to express spiritual fruit without the community. In addition, the exhortation to walk by the Spirit, while originating with the individual, necessarily is conducted in community. Walking by the Spirit requires the community for the experience to be fulfilled.

1 and 2 Thessalonians

New Testament scholarship has generally related the purpose of the Thessalonian Epistles to eschatology in some way. This is due to the large amount of space devoted to issues surrounding the return of Christ.[14] When combined with the high ethical content of both epistles, their purpose can be oriented around Christian living in light of the Lord's soon return.[15]

Karl Donfried orients their purpose toward "God who is present among his elect and suffering people and about a God who is leading them to their promised salvation."[16] This is an attractive thesis given the New Testament propensity to emphasize God's presence among his people through his risen Son (see the earlier discussion in chapters 4 and 5). In addition, this accounts for the emphasis in the Thessalonian Epistles on the example set by the Thessalonian believers in the midst of tribulation. This incarnational aspect of the gospel permeates the epistles and reinforces the role of the community. As a result, the community aspect is present in both epistles.

This is evident in Paul's opening statement of thanksgiving where he commends them for their impact as a community on all the believers in Macedonia and Achaia (1 Thess 1:7). This is just as obvious in his second epistle when he says, "We ought to thank God always for you, brothers and sisters, and rightly so, because your faith flourishes more and more and the love of each one of you all for one another is ever greater" (2 Thess 1:3). In this context several community principles surface.

Effective Outreach is Best Accomplished by the Community (1 Thess 1–2)

The community is the primary means used by God to demonstrate how to live a godly life. "And you became imitators of us and of the Lord, when you received the message with joy that comes from the Holy Spirit, despite great affliction" (1 Thess 1:6). The result of this imitation was that they had become an example to other believers. This is illustrated in the parallelism between verses 6 and 7:

κaὶ ὑμεῖς μιμηταὶ ὑμῶν ἐγενήθητε
And you became imitators of us

ὥστε γενέσθαι ὑμᾶς τύπον
As a result, you became [an example] to all

As noted by Charles Wanamaker, "Τύπον is singular because Paul alludes to the experience of the community as a whole."[17] Their becoming imitators (plural) led to their becoming an example (singular). The impact that they had as a community was powerful and significant precisely because it was community oriented.

In addition, their example was more closely related to how they lived out the gospel in community in the midst of tribulation rather than how they understood it.[18] Paul apparently is using his own life as well as the lives of Timothy and Silas as examples to emphasize their character and behavior as the significant transformational factors that impacted the Thessalonians (1 Thess 1:4–5).[19] It was this that they imitated.[20]

Paul goes on in chapter 2 to expand this idea, both in the example he and his associates had been to them and the resulting impact that occurred. As he makes a transition through the imagery of suffering (1 Thess 2:2), little children (1 Thess 2:7), nursing mother (1 Thess 2:7), diligent workers (1 Thess 2:9), and father (1 Thess 2:11) it becomes obvious that his main point is that they lived among the Thessalonians in such a way as to see them come to know the Lord and to grow in their transformation. This is made clear when Paul says, "As you know, we treated each one of you as a father treats his own children, exhorting and encouraging you and insisting that you live in a way worthy of God who calls you to his own kingdom and his glory" (1 Thess 2:11–12).

Paul's exhortation to live a life worthy of God has a much deeper emphasis than simple obedience. It carries the connotation of the very presence of God. This is supported with the εἰς τὸ περιπατεῖν construction (1 Thess 1:12) which indicates that Paul's purpose for his movement toward them was to produce this worthiness before God precisely because they were associated with his kingdom and glory.[21] The result of this movement was that the Thessalonians had responded to their message (1 Thess 2:13) and had themselves become an example (1 Thess 1:7). At the core of Paul's encouragement is the cycle of faithfulness–imitation–impact. This impact was realized in his conclusion that as they became imitators, they also became faithful participants (1 Thess 2:14).[22]

In the context, the purpose of Paul's (and Silas and Timothy) example was specifically to exhort the Thessalonians to live worthy lives (1 Thess 2:11–12) for the purpose of being an example to others (1 Thess 1:6–7). Here is an example of a smaller community impacting a larger community for transformation and growth. As such, this is a community text that meets the first criterion. It could also be classified as meeting the second criterion, since Paul's commendation (1 Thess 1:6–10) specifically relates to how the faithfulness of the Thessalonian community influenced believers in other communities. Although Paul does not directly identify the nature of the impact, 1 Thess 1:9 implies that it resulted in other communities following their example of faithfulness.

Community Holiness Requires Avoidance of Sexual Immorality and Expression of Genuine Love (1 Thess 4–5)

In discussing the sanctification of the community, Paul states, "For this is God's will: for you to become holy,[23] for you to keep away from sexual immorality, for each of you to know how to possess his own body[24] in holiness and honor, not in lustful passion like the Gentiles who do not know God" (1 Thess 4:3–5). The use of the plural pronouns reveals that Paul is viewing holiness as a community exercise, one which involves sexual purity.

The word used to communicate holiness (ἁγιασμός) is a verbal noun. As such, it expresses action.[25] This is captured by the NET translation "for you to become holy." Otto Procksch helpfully notes, however, that "the operation of ἁγιασμός can be accomplished only by a holy person… so that in the case of self-sanctifying it is always assumed that it is accomplished on the basis of the state of sanctification attained in the atonement."[26] Similarly, David Peterson argues that, rather than a sense of progressive moral transformation, what Paul has in mind is the community's *continuing consecration to his service…* Instead of dishonouring the body by inappropriate sexual behaviour, Christians are to glorify God by treating their bodies as 'consecrated' to his service."[27] This concept is consistent with the view of progressive sanctification argued earlier.

This concept of consecration and glorifying God is supported by the structure of the passage as well.[28]

τοῦτο γάρ ἐστιν θέλημα τοῦ θεοῦ,   ὁ ἁγιασμὸς ὑμῶν (4:3)
For this is God's will: for you to become holy

ἀπέχεσθαι ὑμᾶς… (4:3)
for you to keep away…

εἰδέναι ἕκαστον ὑμῶν... (4:4)
for each of you to know...

τὸ μὴ ὑπερβαίνειν καὶ
No one should violate or

πλεονεκτεῖν... (4:6)
take advantage

Within this structure, ὁ ἁγιασμὸς is understood in apposition to τοῦτο, with the infinitives functioning appositionally;[29] they are defining the behaviors that reveal the continued consecration of the community—sexual purity and avoidance of immorality.

F. F. Bruce argues that this is set in the context of the Greco-Roman world where "there was no body of public opinion" to discourage immorality. As such, "when the gospel was introduced into pagan society, therefore, it was necessary to emphasize the complete breach with accepted mores in this area which was demanded by the new way of life in Christ."[30] The significance of this lies in the community's testimony. By practicing sexual purity, the community has the opportunity to differentiate themselves from pagan society and reflect God's glory to that society.

Paul's emphasis on the individual (ἕκαστον ὑμῶν, 1 Thess 4:4) reveals that individuals play a role as well. For Paul, even though holiness is a community function, it begins with the believers living out their holiness in faithful obedience within that community. Whereas the previous principle was more related to how the Thessalonians' example was spreading among the other communities, this principle is more related to the community growing in progressive sanctification, thus reflecting God's glory through their individual lives.

In 1 Thess 4:1–8 the negative aspect of this consecration is expressed in terms of avoiding sexual immorality. As with the desires of the flesh text (Gal 5:19–21), here is an example of the movement from the individual to the community. The sinful desires discussed here originate with the individual but find expression in the community. There is more than personal holiness at stake. Failure to obey these commands has severe consequences for the community. If Bruce is correct, then one of the consequences is an ineffective testimony before the pagan society. Another consequence is the destruction of unity as believers take advantage of one another. Failure to control sinful desires is more than disobedience. As Paul points out, it represents a blatant disregard of God himself (1 Thess 4:8).[31]

In contrast, 1 Thess 4:9–12 expresses this consecration in positive language. The examples presented by Paul are all bound by the fundamental axiom to "love one another" (1 Thess 4:9). The nature of the command and the context reveal that community is essential to complete this command.[32] This is in keeping with his earlier statements about setting the example for others to follow. Although there is a question as to how the Thessalonians expressed their love for the Macedonian believers, what is clear is that there was an outward focus interrelationally within the community as well as external to the community.[33]

In the context, Paul is exhorting the Thessalonians to maintain community holiness. This consecration involves avoidance of sexual immorality—having sexually pure relationships—and active love for one another. As such, this is a community text that meets the first criterion, since obeying the commands can only be accomplished in the context of community.

1 and 2 Corinthians

However one distills the purpose of the Corinthian Epistles, it must include the concept of relational unity and dealing with factions. Paul makes it clear from the outset of 1 Corinthians that he was writing to address the division that existed when he says, "I urge you, brothers and sisters, by the name of our Lord Jesus Christ, to agree together, to end your divisions, and to be united by the same mind and purpose" (1 Cor 1:10)

It seems that at the core of the divisions was the desire of the various factions to promote and establish their own spirituality (1 Cor 1:12–13).[34] But it does not stop there; it is more deeply rooted in contention. Throughout both epistles contention is evident, not only between the members of the church but between the church and Paul as well (1 Cor 4:14; 5:6; 6:1; 11:21–22; 2 Cor 2:1–4; 7:2–3, 8; 10:9–11; 11:16).[35] The contentions revolve around spirituality, sexuality, litigation, gender confusion, spiritual gift abuse, and clear understanding of the gospel. It is within this context that Paul writes these epistles, foundationally to reestablish unity within the church.[36] As might be expected, there are several significant community texts within these epistles.

Establishing Corporate Unity Requires Active Involvement by Every Believer (1 Cor 1)

Relational involvement within the community is essential to maintain unity within the church. To state it another way, unity is not possible without community. And the beginning point for understanding unity within the church is the person and work of Christ.[57] Paul has this in mind when he states, "God is faithful, by whom you were called into fellowship with his son, Jesus Christ our

Lord" (1 Cor 1:9).[38] The very next verse is a plea to end the divisions. The very existence of the divisions is evidence of self-centeredness and a violation of unity. The existence of divisions and the unity of the church are mutually exclusive concepts in Pauline thought.[39]

This is the context for Paul's question, "Is Christ divided?" (1 Cor 1:13). It is clear from this progression that unity is fundamentally based in Christ.[40] Since Christ cannot be divided, neither should the church. This principle serves as the foundation by which the church is enabled to live out the reality of what Christ has accomplished.

On the continuum of unity discussed earlier, Paul here is arguing between unity that results from being in Christ (union with Christ) and the failure of the church to progress to relational harmony. This progression is in view when he says, "I urge you, brothers and sisters, by the name of our Lord Jesus Christ, to agree together, to end your divisions, and to be united by the same mind and purpose" (1 Cor 1:10). The movement from union to relational harmony requires relational involvement with each other for good rather than evil. This is the movement that Paul has in mind.[41]

All of the clauses in this exhortation reflect a dynamic process wherein individuals living righteously in relationship together productively move the community from one of division to one of unity. As noted by Fee, the construction of this verse is one with three statements following a positive–negative–positive pattern, all being controlled by ἵνα functioning to provide the content of Paul's exhortation.[42]

The first part of the exhortation is that the believers are to all say the same thing. Lexically, λέγω implies expression, so Paul seems to be emphasizing agreement in the way individuals express themselves to one another.[43] Second, believers are to have no divisions among them. Fee argues that by the use of σχίσματα, Paul is referring more to divided opinions than distinctly formed groups.[44] These divided opinions would make "common thought and utterance difficult."[45] Third, believers are to be united by having the same mind and the same purpose. Here, the use of νοῦς and γνώμη refer to their attitudes and purposes.[46] The use of αὐτός as an identifying adjective with the positive statements reveals that what Paul has in mind is total agreement in their expressions, thoughts and purposes.[47]

Each of these points require believers to be actively involved in the community and relationships with each other in such a way so as to develop and maintain unity. Paul's argument from this point forward is a systematic defense of how the church should relate in various situations in order to preserve the unity established by Christ.[48] In addition, as argued earlier, in 2 Cor 3 and 4 Paul will develop the theological idea that Christ, as the image of God, reflects God's glory and, therefore, serves as the model of what believers are becoming as they are transformed. This early exhortation to establish and maintain unity sets the stage for these later discussions, and begins to reveal how the community should reflect God's glory in the way the individuals relate to one another. This is a community text that meets the first criterion, since obeying the commands can only be accomplished in the context of community.

Exercising Spiritual Gifts is a Necessity for Corporate Edification (1 Cor 12–13)

The community is essential for the exercise of spiritual gifts and, therefore, for the maturing process to occur. 1 Cor 12 and 13 provide the clearest examples of this principle. In 1 Cor 12 Paul expands the concept of diversity in unity. Whereas believers are distinct from one another, they are bound together in a way like no other relationship on the earth. And that relationship intrinsically and necessarily involves impacting each other for transformation. This is made clear by Paul's statement, "To each person the manifestation of the Spirit is given for the benefit of all" (1 Cor 12:7). It is within this context that he expands the body imagery introduced earlier in 1 Cor 10 and 11.[49]

While there are many different facets to the body imagery, the community aspects are significant. First of all, true solidarity is located in Christ (1 Cor 12:12). The context reveals that, as unity is generated, it has both ontological and teleological aspects. While baptism probably reflects position, F. W. Grosheide argues that being made to drink "implies a very close communion."[50] Both the preceding and following contexts are highly relational in nature and demonstrate participation together in body life. In other words, the believer's unity is positional (solidarity) as well as practical. Believers are in the body together accomplishing body life functions at both the individual and the community level, all for similar purposes and accomplishment of similar goals. It is impossible to understand or apply this passage without the community aspect.[51]

This is further supported by Paul's statement that "the eye cannot say to the hand, 'I do not need you,' nor in turn can the head say to the foot, 'I do not need you.' On the contrary, those members that seem to be weaker are essential" (1 Cor 12:21–22). Why? So that the divisions in the body are eliminated and unity is secured (1 Cor 12:25). Since the body imagery establishes the conceptual framework for Paul's later statements about the gifts building up the church (1 Cor 14), Paul is here saying that relational involvement in community is essential for Christian growth to maturity.[52] This sets the stage for his expanded teaching on love.

In 1 Cor 13 the discussion of love and how it relates to the exercise of spiritual gifts is significantly expanded. The modifiers used by Paul to describe love are all ultimately community oriented (1 Cor 13:4–8). In other words, Paul's choice of modifiers to describe love all relate to the unity of the community and the elimination of divisions. As described by Paul, community is necessary for the expression of love to occur.

And no matter how one understands the following complex passage involving tongues and prophecy (1 Cor 13:8–13), it is significant for several reasons. Love within community is made effective as believers exercise their gifts within community. The passage is clearly oriented around community and how love expressed through the gifts enables the community to produce maturity (1 Cor 14:1–5, 26).[53] In addition, the movement in the passage relates to the growing maturity of the church and therefore the individual.[54] Since Paul is discussing the superiority of love, the implication is that this new paradigm for relating necessarily includes the exercise of gifts as an expression of love. If the spiritual gifts are designed to build up the community (and thus the individuals within the community), then the community is essential in the maturing process since the gifts are to be expressed within the community.

This is made clear in 1 Cor 14. In his discussion about speaking in a tongue and prophesying, Paul uses several phrases that support his teaching that gifts are meant to build up the body. He talks about building up, encouraging and consoling believers (1 Cor 14:3), and twice mentions building up the church (1 Cor 14:4–5). The implication in these passages is that the community is involved in building up itself as believers share their gifts with one another. And it works in both directions. The individual is built up by being in a community where the gifts are expressed in love, and the community is built up as the individuals express their gifts in love.

Once again, the movement from the individual to the community is clear. Individuals using the gifts for their own personal gain prompted Paul to exhort the Corinthians concerning love (1 Cor 14:1–5). Not only does failure to utilize the gifts in community hinder the maturing process, but the body imagery reveals that it also becomes a cause for division and disunity within the church. This text meets the first criterion since the growth in view can only be accomplished in community.

Romans

At the heart of the argument of Romans lies a sustained discussion explaining and demonstrating the righteousness of God.[55] Paul systematically presents this theme beginning with the need for God's righteousness and concluding with the practical outworking of God's righteousness within the church. Within this context, Paul explains at length and in great detail the justification of the individual believer. As such, much of the argument is oriented toward the individual. However, the community aspect is not absent. In keeping with Paul's tendency, the movement from the indicative (Rom 1–11) to the imperative (Rom 12–16) demonstrates that God's redemptive movement in the life of the individual is as much teleologically oriented as it is ontologically oriented. In other words, the justification of the believer is also effective in generating a teleological effect—moving the believer to maturity. Based on the thematic structure, one could say that the fundamental community principle in Romans is that community is required for the outworking of the individual's justification. And yet, community principles surface at strategic locations in the argument.

Being in Community is Necessary to Offer Oneself in Service to the Lord (Rom 12:1–2)

As Paul begins his transition in Rom 12 to the implications of God's righteousness in the church, he uses temple language, specifically the language of the sacrificial system.[56] The redefinition of this cultural boundary marker discussed earlier is significant in the flow of the argument.

Regarding the believer, Paul has just argued extensively that their justification is based on the work of Christ and is by grace through faith (Rom 3:21–4:25), that they have been transferred from the old order belonging to Adam and now belong to the new order whose solidarity is found in Christ (Rom 5), that they are now freed from the tyranny of sin and the law's dominion (Rom 6–7), and that they are now indwelt by the Spirit. He now moves to sacrificial imagery to communicate their new responsibilities.

The sacrificial system was central to Jewish self-identity.[57] As discussed in chapter 5, Deut 12 defined this self-identity in terms of centralized worship and sacrifice with the focus being community oriented. For Paul to apply this language to the church redefines the concept of sacrificial worship and service from a community perspective.

The primary difference between the concept of sacrifice in the Old Testament and the New Testament lies in the sacrifice itself and its purpose. Whereas in the Old Testament the sin sacrifices involved death, in the New Testament they are oriented toward life. What is being sacrificed is "your bodies." "Therefore I exhort you, brothers and sisters, by the mercies of God, to present your bodies as a sacrifice—alive, holy, and pleasing to God—which is your reasonable service" (Rom 12:1).

The focus has been shifted from sin and atonement to the service of the believer. As argued by James D. G. Dunn, "What he calls for, then, is the offering up of oneself in one's corporeal relationships, in the relationships of every day, made possible by one's being as an embodied person."[58] The location of the sacrifice has been transferred as well. In the language of the temple cult, the sacrifice in the Old Testament was to be accomplished in the holy place. It is now to be offered up in the true temple of God, the church.[59] As such, community is necessary for one to offer themselves up in service to the Lord.

In addition, Paul's words, "alive, holy and pleasing to God" and "...that you may test and approve what is the will of God—what is good and well-pleasing and perfect" (Rom 12:1–2) reveal that God is pleased with the sacrifice of the believer. The double reference to pleasing God emphasizes this aspect.[60] In this context, the will of God is related to the transformation of the believer into Christ-likeness. Therefore, the believers themselves and the process of becoming like Christ please God.

While believers are commanded to offer themselves in service to the Lord, the context in view by Paul is the church. Using the language of sacrifice, Paul is highlighting the outreach aspect discussed earlier—a sacrifice, by definition, is on behalf of another. This reveals that sanctification is accomplished partly for the benefit of others. This text meets the first criterion since the sacrifice in view can only be accomplished in community.

Validating One's Faith Requires Loving Involvement in Community (Rom 12:9–21)

In Rom 12:9–16 Paul moves into the more traditional area of ethics. At the beginning of this section he gives a distinct command related to how believers are to interact within community. "Love must be without hypocrisy" (Rom 12:9). Following David Black's analysis, the emphasis is on the sincerity, or genuineness of love.[61] Black has aptly demonstrated the careful structure of this passage in which Paul reminds his readers that love is "the indispensable ground of all true religion."[62]

After the introductory statement, Paul then proceeds to expand the concept of how genuine love validates one's faith. To begin, Paul sets in parallel the contrasting ideas of what it means to love genuinely when he says, "Abhor what is evil, cling to what is good" (Rom 12:9). These two contrasts are repeated in different ways throughout the passage. For example, he says, "Bless those who persecute you, bless and do not curse" (Rom 12:14). Again he says, "Live in harmony with one another; do not be haughty but associate with the lowly" (Rom 12:19). Finally, he concludes this section with, "Do not be overcome by evil, but overcome evil with good" (Rom 12:21). These series of contrasts provide the reader with a clear picture of how genuine love is expressed.

After this opening, he expands the concept of genuine love within the redeemed community (Rom 12:10–13). The double use of the reciprocal pronoun ἀλλήλων in verse 10 personalizes the concept and reemphasizes the community aspect. In addition, the commands themselves reflect a community orientation.[63] It is difficult to understand Paul's exhortations without the community in mind. In expanding the concept of mutual love the movement within this section is designed to particularize the command to love genuinely. In other words, it is more than description at work. Paul is purposefully arguing in such a way so as to create movement within the community.

Black has argued for a chiastic structure in this section as follows:[64]

Ἡ ἀγάπη ἀνυπόκριτος (12:9)

Love must be without hypocrisy

A   ἀποστυγοῦντες τὸ πονηρόν (12:9)
  Abhor what is evil
 κολλώμενοι τῷ ἀγαθῷ
  Cling to what is good

  B   τῇ φιλαδελφίᾳ εἰς ἀλλήλους φιλόστοργοι (12:10)
    Be devoted to one another with mutual love
   τῇ τιμῇ ἀλλήλους προηγούμενοι
    Showing eagerness in honoring one another
   τῇ σπουδῇ μὴ ὀκνηροί (12:11)
    Do not lag in zeal

    C   τῷ πνεύματι ζέοντες
      Be enthusiastic in spirit
     τῷ κυρίῳ δουλεύοντες
      Serve the Lord

  B'   τῇ ἐλπίδι χαίροντες (12:12)
    Rejoice in hope
   τῇ θλίψει ὑπομένοντες
    Endure in suffering
   τῇ προσευχῇ προσκαρτεροῦντες
    Persist in prayer

A'   ταῖς χρείαις τῶν ἁγίων κοινωνοῦντες (12:13)
  Contribute to the needs of the saints
 τὴν φιλοξενίαν διώκοντες
  Pursue hospitality

Given this, the argument flows from the general introductory statement (Rom 12:9) to the particulars of how that statement is carried out with an emphasis throughout the passage on relational involvement (Rom 12:10–13). As the chiasm moves toward the center, one is caught by the primary theme of mutual love within the community. And the verbal ideas all inherently include passion for others in their action. As is frequent with chiastic structures, as one moves toward the center an emphasis is created. The emphasis in this structure is found with Paul's words, "Be enthusiastic in spirit, serve the Lord" (Rom 12:11). With this construct, it is apparent that genuine love is defined in terms of mutual love within community and reinforced by the exhortation to show enthusiasm and serve the Lord. In other words, loving others is directly tied to serving the Lord. Here is an example of the movement from the individual to the community. The force of the commands requires community for completion.[65] They cannot be obeyed in isolation. Community is required to demonstrate genuine love toward others.

If the previous section emphasized how one is to move toward another with genuine love, Rom 12:14–16 emphasizes relational movement that results in empathy. Responding appropriately when persecuted, sharing with others in their joy and sadness, and living humbly leads to relational harmony. In other words, unity is achieved when believers love one another and share the experiences of daily life. This is further proof of genuine love.

In Rom 12:17–21, the concept of sincere love and proper thinking is extended to those who would hurt the community. This passage is bounded by the word κακός, marking it off as a form of inclusio.[66] As noted by Black,

> if love within the believing community is the dominant Christian virtue, it reaches it climax in the love of enemies. Love is intended not only to permeate the relationship of Christians to one another but to shape their attitudes towards those who even seek their ruin.[67]

And with the initial discussion of sincere love, Paul concludes by noting that love is more than refraining from revenge. It includes the idea of desiring the best for our enemies and taking care of them as much as possible. Here the justice aspect of the law surfaces and the Old Testament quotations support the conclusion that this was God's intention all along.[68]

Christ's locating the heart of the law in the love commands established a new paradigm for carrying out God's purposes. Paul incorporates this new paradigm as a requirement for living the Christian life. For Paul, the expression of love is a validation of genuine faith. Since the believer cannot fulfill these commands apart from community, this text meets the first criterion.

Reaching Society for Christ is a Community Responsibility (Rom 13:1–10)

Romans 12:17–21 serves as a transition passage between how to love sincerely within the redeemed community (Rom 12:9–16) and how to impact the society at-large for Christ (Rom 13:1–10).[69] In Rom 13:1–10 Paul now turns his attention to culture, especially the relationship between the redeemed community and the secular government. In establishing the context for this section, Dunn argues that Paul was aware that the house churches in Rome were in imminent danger and were defenseless because they were associated with Judaism.[70] As such, Paul's concern was that the Roman Christians did not "compartmentalize" their lives and cut themselves off from the "wider community." The ethical behavior required in the church is the same as for those outside of the church (p. 678). In this context, his exhortations are meant to help them navigate through a complex situation in which they could demonstrate genuine love as a community for the purpose of their well-being and safety, and for the purpose of communicating Christ's love to the society at-large.[71]

It is no accident that Paul frames the discussion with the dual commands to love in Rom 12:9 and 13:10. This forms a larger inclusio which sets off the discussion on sincere love, both in community and with those outside, including the government. The summary statement is found when Paul says,

> For the commandments, '*do not commit adultery, do not murder, do not steal, do not covet,*' (and if there is any other commandment) are summed up in this, '*Love your neighbor as yourself.*' Love does no wrong to a neighbor. Therefore love is the fulfillment of the law (Rom 13:9–10).

Here the justice aspect of the law discussed earlier surfaces again. Similar to Jesus, Paul located the heart of the law in the command to love one's neighbor. And, Paul's use here demonstrates that the commands were meant to have an effect within the redeemed community as well as society at-large. In the context, submitting to the government (Rom 13:1–5), paying taxes (Rom 13:6), and paying debts (Rom 13:8) all reflect a genuine desire to demonstrate Christ's love to society. This then becomes a key apologetic for the church in society.[72] The influence that comes from obeying these commands is because it is done at a community level. The testimony of the community is powerful in this regard, to the point that if the community neglected to obey these commands, their testimony would most likely have a negative effect. In other words, the redeemed community is to live in society in such a way so that the culture is drawn to Christ and has no excuse for not turning to the Lord.

Once again, the movement from the individual to the community is present. While the commandments are individually oriented, the power to influence society for Christ lies in the obedience of the larger community. And failure to carry obedience to the community level misses the main point of the passage. This means that the community, in this case the local church, has a responsibility to organize itself such that the individuals within the group understand the influence they are capable of having.

As discussed earlier, the progressive aspect of sanctification necessarily involves an outward focus. This passage demonstrates that the redeemed community, to which all individual believers belong, is designed to impact the culture in which it exists. Therefore, the community is necessary to assist the individual believer in carrying out their God-designed function of impacting the world for Christ. And when individuals work together their impact is more significant than when they work alone. For this reason, this text meets the second criterion.

Protecting the Integrity of the Gospel and the Mission of the Church is a Community Responsibility (Rom 16:17–18)

Paul concludes Romans with a final community principle when he says, "Now I urge you, brothers and sisters, to watch out for those who create dissensions and obstacles contrary to the teaching that you learned" (Rom 16:17). Paul is commanding the community to set in place protective measures to guard against those who would threaten the integrity of the community.[73]

His description reveals not only how to recognize them, but also the destruction that they cause. They create dissension and raise obstacles that counter truth (Rom 16:17). He further indicates that they are selfishly motivated and deceptive (Rom 16:18). This directly contradicts his earlier picture of a community that is demonstrating genuine love. In other words, they destroy the unity of both the church and the gospel and, therefore, prevent the community from carrying out its ultimate purpose on the earth—reaching the rest of the world for Christ. His description, contrasting genuine love with selfish motivation, provides the community with a benchmark for identifying those who would destroy unity. In addition, it heightens the significance of expressing genuine love, since true love reveals true faith.

While outreach is not directly in view, it meets the second criterion for the following reasons. First, protecting the integrity of the church and the gospel is a community responsibility. Second, outreach is indirectly in view since it is a primary responsibility of the church, and the destruction Paul is describing would hinder that mission. Therefore, it is incumbent on the community to organize in such a way so as to recognize those who would destroy unity and deter the group from carrying out its mission.

Prison Epistles

(Ephesians, Philippians, Colossians and Philemon)

In the Prison Epistles,[74] one of the common themes Paul is addressing is the fundamental issue of the unity of the church. In Ephesians he addresses the issue of unity as it relates to the Jews and Gentiles.[75] In Philippians he addresses unity that results from the service of the individual within the community.[76] In Colossians he addresses unity as it relates to theological belief.[77] And in Philemon he addresses unity as it relates to slavery and the result of living in such a way that demonstrates love within that structure.[78] This section is developed following the structure of Ephesians. This is because the theme of Ephesians is directly related to the unity of the church as accomplished between Jew and Gentile based on the finished work of Christ.[79] Because unity is so prominent in the Prison Epistles, the community aspect is strong and community principles surface at strategic and significant locations.

Displaying the Glory and Wisdom of God is the Responsibility of the Community

Ephesians. Paul makes a very interesting statement when he says, "The purpose of this enlightenment is that through the church the multifaceted wisdom of God should now be disclosed to the rulers and the authorities in the heavenly realms" (Eph 3:10). The enlightenment being discussed is the revealed mystery that the Gentiles are included in God's plan of salvation (Eph 3:6). The purpose of revealing the mystery was to demonstrate the wisdom of God to the rest of creation. The medium through which this wisdom is revealed is the church.[80] The context makes it clear that this was God's eternal purpose (Eph 3:11). Here is one of the reasons why the church, and by implication, the individual believer, is to live in obedience to God's commands.

This forms the foundation for Paul's community-oriented prayer in which he asks that the church be strengthened internally with power (Eph 3:16), that Christ may dwell in the hearts of the believers in the church (Eph 3:17), and that the church might be able to comprehend Christ in a deeper way (Eph 3:18–19). Paul's use of the phrase σὺν πᾶσιν τοῖς ἁγίοις (with all the saints, Eph 3:18) reveals that he has the community in mind. What starts with the individual necessarily must find its culmination in community. Failure to carry these principles through to community misses the point Paul is making. Culmination in community is the concept Paul has in mind as he views the church displaying God's wisdom.

Paul's concluding benediction repeats the principle in a slightly different way. He reveals that the glory of God is also revealed in community and in

Christ (Eph 3:21). It is difficult to see how this can be accomplished outside of community. The larger preceding and following context of unity in the new community formed in Christ argues for a community perspective. Part of the believer's purpose is to live in community in such a way as to demonstrate both the wisdom and glory of God. This passage reveals that there is a much larger purpose at work than the life of the individual believer. Part of growing in Christian maturity is recognizing this aspect and living life in community in a way that reveals God's glory and wisdom.

Philippians. In Philippians, a similar pattern emerges in Paul's opening prayer. The use of πάντες ὑμεῖς (you all) throughout this section emphasizes his concern for the unity of the church (Phil 1:1, 4, 7, 8).[81] Within this structure there is a consistent focus on God's involvement with the Philippians and their active obedience and response. This is seen in such concepts as Paul's confidence in God's continuing work in the community (Phil 1:6), their partnership with Paul in the gospel and God's grace (Phil 1:7), and his prayer that their love would abound in knowledge resulting in sincerity and blamelessness (Phil 1:9–10). Each of these concepts is observable and finds fruition in relationship and community. This is what Paul has in mind when he concludes with the expressed wish that all of this would result in glory and praise to God (Phil 1:11).[82]

Similarly, at the end of the epistle, he states, "And my God will supply all that you need according to the riches of his glory in Christ Jesus. May glory be given to God our Father forever and ever. Amen" (Phil 4:19–20). He had just thanked them for their financial gift which he described as "a fragrant offering, an acceptable sacrifice, very pleasing to God" (Phil 4:18). The linkage between community sacrifice and glory emphasizes one of the ways in which the community displays the glory of God. Peter T. O'Brien argues that "the apostle is assuring his readers that their every need will be completely met as they share in God's glory" (p. 548). It is individuals acting within community who display God's glory. These passages meet the second criterion, since Paul makes it clear that it is through the community that the wisdom and glory of God are displayed.

Maintaining Unity within Community is Necessary for Effective Ministry

Ephesians. In Ephesians 4, Paul makes a transition from the "indicatives of the faith" to the "imperatives of the faith." It is significant that his first major emphasis is to "live in unity" (Eph 4:1–16). As discussed earlier, the exhortation to live worthily (Eph 4:1) is clarified with the participial clause, σπουδάζοντες τηρεῖν τὴν ἑνότητα τοῦ πνεύματος ἐν τῷ συνδέσμῳ τῆς εἰρήνης ("making every effort to keep the unity of the Spirit in the bond of peace," Eph 4:3).[83] He goes on to demonstrate that this unity is based on the "one Spirit," "one Lord," "one faith" aspect of the believer's life in Christ.

This passage is significant in the present study for two reasons. First, genuine unity is possible because all believers belong to the community and live and obey the command within the community context. Second, the outward focus resulting from sanctification is clear in this text. Paul is exhorting his readers that, while the foundation to unity is located in the work of Christ, the practical outworking of that unity is located in relationship within the community (p. 513).[84] On the continuum discussed earlier, this represents the movement of the community from union to relational harmony. He exhorts them to live worthily with all humility and gentleness, with patience, and bearing with one another in love (Eph 4:2). All of these modifying phrases are verbal in orientation and require community for both the unity to occur (as defined by Paul) and for unity to be worked out.

The concept of unity is expanded in Eph 4:11–16. Here, as earlier, the unity is related to the equipping of believers for the purpose of ministry (Eph 4). This passage is still in the larger context of preserving unity. Here, though, the idea of ministry is emphasized. The building up of the body of Christ is for the purpose of establishing unity, that is, "a mature person, attaining to the measure of Christ's full stature" (Eph 4:13). The movement in this passage is from the plural to the singular.[85]

Paul's concludes that unity in Christ will result as believers practice the truth in love (Eph 4:15). The reason is because of the work of Christ: "From him the whole body grows, fitted and held together through every supporting ligament. As each one does its part, the body grows in love" (Eph 4:16). Paul is clear that Christ himself is the center that makes everything possible. However, unity in Christ is once again balanced between his present and finished work, and the body which Christ causes to build itself up in love (p. 578).[86] For Paul, while Christ is the center, the members are the instruments of growth in each other's lives (p. 578).[87]

The body imagery and argument in this text emphasizes the interdependent relationships as discussed earlier. This concept of interdependency is captured in the very reason why the gifts were given. Ultimately, they are to build up the body of Christ (Eph 4:13). As discussed earlier, this metaphor has much more in view than simple existence. It captures the living, dynamic aspect of the church as found in relationship. This complex, interdependent, unified, and dynamic body is to work together to produce growth in Christian maturity, ultimately in order to minister together and thus fulfill God's plan. Here, the twin ideas of movement from the individual to the community and of outward focus are clear and profound in this passage.

Philippians. In a similar passage in Philippians, Paul begins his discussion with an exhortation for proper conduct[88] and living in a worthy manner (Phil 1:27).[89] In this context he uses a series of modifiers to communicate the necessity for unity. The believers are to stand firm in one spirit[90] (ἐν ἑνὶ πνεύματι), with one mind (μιᾷ ψυχῇ), contending side by side for the faith (συναθλοῦντες τῇ πίστει; Phil 1:27). Immediately after this, Paul reiterates that believers are to be of the same mind (τὸ αὐτὸ φρονῆτε), share the same love (τὴν αὐτὴν ἀγάπην ἔχοντες), be united in spirit (σύμψυχοι), and share the same purpose (τὸ ἓν φρονοῦντες; Phil 2:2). The use of φρονέω emphasizes the need for unity in thought as well as action.[91] The combination reveals that proper conduct involves unity.

Colossians. The concept of living a worthy life also appears in Colossians when Paul says, "...live worthily of the Lord and please him in all respects" (Col 1:10). While the various terms related to unity are absent, the concept is present. In Col 1:3–8, Paul thanks God for virtues present within the Colossian community. In Col 1:9–14, he prays for virtues missing in the church. Perhaps these missing virtues are necessary for them to work successfully through the problems associated with the heresy.

For example, whereas they knew of the gospel (Col 1:5), they needed deeper spiritual knowledge and understanding (Col 1:10). In a similar way, while the gospel was bearing fruit through them for evangelism (Col 1:6–7), they needed to bear fruit related to Christian growth and transformation (Col 1:11–12). This additional fruit-bearing involved good deeds, growth in knowledge and strengthening in power, all for the purpose of displaying patience and steadfastness (Col 1:11). These are relational terms related to community. Here the concept of movement from the individual to the community is present.

This serves as the background for Paul's discussion on the heresy that threatened to destroy the Colossian church. It seems his point, before he discusses the heresy, is that they needed to invest more into building unity. Dealing with a complex theological problem that has the potential to destroy unity would require a strong and unified group.

Philemon. Finally, Philemon is a letter rooted in issues involving unity. The circumstances surrounding slavery in the first century created a drama between Paul, Philemon and his family, and Onesimus in which there was divergence in social class that tended toward relational disunity. With the advent of Christianity and life in the Spirit, these class and relational distinctions posed a threat to spiritual unity within the church. As such, Paul's letter to Philemon represents a plea to live within the social structure of slavery in such a way that each person in the differing classes could demonstrate genuine love and thus create true spiritual unity, even with human ownership.[92] As noted by Bruce, while the epistle itself provides little formal teaching on the subject of slavery, it does "bring us into an atmosphere in which the institution could only wilt and die."[93]

Within this context, there are several aspects of community life and associated implications that relate to unity. First, the tone of the letter is such that Paul refrains from giving Philemon demands about Onesimus, other than the appeal to love (Phlm 9, 14). Rather, he places the matter completely under Philemon's control.[94] The implication is that spiritual unity results from one individual moving toward another in genuine love. Second, while the social structure of slavery identified Onesimus as a runaway slave, Paul identified him as a fellow believer (Phlm 16). The implication is that spiritual unity results when a believer in a position of authority acts toward another to lift them up in equality in Christ. Finally, Paul assumed the consequences for the criminal acts of Onesimus, to the point of assuming the debt created by Onesimus' fraud (Phlm 18). The implication is that spiritual unity results when a believer moves toward another believer to assume or share the burden created by their position or immaturity.

What this epistle reveals is that community is necessary to live in unity. As discussed earlier, the very heart of unity involves relationship and movement within relationship such that another's best interests are exalted and protected. In addition, the context of the epistle reveals that what Paul was asking Philemon to do had a public aspect to it.[95] In other words, it was observable. What Paul did of his own accord and what he was asking of Philemon was exactly what Christ did for the church—he put the interest of others before himself as an expression of love.[96]

Confronting Deeds of Darkness and Bearing Fruit is a Community Responsibility

In Eph 5:8 Paul exhorts the Ephesians to "walk as children of light." The metaphor "light" is a consistent Pauline metaphor that is contrasted with darkness and night.[97] The point of comparison for this metaphor has to do with both ontology and teleology. Believers are considered to be light because of their association with and regeneration in Christ.[98] It also involves behavior and the way believers live their life, that is, the character of the fruit they bear.[99]

The distinction between light and darkness implies a contrast in worlds (1 Thess 5:1–11). These metaphors function as "spheres or qualifying forces."[100] And, the metaphors carry a strong behavioral nuance. "Being light is worked out in conduct."[101] This is in view here. O'Brien argues that these metaphors are continuing the previous discussion concerning the old humanity and the new humanity (Eph 4:22–24; discussed earlier). This means that they carry an eschatological orientation as well. Whereas darkness represents what believers once were, light represents what they presently are, and are becoming in Christ as they are transformed.

Whereas darkness represents "ignorance, error, and evil," light represents "truth, knowledge, and now holiness."[102] As such, walking in the light is most likely metaphorical for transformation; the progressive idea being captured by "trying to learn what is pleasing to the Lord" (Eph 5:10). In the context, walking in darkness involves indulging the desires of the flesh, that is, the "unfruitful deeds of darkness." In contrast, walking in light involves bearing the fruit of "goodness, righteousness, and truth" (Eph 5:9). In this context, believers are to "walk as children of the light" (Eph 5:8).

But the metaphor is more complex than individual choice and avoiding destruction and engaging in righteousness. Paul goes on further to say, "Do not participate in the unfruitful deeds of darkness, but rather expose them" (Eph 5:11). Exposing the deeds of darkness involves showing someone their sin and calling them to repentance.[103] While there is debate about whether the exposing is internal or external, it is possible that both are in view.[104] To be sure, exposing sin is the responsibility of the Holy Spirit (John 16:8) and, therefore, it is an unusual role for the church. As was argued earlier, this passage is in a longer context in which the preservation of unity is the main point (Eph 4:1–3). This supports the idea that, with the exhortation in Eph 5:11 to expose sin, God has assigned this responsibility to the community. However, while the community is to expose the deeds, *who* is responsible for the deeds?

The beginning of this section begins with an imperative to "let nobody deceive you with empty words, for because of these things God's wrath comes on the sons of disobedience" (Eph 5:6). The phrase "sons of disobedience" appeared in Eph 2:2 where they are identified as unbelievers. Regarding these individuals, Harold W. Hoehner argues that the terminology as well as the context in both occurrences reveals that "unbelief is more than absence of trust—it is a defiance against God."[105] Although Eph 5:6 does not specify who originates the deceptive and empty words, the reference to the sons of disobedience implies that they were involved. This explains Paul's command to not be partakers with them (Eph 2:7). With this background, the ones who are responsible for the deeds that need to be exposed are identified as those who deceive the community and destroy the unity—the sons of disobedience. Unity must be preserved and sin exposed whether it is challenged from inside the church or outside.

Living Wisely Requires Community Involvement under the Control of the Spirit

Ephesians. In Eph 5:15–16, Paul exhorts the Ephesians to "be very careful how you live—not as unwise but as wise, taking advantage of every opportunity, because the days are evil" (Eph 5:15–16). In this context, there are three sets of parallel ideas to explain what it means to live in wisdom:

Βλέπετε οὖν ἀκριβῶς πῶς περιπατεῖτε . . .
Therefore, be careful how you live

μὴ ὡς ἄσοφοι	ἀλλ'	ὡς σοφοί (5:15)
Not as unwise	but	as wise
μὴ γίνεσθε ἄφροντες	ἀλλὰ	συνίετε τί τὸ θέλημα τοῦ κυρίου (5:17)
Do not be foolish	but	[be wise] by understanding what the will of the Lord is
μὴ μεθύσκεσθε οἴνῳ	ἀλλὰ	πληροῦσθε ἐν πνεύματι (5:18)
Do not get drunk with wine	but	be filled by the Spirit

The structure demonstrates that there is linkage between wisdom, understanding God's will and being filled by the Spirit.

There are several features that reveal that Paul has community in mind throughout his section. First, the verbs and participles applied to the recipients are all plural throughout this first section. Second, the following series of participles (Eph 5:19–21) are all community-oriented as follows:

λαλοῦντες ἑαυτοῖς ἐν ψαλμοῖς καὶ ὕμνοις καὶ ᾠδαῖς πνευματικαῖς (5:19)
Speaking to one another in psalms, hymns, and spiritual songs

ᾄδοντες καὶ (5:19)
Singing and...

ψάλλοντες τῇ καρδίᾳ ὑμῶν τῷ κυρίῳ (5:19)
Making music in your hearts to the Lord

εὐχαριστοῦντες πάντοτε ὑπὲρ πάντων ἐν ὀνόματι τοῦ κυρίου ἡμῶν (5:20)

Always giving thanks… for each other in the name of our Lord Jesus
Christ

ὑποτασσόμενοι ἀλλήλοις ἐν φόβῳ Χριστοῦ (5:20)
Submitting to one another out of reverence for Christ

The use of the reflexive pronoun ἑαυτοῦ (one another) and the reciprocal pronoun ἀλλήλων (one another) serve to frame the series as a text oriented toward
relationship and confirm that Paul has the community in mind.[106]

Third, the following section (Eph 5:22–6:9) expands this last participle and
demonstrates how the community is to live wisely at the foundational levels of
relationship: the marriage and family relationships. "Paul's injunction to be
filled by the Spirit extends beyond merely a church service or a casual gathering
to the believer's life at home and at work where he or she will be observed
twenty-four hours a day."[107] Fourth, as noted by O'Brien,

> The passage further explains what it means to *live a life worthily of the calling you have received*
> (4:1), the opening admonition and 'topic sentence' of the lengthy exhortatory material
> that extends from 4:1 to 6:9.[108]

The community orientation of Eph 4 has already been established. Paul is here
completing the "walking" series that he started in Eph 4:1.

In this passage, walking in wisdom is discussed in terms of knowing the will
of the Lord.[109] The command here is not implying that the Ephesians do not
know God's will, for he had already made it known (Eph 1:9). Rather, with the
use of the verb συνίημι, Paul is admonishing the Ephesians to "appropriate
it."[110] Understanding implies a changed thought-process resulting in changed
behavior.[111] The secret mystery that had been revealed was the inclusion of
Gentiles into the new humanity (Eph 2:15–16; 3:6). It is this revealed mystery
that forms the foundation for Paul's imperatives in Eph 4–6. Since they are part
of the new humanity, they should think and act accordingly.

As the structure demonstrates, walking in wisdom is also discussed in terms
of being filled with the Spirit. At issue here is the construction ἐν with the dative; does it imply content? Daniel Wallace notes that there are no clear New
Testament examples where this construction indicates content. Rather, he argues that this construction is inferring means; the Holy Spirit is the means by
which believers are filled.[112]

Placing the Holy Spirit textually in contradistinction to drunkenness, although surprising, orients the role of the Holy Spirit more toward control.[113]
Just as drunkenness results in a loss of control, so being filled with the Spirit
indicates living under control. "If drunkenness leads to dissolute behaviour,

then Spirit-filled Christians whose lives are characterized by singing, thanksgiving, and submission present a very different picture" (p. 394). As just described by O'Brien, the five participles describe life for a community that is filled by the Spirit. This understanding classes these participles as result participles; they express the condition that results from being filled by the Spirit.

To summarize, the exhortation to walk wisely means understanding the will of God. Contextually, his will is related to what he has already accomplished by creating the new humanity and how individuals are to live within that new humanity. The way believers walk wisely is by being filled with the Spirit; being under the control of the Spirit, such that their expressions are characterized by singing, thanksgiving, and submission. Relating this back to the original exhortation in Eph 4:1–3, being filled with the Spirit is an essential step in guarding the unity of the Spirit in the bond of peace.

From a community perspective, the following context reveals several significant concepts. First, the principles of being filled with the Spirit are applied to the lowest level of solidarity,[114] namely, relationship between two people.[115] While individuals are addressed, they are addressed in the context of how to be integrally involved in mutually edifying, life-changing relationships that guard the unity of the Spirit.

Second, in each passage, unity is an observable characteristic. This is that aspect of unity discussed earlier in which the church is growing together into the new humanity by obeying Christ as a community. The emphasis is on the outward focus that results from our sanctification and relating to others, rather than a state of being. While grounded in the work of Christ, unity is, at the core, a community exercise involving outward movement into each other's lives for the purpose of serving and putting their interests first. This seems to be the central message Paul is communicating by the series of "walking" commands which are to preserve the unity of the Spirit (Eph 4:1, 17; 5:2, 8, 15).[116] This outward movement is what is observable from the perspective of the world.

Third, this passage demonstrates in real and tangible ways what was discussed in chapters 3 and 4, namely, that holiness—reflecting God's glory—is more than separation from something bad; it is also dedication to something good and ultimately attainable.

These ideas (and those discussed in the earlier chapters) are seen in the marriage text where Paul compares the union of marriage with the relationship of Christ to the church.

> Husbands, love your wives just as Christ loved the church and gave himself for her to sanctify her by cleansing her with the washing of the water by the word, so that he may present the church to himself as glorious—not having a stain or wrinkle, or any such blemish, but holy and blameless (Eph 5:25–27).

Christ's sacrificial acts toward the church are the primary example in this passage of how spouses are to relate to one another.[117] Their involvement in each other's life is to produce a dynamic quality that results in growth to maturity. In other words, marriage is as much related to the holiness of the believer as it is their happiness.

In addition, the dynamic view of the image of God discussed in chapter 4 is seen in how believers relate to each other. If progressive sanctification is observable in relationships, then it follows that image-bearing is also observable in relationships. In other words, believers model the image of God best and clearest when they relate to one another in such a way that holiness is protected and love is generated.

Colossians. In a related passage, Paul states, "We proclaim him by instructing and teaching all people with all wisdom so that we may present every person mature in Christ" (Col 1:28). There are several features in this passage that reveal that this is a community text involving wisdom. The passage is oriented toward the church at-large (ὑπὲρ τοῦ σώματος αὐτοῦ, ὅ ἐστιν ἡ ἐκκλησία) and the Colossian church in particular (ὑπέρ ὑμῶν) (Col 1:24).[118] His goal for bringing up his sufferings is that they would be encouraged as they grew in their understanding of the mystery of Christ and the ensuing treasures of wisdom and knowledge (Col 2:2–3).

It is in this context that Paul writes Col 1:28. What is significant from this verse is that the very act of helping another believer grow in maturity is relational in nature. Christian maturation, or the progressive aspect of sanctification, is the core of what is being addressed in this study. Here Paul reveals a very clear principle that community (found at the lowest level of solidarity—one-on-one relationship) is fundamental to growth in maturity. Here is seen the movement from the individual to the community. It is the individual (Paul) who is instructing and teaching[119] the community such that all people within the community grow in maturity (p. 88).[120] That Paul had community in mind is further clarified later when he says, "Let the word of Christ dwell in you richly, teaching and exhorting one another with all wisdom" (Col 3:16).[121]

These texts reveal that living in wisdom necessarily involves community.[122] Specifically, it involves relationship. Applying the principles of unity to relationship makes progressive sanctification, at its core, a relational activity. Community is necessary to live in wisdom.

Preserving the Unity of the Spirit Requires the Community Fighting the Spiritual Battle Together

Paul concludes Ephesians with the exhortation, "Finally, be strengthened in the Lord and in the strength of his power. Clothe yourselves with the full armor of

God so that you may be able to stand against the schemes of the devil" (Eph 6:10–11). This entire section (Eph 6:10–20) has traditionally been interpreted individualistically, with the battle scene oriented between the individual and Satan.[123] The entire discussion typically revolves around how the individual is to put on the full armor of God. However, as concluded above, Ephesians represents a sustained argument demonstrating how the Jews and Gentiles have been united in one body in Christ, and are therefore to live in unity within this new community. With the strong community emphasis in Ephesians, it is not surprising that the force of the commands in the last section is community-oriented as well. In other words, guarding the unity of the Spirit (Eph 4:3) is a community activity wherein believers fight the spiritual battle together.

As with the rest of Ephesians, the plural imperatives orient the discussion toward community.[124] Of particular interest is the command for members of the community to "clothe" themselves with the full armor of God (Eph 6:11). The earlier use of this verb in Eph 4:24 commands the Ephesians to "put on" the new humanity. Both this passage and the parallel passage in Col 3:10 were evaluated in chapter 4 and it was argued that this is a reference to the new humanity formed in Christ. In both contexts putting off the old person and putting on the new is a metaphor for the conversion and baptism experience found in Christ. As such, the "putting off" and "putting on" imagery reflects an exchange of identities.

In addition, the linkage regarding the heavenly realm (Eph 6:12) was also evaluated previously and it was concluded that this refers to the location where God, Christ, all believers, and the heavenly host dwell. As such, it is directly related to the new spiritual temple as God's dwelling place (Eph 2:20–22). The imagery of the new humanity and the temple are both community metaphors to describe how believers relate to Christ and what they are becoming in Christ.

In addition, the language used to describe the armament itself and the corresponding strategies employed by the Roman army in warfare support a community orientation. With the use of θυρεός to describe the broad shield (Eph 6:16), Paul is picturing the Roman infantry soldier.[125] The soldier's armament, especially the use of the broad shield, was designed to be used against an enemy in a line of battle, rather than as an individual.[126] However, the individual emphasis is not lost. Preparing for battle is as much an individual exercise as it is a community endeavor. Each believer must prepare for the battle. The point is that the battle is to be fought as the new humanity stands firm together against Satan. This final section reveals the ultimate defense against the attack on the unity of the church—the community standing together against Satan.

Pastoral Epistles (1 and 2 Timothy, Titus)

Among the consistent proposals for the theme of the Pastoral Epistles is the idea that Paul is providing instructions to Christians in Asia Minor and Crete regarding Christian living and church life. I. Howard Marshall states, "The letters introduce new concepts to describe the nature of Christian conduct."[127] As such, the community plays a significant role in the development of godly leaders.

Developing Godly Leaders Requires Involvement in Community

One of the major themes in the Pastorals is the development of leadership. Marshall notes that approximately one sixth of these epistles are devoted to leadership and related matters (1 Tim 3:1–12; 2 Tim 2:1–7; Tit 1:5–9).[128] Growing in leadership capability is directly related to progressive sanctification since the very heart of the matter involves Christian maturity. As such, the passages in the Pastorals related to leadership have several statements concerning the role of the community.

In the qualifications for elder there are several points at which community and relationship play a dominant role in preparing one for leadership. Elders must manage their own household well and keep their children under control. The implications of this are significant and related to the experience necessary for managing the church (1 Tim 3:4–5; Titus 1:6). Accomplishment of this reveals one's priorities, one's ability to lead others well, commitment to endurance, and commitment to God's Word in the family. It is within this relational nucleus that leadership qualities are developed and revealed.

In addition, the elder must be well thought of by non-believers. The immediate reason is so that they will avoid disgrace with the unchurched (1 Tim 3:7). These two spheres, the community and the culture, ensure that a leader growing in maturity has a consistent pattern of integrity.[129] It is difficult to fool both the community and their relationships with unbelievers. The leader's reputation in both arenas ensures that godly leadership qualities have been developed and verified.

In addition, both spheres imply outward relational movement and focus on the part of the leader. As discussed in chapters 3 and 4, sanctification involves an outward focus. The outward focus in the family has to do with the well-being of the individual family members. The outward focus in the culture has to do with evangelism and maintaining a godly witness. In discussing this verse, Marshall notes, "The health (good witness) of the church and its leaders impinge on the acceptance of the gospel by those outside" (p. 484).

In 2 Timothy, Paul provides another reason community is necessary for developing leaders when he says, "And what you heard me say in the presence of many others as witnesses entrust to faithful people who will be competent to teach others as well" (2 Tim 2:2). The strong emphasis on teaching in the Pastorals (e.g., 2 Tim 4:1–5) is here related to the development of mature leaders. "Passing the torch" is a necessary element in maintaining continuity and helping the less mature grow in their desire to serve Christ and their understanding of the truth (p. 725).[130] In this regard, the community becomes the channel for teaching the truth and developing leaders.

Summary

After reviewing the Pauline corpus, the following concluding observations are made regarding the role of the community in the progressive sanctification of believers. First, the concept of solidarity as it was originally conceived of in Israel reflects development in the New Testament. The most radical redefinition occurred through the life and ministry of Christ as was concluded in chapter 5. In addition, for Paul, while it is true that solidarity is centered in Christ, Christ also is the true human—the image of God—and the one who created the new humanity. As such, Christ's dynamic involvement with the new humanity generates true spiritual unity wherein believers are engaged with each other in the transformation process.

Second, for Paul, the cultural markers originally given to Israel all point to a spiritual reality found only in Christ and experienced only in community. As the true human, Christ has created the new order to which every believer belongs. By fulfilling the law, he has freed believers from the tyranny of the law and sin and has enabled every believer to love others. By creating the new spiritual temple, he has redefined the individual's identity—their values, well being, and actions—such that they now participate in a community life of holiness and find significance through the building of the temple.

Finally, for Paul, progressive sanctification is that process wherein believers are experiencing transformation into the image of God, thus increasing their capacity to reflect his glory to others. This process is accomplished as believers engage in the community and obey the commands of God together. As they obey God's commands and reflect his glory, the community grows together and impacts the world for Christ.

NOTES

1 F. F. Bruce, *Paul: Apostle of the Heart Set Free* (Grand Rapids: Eerdmans, 1977), 475. The epistles are examined in the chronological order identified by Bruce.

2 David S. Dockery, "Fruit of the Spirit," in *DPL*, 317.

3 As discussed in earlier, this study assumes the South Galatian view of Galatians. Herman N. Ridderbos, *The Epistle of Paul to the Churches of Galatia: The English Text with Introduction, Exposition and Notes*, trans. Henry Zylstra, NICNT, ed. N. B. Stonehouse (Grand Rapids: Eerdmans, 1953; reprint, 1981), 18; F. F. Bruce, *The Epistle to the Galatians: A Commentary on the Greek Text*, NIGTC, ed. I. Howard Marshall, and W. Ward Gasque (Grand Rapids: Eerdmans, 1982), 3.

4 Note the use of the reciprocal pronoun ἀλλήλοις in verses 13 and 26. This appears to set the passage off in a form of inclusio. Walt Russell calls this combination a "bookend in Paul's argument." Walt Russell, "The Apostle Paul's Redemptive-Historical Argumentation in Galatians 5:13–26," *Westminster Theological Journal* 57 (fall 1995): 337. Although Bruce does not identify it as an inclusio, he identifies it as a distinct pericope resuming the discussion started in verse 6. Bruce, *Galatians*, 239–40. See also Moisés Silva, *Interpreting Galatians: Explorations in Exegetical Method*, 2d ed. (Grand Rapids: Baker, 2001), 98–99.

5 As community was defined earlier, it can be accomplished with unbelievers as well. However, the context here reveals that Paul had the Christian community in mind with a view to stating the purpose of the fruit of the Spirit.

6 ἀγάπη-ἀγαπάω; χαρά-χαίρω; εἰρήνη-εἰρηνεύω; μακροθυμία-μακροθυμέω; χρηστότης-χρηστεύομαι; ἀγαθωσύνη-ἀγαθοποιέω; πίστις-πιστεύω; πραΰτης-ταπεινόω (synonym; Friedrich Hauck and Siegfried Schulz, "πραΰς, πραΰτης," in *TDNT*, 646); ἐγκράτεια-ἐγχρατεύομαι.

7 Dockery, "Fruit of the Spirit," in *DPL*, 318.

8 Michael Parsons, "Being Precedes Act: Indicative and Imperative in Paul's Writing," *EvQ* 60 (April 1988): 121–22. He argues persuasively that the first class condition in Gal 5:25 reveals that, for Paul, believers do live by the Spirit. As such, the exhortation in the apodosis is more than encouragement. It reflects that the Spirit is the "author of their new creation and new life" and the one who "makes possible the life which he demands." It is this imperative quality that makes the community essential to obedience.

9 Although God used Balaam and his donkey (Num 22:22–35), the pattern is still consistent and clear. Examples include Nathan and David (2 Sam 12:1–14), Samuel and Saul (1 Sam 28:3–19), and Paul and Peter (Gal 2:11–14). Nor is it to downplay the role of the Spirit in the exposure of sin. It is the work of the Spirit in and through the community that often exposes the sin in individuals. The emphasis in these examples is exposure of sin and helping another come to the realization of the existence of some sin.

10 Silva, *Exegetical Method*, 182–83. See also, Thomas R. Schreiner, "Law of Christ," in *DPL*, 542–43, who defines the law of Christ as "the moral norms of the OT Law, focusing particularly on the commandment to love one's neighbor." Bruce W. Longenecker, "Defining the Faithful Character of the Covenant Community: Galatians 2.15–21 and Beyond," in *Paul and the Mosaic Law*, ed. James D. G. Dunn (Grand Rapids: Eerdmans, 2001): 91–93, argues that in this passage, the Mosaic law comes to its fullest expression and represents a redefinition of the law by Paul. As such, it is now related to the Spirit and community of Christ. Morna D. Hooker, "'Heirs of Abraham': The Gentiles' Role in Israel's Story," in

Narrative Dynamics in Paul: A Critical Assessment, ed. Bruce W. Longenecker (Louisville, KY: Westminster John Knox, 2002) 94, similarly states, "The law might not have been able to give the life it promised (3:12), but it pointed clearly enough to what God required of God's people—the love for others that is now realized in the lives of those who 'live by the Spirit' (5:16)."

11 The issue of βάρος (Gal 6:2) versus φορτίον (Gal 6:5) is well documented in New Testament scholarship. As noted by Silva, identifying the difference as being between an "oppressive burden" and a "light load" may be pressing the semantic distinction too far. Allowing for a paradox does not eliminate the community orientation. It is possible that the believer is carrying his own load while looking to carry the load of others as well. In contrast, looking to others to carry one's load violates the intent of the command. Silva, *Exegetical Method*, 56–57. These two verses, when placed together, may reflect a healthy tension that balances between avoiding an entitlement mentality (Gal 6:5) and an individualistic arrogance about one's own abilities (Gal 6:2).

12 This is the view taken by Bruce, *Galatians*, 265.

13 Russell, "Redemptive-Historical Argumentation," 338. "Paul's argument takes a strong relational turn in Gal 5:6 that continues through 6:16." He focuses his discussion on the contrast between σάρξ and πνεῦμα and notes that this represents a new "relational standard" in the church.

14 F. F. Bruce, *1 & 2 Thessalonians*, WBC, ed. David A. Hubbard, Glenn W. Barker, and Ralph P. Martin, vol. 45 (Waco, TX: Word, 1982), xxxvi–xxxix; Leon Morris, *The First and Second Epistles to the Thessalonians: The English Text with Introduction, Exposition and Notes*, NICNT, ed. F. F. Bruce (Grand Rapids: Eerdmans, 1959), 22–24; D. Edmond Hiebert, *The Thessalonian Epistles: A Call to Readiness* (Chicago, IL: Moody, 1971), 23, 263–64.

15 Wayne McCown, "God's Will for You: Sanctification in the Thessalonian Epistles," *Wesleyan Theological Journal* 12 (spring 1977): 26. He argues that the sanctification texts provide the literary framework for understanding these epistles as well as the major thematic motif.

16 Karl Paul Donfried, *Paul, Thessalonica, and Early Christianity* (Grand Rapids: Eerdmans, 2002), 120.

17 Charles A. Wanamaker, *The Epistles to the Thessalonians: A Commentary on the Greek Text*, NIGTC, ed. I. Howard Marshall, and W. Ward Gasque (Grand Rapids: Eerdmans, 1990), 82.

18 Robert Banks, *Paul's Idea of Community: The Early House Churches in Their Historical Setting*, rev. ed. (Peabody, MA: Hendrickson, 1994), 184; Donfried, *Thessalonica*, 149. Donfried argues that the Thessalonians became an "actualization" of the gospel through their living out the gospel.

19 Paul is using the first person plural pronouns throughout this section most likely as an exclusive "we" since both Timothy and Silas were with him when he visited Thessalonica (Acts 16:3; 17:4). Here is an example of how a smaller community can impact a larger community for their transformation.

20 Wanamaker, *Thessalonians*, 80, raises the possibility that Paul understood his own life as "a form of mediation between Christ and his converts." In other words, his life became a model of Christ-likeness for new converts. This does not violate the context and allows for an even stronger bond between outward focus and example.

21 Preben Vang, "Sanctification in Thessalonians," *SwJT* 42 (fall 1999): 54. See also, Bruce,

Thessalonians, 37–38, who raises the possibility that Paul's reference to the kingdom and glory in this verse might have present implications, since Paul refers to the kingdom in terms of the present life in the Spirit in Rom 14:17 and 1 Cor 4:20. What is clear is the future aspect of his reference to the kingdom and glory. In addition, earlier it was argued from 2 Cor 3:18 that the beholding of glory implies reflection. In the context, Paul contrasts selfish motives—not seeking glory from people (1 Thess 2:6)—with righteous motives—encouraging others to live worthy lives. In both contexts, Paul utilizes the glory concept to illustrate these motives. Whether he meant to imply the idea of reflection directly in his use of glory is not clear. However, his examples all demonstrate how living in godliness is a community exercise, and which is part of reflecting God's glory.

22   The context indicates that they were imitators of the churches in Judea (1 Thess 2:14). However, the impact is related to apostolic leadership for several reasons. First, as noted earlier Paul begins his argument by indicating that they had imitated both him (and others) and God (1 Thess 1:6). Second, as argued by Bruce, their knowledge of the Judean churches was hearsay at best. See Bruce, *Thessalonians*, 45. As a result "the experience of the Judean churches was reproduced in the Thessalonian church" and they imitated the faithfulness and responsiveness that they had heard about in the Judean churches. According to Acts 8:1–2, these churches probably originated out of the Jerusalem church and were now "in dispersion." Here is an example of how whole communities impact other communities. See also Wanamaker, *Thessalonians*, 112–13.

Marcus Barth, *The People of God, JSNTSup*, vol. 5 (Sheffield, England: JSOT, 1983), 16, in an attempt to demonstrate that Paul was anti-Semitic, raises an interesting observation. In this passage, Paul is using the Jews as a "negative foil" to Christianity. While this study does not take the position that Paul was anti-Semitic, it is conceivable that Paul was using Judaism as a negative foil to illustrate that the true intent of the law involved loving others, and that the gospel was intended to be lived out as an example to all peoples. This idea is consistent with the redevelopment by Jesus of the symbol of law presented in chapter 5.

23   Donfried, *Thessalonica*, 122–23, notes that the term ἁγιασμός appears three times here (1 Thess 4:3, 4, 7) and only three other times in the remainder of the Pauline corpus. This concentration in 1 Thessalonians supports the emphasis on sanctification. "If for Paul suffering was an advertisement for God then it followed especially that the situation of persecution was no excuse for moral laxity or any behavior which would allow the non-Christian world to ridicule the work of God in Thessalonica" (p. 123). This is an example of the outward focus of sanctification discussed earlier.

24   The issues surrounding σκεῦος are well known in New Testament scholarship. Whether one sees it as referring to one's own body or one's own wife does not obscure the need for continual holiness. The context reveals sexual purity as the primary topic under discussion. Therefore, holiness here is framed by the need for sexual purity in the believer's life. For further review of this issue see, Jouette M. Bassler, "Skeuos: A Modest Proposal for Illuminating Paul's Use of Metaphor in 1 Thessalonians 4:4," in *The Social World of the First Christians: Essays in Honor of Wayne A. Meeks* (Minneapolis, MN: Fortress, 1995): 53–56; Torleif Elgvin, "'To Master His Own Vessel': 1 Thess 4:4 in Light of New Qumran Evidence," *NTS* 43 (October 1997): 604–19; William L. Lane, "Vessel, Pot, Potter, Mix," in *NIDNTT*, 3:910–13; Christian Maurer, "σκεῦος," in *TDNT*, 7:358–67; Jay E. Smith, "1 Thess 4:4–Breaking the Impasse," *BBR* 11, no. 1 (2001).

25   F. Blass and A. Debrunner, *A Greek Grammar of the New Testament and Other Early Christian Literature*, trans. Robert W. Funk (Chicago: University of Chicago Press, 1961), § 109, 58–59; Bruce, *Thessalonians*, 82.

26   Otto Procksch, "ἁγιασμός," in *TDNT*, 1:113.

27   David Peterson, *Possessed by God: A New Testament Theology of Sanctification and Holiness*, NSBT, ed. D. A. Carson (Downers Grove, IL: InterVarsity, 1995), 81.

28   William Hendriksen, *Thessalonians, Timothy and Titus*, New Testament Commentary (Grand Rapids: Baker, 1957), 100.

29   Daniel B. Wallace, *Greek Grammar Beyond the Basics* (Grand Rapids: Zondervan, 1996), 606.

30   Bruce, *Thessalonians*, 82.

31   Vang, "Sanctification," 59.

32   Wanamaker, *Thessalonians*, 160, states, "Paul's emphasis on mutual love for fellow Christians was intended to create a new sense of identity and commitment among people who had no basis for a mutual relation prior to their conversion to Christ." Similarly, Morris, *Thessalonians*, 129, notes that the command to love one another is the primary means by which people are drawn to community and, therefore, obedience. In this context love is an essential action designed for the maturing of the individual and the community.

33   Hiebert, *Thessalonian Epistles*, 179.

34   Marion L. Soards, *1 Corinthians*, New International Biblical Commentary, ed. W. Ward Gasque (Peabody, MA: Hendrickson, 1999), 6.

35   Colin G. Kruse, *Paul, the Law, and Justification* (Peabody, MA: Hendrickson, 1996), 117. Beneath the surface there was a "criticism of Paul's gospel, style of speaking, spirituality, and integrity."

36   Hans Conzelmann, *1 Corinthians: A Commentary on the First Epistle to the Corinthians*, trans. James W. Leitch, Hermeneia, ed. George W. MacRae (Philadelphia: Fortress, 1975), 9, notes, "The great attraction of 1 Corinthians, however, lies in the fact that here Paul is practicing applied theology… Theology here is translated into an illumination of the existence of the church and of the individual Christian in it."

37   Miriam Francis Perelewitz, "The Unity of the Body of Christ," *TBT* 18 (November 1980): 395.

38   Conzelmann, *First Corinthians*, 29. "The understanding of our fellowship with Christ is also determined by the idea of calling. It is not understood as an experience of mystical communion, but in terms of belonging to the Lord until his parousia." Anthony C. Thiselton, *The First Epistle to the Corinthians*, NIGTC, ed. I. Howard Marshall and Donald A. Hagner (Grand Rapids and Cambridge: Eerdmans, 2000), 104, refers to this as "communal participation in the sonship of Jesus Christ."

39   Stig Hanson, *The Unity of the Church in the New Testament: Colossians and Ephesians*, ASNU, ed. A. Fridrichsen, vol. 14 (Uppsala: Almquist & Wiskells Boktryckeri, 1946; reprint, Lexington, KY: American Theological Library Association, 1963), 74.

40   This is also in view in 2 Corinthians when Paul states, "But it is God who establishes us together with you in Christ" (2 Cor 1:21).

41   Thiselton, *First Corinthians*, 111. He refers to this verse as "the thesis statement of the entire discourse."

42   Gordon D. Fee, *The First Epistle to the Corinthians*, NICNT, ed. F. F. Bruce (Grand Rapids: Eerdmans, 1987), 52.

43   BDAG, "λέγω," 588.

44 Fee, *First Corinthians*, 54.

45 Christian Maurer, "σχίζω, σχίσμα," in *TDNT*, 7:964.

46 BDAG, "νοῦς," 680; and "γνώμη," 202. Thiselton, *First Corinthians*, 118, argues for the translation, "that you all take the same side."

47 C. F. D. Moule, *An Idiom Book of New Testament Greek*, 2d ed. (Cambridge: Cambridge University Press, 1959), 122.

48 F. W. Grosheide, *Commentary on the First Epistle to the Corinthians: The English Text with Introduction, Exposition and Notes*, NICNT, ed. Ned B. Stonehouse (Grand Rapids: Eerdmans, 1953), 38. He argues that the divisions were the greatest sin of the Corinthian church and the one that Paul consistently rebuked.

49 James D. G. Dunn, *The Theology of Paul the Apostle* (Grand Rapids: Eerdmans, 1998), 550, observes that the linkage to chapter 10 is not so much bread—body of Christ—as it is, "*one* bread, therefore *one* body." He goes on to argue that the language of body is drawn from the "body politic" found in nation-state thinking. In a nation state such as Israel the community is identified by ethnic and other traditional boundary markers. In employing this imagery for the church Paul eliminates the traditional boundary markers, such as different ethnic backgrounds and various social strata, as well as geographical boundaries or political affiliations, as identifying factors and focuses instead on spiritual unity. Borrowing from this thinking, the church cannot be distinguished by ethnic, gender or other traditional boundary markers (e.g., Gal 3:28). Craig S. Keener, *1–2 Corinthians*, New Cambridge Bible Commentary, ed. Ben Witherington, III (Cambridge: Cambridge University Press, 2005), 102-5, argues similarly.

Contra Dunn and Keener, Herman Ridderbos, *Paul: An Outline of His Theology*, trans. John Richard de Witt (Kampen, The Netherlands: JH Kok, 1966; reprint, Grand Rapids: Eerdmans, 1975), 369–71, challenges the view that body imagery originates from "human society." Rather, the language and concepts used by Paul show that this metaphor has deeper roots in the body of Christ. This is supported by his linkage with the communion supper. As such, since the church is the body of Christ, it is to conduct itself as a body, rather than growing from relationships into a body. In other words, feet and hands do not "rise up" to form a body. Rather, a body has feet and hands to employ.

50 Grosheide, *First Corinthians*, 293.

51 Thiselton, *First Corinthians*, 997–98, argues that, "Any theology that might imply that this one baptism in 13a in which believers were baptized by (or in) one Spirit might mark off some postconversion experience or status enjoyed by some Christians attacks and undermines Paul's entire argument and emphasis. Paul's constant use of ἕν, one, and πάντες, all, constitutes a direct onslaught against categorization or elitism within the church."

52 That Christian growth is in view is also captured by the ἵνα clause of 1 Cor12:25. The purpose for God's blending the various parts of the body together includes having mutual concern for one another. The result is true solidarity, "If one member suffers, everyone suffers with it. If a member is honored, all rejoice with it" (1 Cor 12:26).

53 The use of singular verbs in verses 11 and 12 are metaphorical to explain the church's movement from immaturity to maturity.

54 This is also captured by the imagery and distinctions between child and adult and mirror and face-to-face metaphors (1 Cor 13:11–12).

55 C. E. B. Cranfield, *The Epistle to the Romans*, vol. 1, ICC on the Holy Scriptures of the Old

and New Testaments, ed. J. A. Emerton and C. E. B. Cranfield (Edinburgh: T&T Clark, 1975), 87–102; James D. G. Dunn, *Romans 1–8*, WBC, ed. David A. Hubbard, Glenn W. Barker, and Ralph P. Martin, vol. 38A (Dallas, TX: Word, 1988), 36–49; Douglas J. Moo, *The Epistle to the Romans*, NICNT, ed. Gordon D. Fee (Grand Rapids: Eerdmans, 1996), 63–79; N. T. Wright, *What Saint Paul Really Said: Was Paul of Tarsus the Real Founder of Christianity?* (Grand Rapids: Eerdmans, 1997). The question arises as to the meaning of the righteousness of God. There are several possibilities. If the genitive is taken as possessive, it would be referring to that righteousness that belongs to God—an attribute of God. If it is genitive of source, it would be referring to that righteousness that comes from God—a standing with God which is given by him as a gift to believers. If it is a subjective genitive, it would be referring to God as the one who makes righteous—the activity whereby God puts right what is wrong. As noted by Moo, the difficulty lies in the fact all three are true and Paul uses the phrase in various ways. As such, he notes that it is a relational concept, specifically describing the relationship between God and man. He defines it as "the act by which God brings people into a right relationship with himself" (74).

56   BDAG, "θυσία," 462; Johannes Behm, "θυσία," in *TDNT*, 3:183. "The concept of sacrifice in the OT is rooted in the reality of the covenant order into which God's historical revelation has integrated the people of Israel… its characteristic distinctiveness… is always oriented to the presence of God in grace and judgment."

57   Dunn, *Theology of Paul*, 543. The "sacrificial cult" and the corresponding obligations "were characteristic of all sects and religions that focused on a temple and the worship offered there." See also C. E. B. Cranfield, *The Epistle to the Romans*, vol. 2, ICC, ed. J. A. Emerton and C. E. B. Cranfield (Edinburgh: T&T Clark, 1979), 599; Moo, *Romans*, 750–51.

58   Dunn, *Theology of Paul*, 544.

59   Contra Moo, *Romans*, 751, who sees the sacrifice as primarily oriented toward the world, with all of its "harsh" aspects.

60   Cranfield, *Romans*, 2:601. More than pleasing, it also has the idea of desire on the part of God to receive the sacrifice.

61   David Alan Black, "The Pauline Love Command: Structure, Style, and Ethics in Romans 12:9–21," *Filologia Neotestamentaria* 1 (May 1989): 6. BDAG, "ἀνυπόχριτος," 91, defines it as, "pert. to being without pretense, genuine, sincere." See also, Moo, *Romans*, 769–774, who follows Black's structural scheme.

62   Black, "Pauline Love Command," 15. He sees the use of chiasm in Rom 12:9–13 and basic stichometry in Roman 12:14–16, both of which emphasize the particulars of what it means to love genuinely. The third section (Rom 12:17–21) is not as structured and represents a more traditional Pauline style emphasizing how believers are to demonstrate their genuine love to all of humanity.

63   The commands represent a series of participles and adjectives interchangeably functioning with imperatival force. The debate over whether these reflect a common Semitic idiom or are simply a series of participles functioning as imperatives need not concern us here. What is significant is that Paul is not simply providing descriptions of genuine love. For further discussions of this participial-adjectival construction see Stanley E. Porter, *Idioms of the Greek New Testament*, 2d ed. (Sheffield: Sheffield Academic and JSOT, 1996), 185–86; Moule, *Idiom Book*, 179–80; BDF, 245–46; Black, "Pauline Love Command," 16–17.

64   Ibid., 5–9. This is attractive given the textual features of (1) the symmetry of A and A' where the first and second lines of A end with an accusative and a dative noun, respectively, and the first and second lines of A' begin with an accusative and dative article, re-

spectively, (2) the parallel dative structures of B and B', (3) the thematic cohesion within the chiastic sub-parts, (4) the parallel ideas in C and, (5) the sound repetitions which begin and end the lines. Black lists more features, but these are the primary ones. See also Moo, *Romans*, 770–71.

65 Ridderbos, *Paul*, 297. In discussing this passage, he states, "These virtues… in Paul's epistles are always brought under the viewpoint of brotherly communion and the upbuilding of the church… they are always understood therefore as the fulfillment of the requirement of love and thus approached from the liberty and obedience in Christ."

66 Moo, *Romans*, 789.

67 Black, "Pauline Love Command," 18.

68 Dunn, *Romans*, 2:756.

69 R. David Kaylor, *Paul's Covenant Community: Jew and Gentile in Romans* (Atlanta, GA: John Knox, 1988), 195, states, "Paul's theology is grounded in God's initiative toward the world; it ends not in pious speculation about dream worlds yet to be, but in admonitions to let the new world of the future transform present human community. The earthly conduct of the believing community is to proclaim the message of God's salvation. Faith is proclaimed through the community of faith not as an abstract truth stated in propositional terms but as lived truth expressed through the active life of the community."

70 Dunn, *Theology of Paul*, 674–75. Specifically, the Roman government was suspicious of "clubs and societies," and Paul anticipated "further imperial rulings against the Jews."

71 Contra Moo, *Romans*, 790–91, who states, "This argument comes on the scene quite abruptly, with no explicit syntactical connection with what has come before it – and not much evidence of any connection in subject matter either."

72 Dunn, *Theology of Paul*, 79. This is what he refers to as "political quietism." See also, Jon M. Isaak, "The Christian Community and Political Responsibility: Romans 13:1–7," *Direction* 32 (spring 2003): 43, who argues that this the central responsibility of community.

73 Moo, *Romans*, 930, notes that the construction τοὺς τὰς διχοστασίας indicates that Paul had a specific group in mind; however it is not revealed in the text. This implies that the Roman Christians would recognize this group if and when they appeared. As such, they are probably to be recognized on the strength of the description given here by Paul.

74 The Prison Epistles are treated as a unit because much of the community material overlaps contextually and theologically.

75 F. F. Bruce, *The Epistles to the Colossians, to Philemon, and to the Ephesians*, NICNT, ed. F. F. Bruce (Grand Rapids: Eerdmans, 1984), 241. The purpose of Ephesians involves "an extended benediction and prayer, constituting the framework for a celebration of God's accomplishment in Christ of his eternal purpose, which embraces the incorporation into one divine society of Gentiles and Jews on an equal footing."

Elna Mouton, *Reading a New Testament Document Ethically*, SBL: Academia Biblica, ed. Mark Allan Powell, vol. 1, (Leiden: Brill, 2002), 185–86, notes, "The narrative of the Ephesians communities can therefore be described as a story about *community life* radically formed and transformed by the empowering experience of God, Christ, and the Spirit. Their story witnesses to the reality that they did not so much *have* a social ethic as that they *were* a social ethic in the process of formation."

76 Moisés Silva, *Philippians*, Wycliffe Exegetical Commentary, ed. Kenneth Barker (Chicago: Moody, 1988), 19–21. He locates the purpose within the sphere of sanctification stating

that the believer's duty is to grow in holiness. It seems his primary reason is because of the focus on Christ in 2:6–11. I disagree with his treatment and see the focus on Christ as the *primary* example, not of growing in holiness, but in serving others. For this reason, I orient the purpose around service within the church and the unity that results.

Davorin Peterlin, *Paul's Letter to the Philippians in the Light of the Disunity of the Church*, Nov-TSup, ed. A. J. Malherbe and D. P. Moessner, vol. 79 (Leiden: Brill, 1995), 6–10. He argues that the primary theme of Philippians is to be understood against the background of disunity within the church and, therefore, the theme of unity "is even more widespread than is usually acknowledged, and that it underlies the whole of Phil" (p. 9).

77 Bruce, *Colossians, Philemon, Ephesians*, 30. "Not only the living fellowship among the members but the dependence of all the members on Christ for life and power is vividly brought out, and the supremacy of Christ is vindicated against a system of thought which threatened to cast him down from his excellency."

Peter T. O'Brien, *Colossians, Philemon*, WBC, ed. David A. Hubbard, Glenn W. Barker, and Ralph P. Martin, vol. 44 (Waco, TX: Word, 1982), xxx. "But probably the main reason for [Epaphras'] visit was to seek advice from Paul as to how to deal with the false teaching which had arisen in Colossae and which, if it was allowed to continue unchecked, would threaten the security of the church. Paul's letter is then written as a response to this urgent need."

78 Bruce, *Colossians, Philemon, Ephesians*, 192. "The letter to Philemon suggests that perhaps Onesimus and his master were temporarily separated in order that they might be united and belong to each other forever, no longer as slave and master but as loving brothers in Christ."

Tom Wright, *Paul for Everyone: The Prison Epistles Ephesians, Philippians, Colossians and Philemon* (London: SPCK, 2002), 201. In discussing the gospel, and its effects on social hierarchy, he says, "As it does its work, it produces new things, good things, new ways of living for individuals, households and communities."

79 In Eph 2:2 Paul explains that unbelievers are "dead" in their sins. He describes these sins as ἐν αἷς ποτε περιεπατήσατε κατὰ τὸν αἰῶνα τοῦ κόσμου τούτου. And then he reveals that the believer is alive and is responsible to carry out the good works which God has prepared beforehand ἵνα ἐν αὐτοῖς περιπατήσωμεν (Eph 2:10). Paul picks up this theme of "walking" again in chapters 4–6 to demonstrate in expanded detail what it means for the believer to carry out the good works of God. Note the following:

> …ἀξίως περιπατῆσαι τῆς κλήσεως ἧς ἐκλήθητε (4:1)
> …μηκέτι ὑμᾶς περιπατεῖν, καθὼς καὶ τὰ ἔθνη περιπατεῖ (4:17)
> …καὶ περιπατεῖτε ἐν ἀγάπῃ (5:2)
> …ὡς τέκνα φωτὸς περιπατεῖτε (5:8)
> …βλέπετε οὖν ἀκριβως πῶς περιπατεῖτε μὴ ὡς ἄσοφοι ἀλλ' ὡς σοφοί (5:15)

This last command is expanded in greater detail and covers Eph 5:15–6:9. He then wraps up his discussion with the exhortation, τοῦ λοιποῦ, ἐνδυναμοῦσθε ἐν κυρίῳ καὶ ἐν τῷ κράτει τῆς ἰσχύος αὐτοῦ (Eph 6:10). Since the theme of Ephesians is related to the unity of the new body of Christ, composed of both the Jews and the Gentiles, these divisions relate practically to protecting this unity (cf. Eph 4:3). This last section is strategically related to this protection in that the ultimate cause of disunity is satanic in nature. As will be concluded, community is essential to carry out the commands in each of these sections.

80 Note the use of διὰ τῆς ἐκκλησίας, rather than ἐν ἐκκλησία. This implies that the wisdom is demonstrated by how the church functions, rather than in its existence. For further

treatment of this, see Wallace, *Greek Grammar*, 434; Harold W. Hoehner, *Ephesians: An Exegetical Commentary* (Grand Rapids: Baker, 2002), 460. For a contrasting view, see Andrew T. Lincoln, *Ephesians*, WBC, ed. David A. Hubbard and Glenn W. Barker, vol. 42 (Dallas, TX: Word, 1990), 187–88.

81   Peterlin, *Paul's Letter to the Philippians*, 19; Silva, *Philippians*, 42; Peter T. O'Brien, *The Epistle to the Philippians: A Commentary on the Greek Text*, NIGTC, ed. I. Howard Marshall and W. Ward Gasque (Grand Rapids: Eerdmans, 1991), 58.

82   Ibid., 82. "God's saving work among the Philippians eventually rebounds to the divine glory." He further argues that this sets the stage for the emphasis on glory in the "Christ-hymn" (Phil 2:10–11).

83   Hoehner, *Ephesians*, 511–12. He classifies τοῦ πνεύματος as either a genitive of author, originating cause, or production/producer. In all cases, the Spirit is the one who produces the unity.

84   "Believers are to make every effort to preserve the unity which has its origin in the Holy Spirit."

85   Note the conceptual transitions from the plural to the singular: from believers to unity, (immature) children to a mature person, the trickery of people to the truth, from waves and every wind of teaching to sound doctrine. Also note the parallel passage in Col 2:6–7 where Paul says, "Therefore, just as you received Christ Jesus as Lord, continue to live your lives in him, rooted and built up in him and firm in your faith just as you were taught, and overflowing with thankfulness." The community emphasis is just as strong in this passage as well.

86   He notes that "the reciprocal pronoun (ἑαυτοῦ) emphasizes the body's own activity of growth."

87   "Love among members is another prerequisite for growth. Earlier in the verse Paul spoke of the interconnectedness between members of the body of Christ. He now makes clear that love must be an integral part of this dynamic in order for growth to occur." It is interesting that in a parallel verse in Colossians 3:14, the Western Texts (D* F G) read σύνδεσμος τῆς ἑνότητος, rather than σύνδεσμος τῆς τελειότητος, to complete the picture that love is related to unity. While the support for this variant is not substantial enough to warrant inclusion, it does reflect the fact that part of the early church may have viewed the concept of forgiveness leading to love as related to the unity of the body.

88   Peterlin, *Paul's Letter to the Philippians*, 55. He argues that πολιτεύεσθε has more than simply conduct in mind. Inherent in the term is the "universal community" of believers and how they are to live in light of the New Covenant. Accordingly, "What is important is that the term requires that individual Philippians should act responsibly within, and as members of, their given community. Their action is corporate in character and... the proper framework is their church" (p. 55). For a fuller treatment see Ernest C. Miller, "Πολιτεύεσθε in Philippians 1:27: Some Philological and Thematic Observations," *JSNT* 15 (1982): 86–96.

89   It is significant that in a book dealing with service and ministry, the very first command is, "Μόνον ἀξίως τοῦ εὐαγγελίου τοῦ Χριστοῦ πολιτεύεσθε" (Phil 1:27). Obviously the start of proper service in the church begins with a life worthy of the good news brought about by Christ.

90   Gordon D. Fee, *Paul's Letter to the Philippians*, NICNT, ed. Gordon D. Fee (Grand Rapids: Eerdmans, 1995), 166. He correctly notes that the Spirit is the key to unity in the church. But this is conjoined with στήκετε, thus emphasizing the partnership between God and

believers. Each play a significant role in ensuring that unity is accomplished and protected.

91   Georg Bertram, "φρήν," in *TDNT*, 9:233. "The fundamental demand of Pauline exhortation is a uniform direction, a common mind, and unity of thought and will."

92   O'Brien, *Colossians, Philemon*, 269–70.

93   Bruce, *Paul*, 401.

94   Eduard Lohse, *Colossians and Philemon*, trans. William R. Poehlmann, and Robert J. Karris, Hermeneia, ed. Helmut Koester (Philadelphia: Fortress, 1971), 187.

95   For a discussion of Philemon's position in the church, see Bruce, *Paul*, 401–6; Lohse, *Colossians and Philemon*, 186–87; O'Brien, *Colossians, Philemon*, 265–68.

96   Lohse, *Colossians and Philemon*, 188.

97   For example, note 1 Cor 4:5 and 1 Thess 5:5.

98   Rudolf Schnackenburg, *Ephesians: A Commentary*, trans. Helen Heron (Edinburgh: T&T Clark, 1991), 222.

99   Lincoln, *Ephesians*, 327. This is also captured by the move from the indicative (ἦτε γάρ ποτε σκότος, νῦν δὲ φῶς ἐν κυρίῳ) to the imperative (ὡς τέκνα φωτὸς περιπατεῖτε).

100 Hans Conzelmann, "φῶς," in *TDNT*, 9:346.

101 Ibid., 9:347.

102 Peter T. O'Brien, *The Letter to the Ephesians*, Pillar New Testament Commentary, ed. D. A. Carson (Grand Rapids: Eerdmans and Apollos, 1999), 365–66. This imagery is reminiscent of the glory language used in 2 Cor 3 (discussed earlier).

103 Freidrich Büchsel, "ἐλέγχω," in *TDNT*, 2:474. See also Hans-Georg Link, "Guilt," in *NIDNTT*, 2:141–42.

104 Lincoln, *Ephesians*, 329–33. For a contrasting view see Hoehner, *Ephesians*, 678–80.

105 Hoehner, *Ephesians*, 316.

106 While the imperative (and associated participles) are typically obeyed in the context of a local church, it is not essential to limit it to the "gathered" community of believers. These are modifiers that should characterize believers in the community at large, and should reflect their relationships with each other no matter the location or environment.

107 Hoehner, *Ephesians*, 720.

108 O'Brien, *Ephesians*, 379.

109 The term "will of the Lord" is unusual since Paul typically refers to God's will (Eph 1:1, 5, 9, 11; 6:6). The similar expression in Rom 12:2 might provide some interesting parallels since the issue of transformation also results in changed behavior.

110 O'Brien, *Ephesians*, 385.

111 Hans Conzelmann, "συνίημι," in *TDNT*, 7:895, states, "Understanding and conduct are an indissoluble unity. To be without understanding is not just a partial deficiency which might be overcome; it is total darkening." This is continuous and consistent with the previous passage (Eph 5:6–14) where believers are exhorted to walk in the light and avoid deeds of darkness.

112 Wallace, *Greek Grammar*, 375. Conversely, he argues that the content of the filling is found earlier when Paul says, "I pray that according to the wealth of his glory he may grant you… to know the love of Christ that surpasses knowledge, so that you may be filled up to all the fullness of God" (Eph 3:16, 19). The fullness may be a reference to God's moral attributes.

113 O'Brien, *Ephesians*, 393.

114 The use of the term "level" is meant to communicate that, whereas solidarity occurs because one belongs to the community, unity can occur in all situations in which believers are present. At one end of the continuum is the church universal. At the other end might be one-on-one relationships. In between are a series of possibilities, namely, local churches, Sunday schools, small groups, discipling groups, friendships, etc.

115 Note the parallel passage in Colossians 3:18–4:1 where the same argument is presented in the same order but in summarized form.

116 It is also seen in Phil 2 where service and putting others first leads to unity—patterned after the example of Christ.

117 This is not a commentary on gender roles or issues of gender equality. This passage is simply being used to illustrate how important relationship is to the process of sanctification in the life of the believer.

118 O'Brien, *Colossians, Philemon*, 80. The complexities of this passage notwithstanding, O'Brien argues that it is necessary for the church, as a community, to share in the sufferings of Christ. Accordingly, Paul is here arguing that his contribution to the total sufferings of the church reduces the need for others to suffer. "The more of these sufferings he personally absorbed, as he went about preaching the gospel, the less would remain for his fellow Christians to endure" (p. 80). If this is a correct understanding of this passage, the implications for the essentiality of community especially as it relates to suffering are tremendous, since believers can "absorb" suffering on behalf of others as Paul did. This is a great and personal sacrifice. In any event, within the complexity is the clear idea that Paul had community in mind.

119 These are seen as participles of means. Instructing and teaching are the means by which Paul presents everyone complete in Christ.

120 The thrice repeated πάντα ἄνθρωπον reflects Paul's dual focus on community as well as the individuals within community.

121 Lohse, *Colossians and Philemon*, 77.

122 O'Brien, *Colossians, Philemon*, 280. Perhaps this idea is also included in Phlm 1:6, "I pray that the faith you share with us may deepen your understanding of every blessing that belongs to us in Christ." While complex to translate, this verse carries the idea that "the intercessory request of the apostle was that Philemon's liberality… might lead him effectively… into a deeper understanding… of all the blessings that belonged to him in Christ." The active force related to ἡ κοινωνία τῆς πίστεώς σου ἐνεργὴς γένηται reveals that active involvement in community has implications on wisdom and living life. This idea is validated when Paul attributes his own joy to the faithfulness of Philemon (Phlm 1:7). See also Bruce, *Colossians*, 209.

123 Hoehner, *Ephesians*, 824. He notes, for instance, "Paul exhorts believers to put on the full armor of God for the purpose of being able to stand firmly against the lying strategies of the devil." Although he allows for a community orientation with the plural reference to "believers," he does not explicitly orient this toward community action. See also Lincoln, *Ephesians*, 441. Similarly, while he refers to "believers" throughout his argument, he does

not explicitly orient this toward community action. He summarizes this section with, "The portrait of Paul with his desire to proclaim the gospel boldly and openly even in the adversity of imprisonment reflects what the writer wishes for both himself and his readers – the fearless living out of Christian existence in the midst of a hostile world" (p. 441). He does note that the form of this section is similar to the "speeches of generals before battle, urging their armies to deeds of valor in face of the impending dangers of war" (433).

124   Note ἐνδυναμοῦσθε (Eph 6:10); ἐνδύσασθε (Eph 6:11); ἀναλάβετε (Eph 6:13); στῆτε (Eph 6:14); and δέξασθε (Eph 6:17).

125   Albrecht Oepke, "θυρεός," in *TDNT*, 5:312–14. He notes that this shield was a "four-cornered long shield which covers the whole man like a door." This was the primary shield used in the Roman army from c. 340 B.C. until the age of Constantine. He thinks that the shield did not actually extinguish flaming arrows, but caused them to fall to the ground. See Hoehner, *Ephesians*, 848. Contra Oepke, Hoehner has gathered impressive evidence that the θυρεός did, in fact, extinguish the flaming arrows, thus validating Paul's use of the metaphor. Perhaps the best perspective in this passage is believer with believer, side-by-side, fighting together against the enemy. This ensures that the integrity of the battle line is protected and the ground gained is held.

126   *Gladiator*, prod. and dir. Ridley Scott, Universal Pictures and Dreamworks, 2000, motion picture. This motion picture graphically portrays how the armament of the Roman army was designed to work together. In the opening scene, the Roman army is organized in a battle line strategy and the soldiers use their shields in a side-by-side orientation to protect one another from the onslaught of the enemy's flaming arrows. Similarly, later in the coliseum, the gladiators form into a group and fight together in what they refer to as the "turtle maneuver." In this scene, one of the gladiators separates from the group and is cut down and killed by the charioteers. This scene graphically portrays what happens when one individual isolates himself from the group while in the middle of the battle.

127   I. Howard Marshall, *A Critical and Exegetical Commentary on the Pastoral Epistles*, ICC, ed. J. A. Emerton, C. E. B. Cranfield, and G. N. Stanton (Edinburgh: T&T Clark, 1999), 103. See also George W. Knight, *The Pastoral Epistles: A Commentary on the Greek Text*, NIGTC, ed. I. Howard Marshall, and W. Ward Gasque (Grand Rapids: Eerdmans, 1992), 10; Gordon D. Fee, *1 and 2 Timothy, Titus*, New International Biblical Commentary, ed. W. Ward Gasque, vol. 13 (Peabody, MA: Hendrickson, 1988), 17–18.

128   Marshall, *Pastoral Epistles*, 52.

129   In 1 Tim 5:17–25, the elder who leads well is contrasted with the one who needs public censure and rebuke. It is interesting that Paul concludes this contrast with the statement, "Do not lay hands on anyone hastily and so identify with the sins of others" (1 Tim 5:22). He goes on to say that both sins and good works are obvious (1 Tim 5:24–25). The community is necessary to expose the pattern of integrity developed in the leader's life.

130   Μαρσηαλλ αργυεσ τηατ τηε πηρασε διὰ πολλῶν μαρτύρων implies a strong public element in which many people could attest to Paul's words to Timothy. "This would be at once a warning against any attempt to falsify what Paul had said, a reminder that any lapses of memory could be remedied by appeal to such witnesses, but also an encouragement to Timothy that what he preaches as the gospel received from Paul is backed up by many other people." See also Knight, *Pastoral Epistles*, 390; William D. Mounce, *Pastoral Epistles*, WBC, ed. Bruce M. Metzger and Ralph P. Martin, vol. 46 (Nashville, TN: Thomas Nelson, 2000), 505–6.

CHAPTER 8

Conclusion

This study began with a quest to identify the role of the community in the progressive sanctification of the individual believer. In chapter 1, it was stated that the primary thesis of this study is that the redeemed community, at all levels of personal relationships, is an essential element in the process of growing in Christ. In chapter 2 the various theological approaches to understanding progressive sanctification were surveyed. It was concluded that, while there is general agreement in evangelicalism that the Holy Spirit and the Word of God are essential means used by God to grow the believer, there is little consensus regarding the role of the community.

If there is a pattern of consistency, it is that the growth of the believer is largely an individual effort. This seems to reflect the influence of Western individualism. And yet, the quest for growth evidenced by the various traditions reflects a deep and genuine optimism about what God has in store for the redeemed. There is a consistent hope for relief from the struggles of life that is not found as one engages life alone. Is the primary problem that the maturing process is approached individualistically when God intended otherwise? Asked another way, does community play a necessary role in the process of growing in Christ?

To begin to answer these fundamental questions, a method of approaching the biblical data was developed that moved from broad theological categories to the more focused aspect of Pauline theology as it relates to community. To begin the study, in chapter 3 basic definitional considerations were considered which surfaced community related points intrinsic to the understanding of sanctification. In both the Old and New Testaments, the basic language of sanctification involves the idea of holiness. And while the believer's holiness is the result of the finished work of Christ on the cross, there is a consistent and pervasive aspect in Scripture wherein the believer lives out that holiness within the context of community such that they grow in their spiritual maturity—an aspect of progressive sanctification. As such, holiness was defined as the unique status given by God to the redeemed for the purpose of impacting others for his glory.

To articulate this process of growing in progressive sanctification, the authors of Scripture use a variety of sanctification related terms. Of particular interest in this study are the terms related to the temple system—the sacrificial system, priesthood and law. These terms demonstrate continuity between the Old and New Testaments and reflect a strong community orientation. In other words, these terms inherently require community for them to be understood properly and integrated into the life of the redeemed. These terms all find their fundamental meaning in the context of relationship.

Chapter 4 considered the pattern of how God himself relates to the redeemed as an example for identification and validation of community related principles. There it was shown that both the Old and New Testament authors consistently present God as initiating relationship with the community. Of particular interest to this study was the initiation by God to transform believers into his image. There it was argued that Christ is the image of God—the true human—who reflects God's glory to creation. Since he is the image of God, he is the perfect revelation of God and represents what the community of believers is destined to become in eternity. In this regard, believers together represent the new humanity—the new person—brought about by the death of Christ. In the "already-not yet" Pauline eschatological scheme, this future aspect represents the "not yet" phase. The "already" phase—the primary concern of this study—wherein the believer is being conformed into the image of Christ involves transformation—an aspect of progressive sanctification.

The pattern of God initiating relationship with his creation forms the basis and example in the New Testament for how the community is to act toward one another. God's normal method of moving his people to righteous living is through the catalytic effect of believers relating to one another in authentic ways. This catalytic effect is apparent on a continuum from exposure and confrontation of sin to genuine loving encouragement for holy living. Since these actions are all designed to help one grow in Christian maturity, it was concluded that growing in Christ-likeness involves learning to initiate actively toward believers in order to help them grow in Christ-likeness and be transformed into the image of Christ—the basic definition of progressive sanctification. As such, the community plays a significant and essential role in the progressive sanctification of the believer.

Chapter 5 considered theological development in the biblical understanding of community under the New Covenant era and how that development impinges on transformation and Christian growth. During the first advent of

Christ, the cultural factors that generated solidarity within Israel were radically redefined around Christ himself. Specifically, the temple system and law were redefined in such a way that they pointed to Christ as the true unifying factor for the redeemed. Whereas Israel had developed their identity around these cultural symbols, Christ radically attacked this understanding and reshaped unity around himself. This had significant impact on the biblical understanding of community. With the inauguration of the New Covenant, true community was now understood in spiritual terms.

This radical development reshaped the way the community viewed itself. Since the time of Christ, the identity of the individual believer is now located in his person and work. Since the original cultural symbols were given as a gift by God himself, this redefinition reinforced the high value of the redeemed community. In addition, understanding the cultural symbols in terms of community, sanctification and outreach reoriented the role of the community toward ministry and relationships with one another and the world. As such, under the New Covenant unity is a gift from God and necessarily involves interrelationships that must occur for the community to carry out its responsibility to grow in Christ-likeness and impact the world for the glory of God.

With this as a background, in chapter 6 the Pauline corpus was studied to determine if the community texts revealed theological development regarding solidarity and the person of Jesus. Prior to studying the Pauline Epistles a basic definition of unity was developed. Based on the conclusions drawn in chapters 3–5, unity was identified as a broad and multi-faceted concept that ranged on a continuum from union with Christ to relational harmony within the community. In this chapter, it was concluded that all three symbols—the Messiah, the law, and the temple—come together in the person and ministry of Jesus. Paul understood this as he viewed these symbols christologically. It is these three symbols, operating together, that form the basis for the identity of the individual and unity within the church. It is the work of the Spirit in the community that makes possible the growth to maturity and impact in the world as the community together represents the Lord. This forms the basis for the remainder of Paul's teaching involving the community.

Chapter 7 reviewed the remainder of the Pauline corpus to identify any community or relational features on which the progressive sanctification of the believer depends. Of particular interest to this study was that aspect of unity wherein movement from union with Christ to relational harmony is achieved. It was argued that this movement requires active involvement by the community to grow together in progressive sanctification. This active involvement takes the primary form of being a catalyst for transformation and growth—the basic definition of progressive sanctification.

As a result of the study of the Pauline Epistles, several significant conclusions were drawn. First, Paul continues the temple, law and sacrificial imagery. However, he combines it with the idea of participation of the redeemed in Christ. The blending of this imagery produces a richness in community thinking. Whereas Paul locates the identity of the individual believer in Christ, the reality of this identity is "fleshed out" within the community. In other words, Paul inseparably integrates participation in Christ with participation in community. This forms the basis for the Pauline teaching on growth to Christian maturity. It is in community that the believer experiences progressive sanctification and it is in community that believers find significance and fulfillment as they obey the New Testament.

Second, the concept of solidarity is a strong unifying factor in Pauline theology for understanding the community and its role in progressive sanctification. For Paul, progressing in sanctification necessarily involves living in community and loving others. His consistent pattern is to take the demands of holy living to the lowest level of solidarity—marriage, family, slavery and friendship relationships. It is in these relationships that the foundational requirement to love others is lived out. In Pauline theology, not only is the community necessary for holy living, it is impossible to live holy lives without involvement with community.

Third, the example of God initiating relationship with the redeemed is the primary example for how the community is to relate to one another. God's acts in the Exodus event play a major role in explaining what it means to love one another. His movement in love is repeated in a grand way through the ministry of his Son. The supreme sacrifice of Christ to lead the unregenerate out of the bondage of sin becomes the predominant example of how believers are to serve to one another.

Fourth, the language of sanctification necessarily involves an outreach focus. This outreach focus is present at several levels in Pauline theology. First is the consistent movement from the individual to the community. Obedience of the Pauline imperatives, while often originating with the individual, finds its expression in community. In fact, in several passages, the imperatives are impossible to obey without the community. Second is the movement from the community to culture. Two of Paul's consistent themes involved protecting the integrity of the gospel and impacting the culture for Christ. For Paul, failure to carry the imperatives through to cultural impact was inconceivable. What this reveals is a pattern wherein the individual impacts the community for growth and transformation and the community impacts the culture for evangelism—reflecting God's glory at every step. It reflects a strong outward focus wherein individuals are consistently moving toward others in a selfless and loving way—

the fundamental intent of the law. And since outreach is inherent in the concept of sanctification, the community is essential in helping the individual carry out this aspect of their Christian responsibility.

Finally, obedience is at the heart of sanctification. Learning to think and live like Christ—growing in Christ-likeness—is the fundamental definition of progressive sanctification. For Paul, this process necessarily involves community. In Pauline theology, community becomes both a cause and a means of progressive sanctification. It cannot occur in isolation without the community.

At its core, this study asked the question, "Is it possible to grow to maturity in Christ without the believing community?" The answer, found in the preceding pages, is "no." In a very real way, believers need one another. No longer is it simply desirable to have mutually edifying relationships—it is essential. No longer is it optional to belong to a Christian community—it is essential. And finally, no longer is it a dream to have lasting and significant impact in the lives of others and the world—it is essential. This is the way God designed it and Paul envisioned it.

BIBLIOGRAPHY

Adewuya, J. Ayodeji. *Holiness and Community in 2 Cor 6:14–7:1: Paul's View of Communal Holiness in the Corinthian Correspondence.* Studies in Biblical Literature, ed. Hemchand Gossai, vol. 40. New York: Peter Lang, 2001.

—————. *The Pursuit of Godliness: Sanctification in Christological Perspective.* Lantham: MD: University Press of America, 1999.

Alexander, T. Desmond et al., eds. *New Dictionary of Biblical Theology: Exploring the Unity & Diversity of Scripture.* Downers Grove, IL: InterVarsity, 2000.

Allen, Thomas G. "Exaltation and Solidarity with Christ: Ephesians 1.20 and 2.6." *JSNT* 28 (October 1986): 103–20.

Anthropological Approaches to the Old Testament. Issues in Religion and Theology, ed. Bernhard Lang, vol. 8. Philadelphia: Fortress, 1985.

Arnett, William M. "Entire Sanctification." *Asbury Seminarian* 30 (October 1975): 24–49.

Attridge, Harold W. *The Epistle to the Hebrews.* Hermeneia, ed. Helmut Koester. Philadelphia: Fortress, 1989.

Banks, Robert. *Paul's Idea of Community: The Early House Churches in Their Historical Setting.* Rev. ed. Peabody, MA: Hendrickson, 1994.

Barabas, Steven. *So Great Salvation: The History and Message of the Keswick Convention.* London: Marshall, Morgan & Scott, 1952.

Barker, Glenn W. "1 John." In *Expositor's Bible Commentary*, ed. by Frank E. Gaebelein, vol. 12, 291–358. Grand Rapids: Zondervan, 1981.

Barnett, Paul. *The Second Epistle to the Corinthians.* NICNT, ed. Gordon D. Fee. Grand Rapids: Eerdmans, 1997.

Barrett, C. K. *A Commentary on the First Epistle to the Corinthians.* BNTC, ed. Henry Chadwick. London: Adam & Charles Black, 1968. Reprint, Peabody, MA: Hendrickson, 1987.

—————. *From First Adam to Last: A Study in Pauline Theology.* London: Adam and Charles Black, 1962.

—————. *On Paul: Aspects of His Life, Work and Influence in the Early Church.* London: T&T Clark, 2003.

—————. *Paul: An Introduction to His Thought.* Louisville, KY: Westminster John Knox, 1994.

Barth, Karl. *Church Dogmatics.* Edited by. G. W. Bromiley and T. F. Torrance. Translated by G. W. Bromiley, vol 4. Edinburgh: T&T Clark, 1958.

Barth, Markus. *Ephesians 1–3.* AB, ed. William Foxwell and David Noel Freedman, vol. 34. Garden City, NY: Doubleday, 1974.

—————. *Ephesians 4–6.* AB, ed. William Foxwell and David Noel Freedman, vol. 34A. Garden City, NY: Doubleday, 1974.

————. *The People of God. JSNT*, vol. 5. Sheffield: JSOT Press, 1983.

Barton, Stephen C. *Life Together. Family, Sexuality and Community in the New Testament and Today.* Edinburgh: T&T Clark, 2001.

Bassler, Jouette M. "Skeuos: A Modest Proposal for Illuminating Paul's Use of Metaphor in 1 Thessalonians 4:4." In *The Social World of the First Christians : Essays in Honor of Wayne A. Meeks*, ed. L. Michael White and O. Larry Yarbrough, 53–66. Minneapolis, MN: Fortress, 1995.

Bauckham, Richard J. *Jude, 2 Peter*. WBC, ed. David A. Hubbard, Glenn W. Barker, and Ralph P. Martin, vol. 50. Waco, TX: Word, 1983.

Bauer, W., F. W. Danker, W. F. Arndt, and F. W. Gingrich. *Greek-English Lexicon of the New Testament and Other Early Christian Literature.* 3d ed. Chicago, 2000

Beale, G. K. *The Book of Revelation.* NIGTC, ed. I. Howard Marshall and W. Ward Gasque. Grand Rapids: Eerdmans, 1999.

————. *The Temple and the Church's Mission: A Biblical Theology of the Dwelling Place of God.* NSBT, ed. D. A. Carson. Downers Grove, IL: InterVarsity and Apollos, 2004.

Beasley-Murray, George R. *John.* WBC, ed. Glenn W. Barker, David A. Hubbard, and Ralph P. Martin, vol. 36. Waco, TX: Word, 1987.

Beck, James R. "Sociopathy and Sanctification." *Journal of Psychology and Christianity* 14 (spring 1995): 66–73.

Berg, Jim. *Changed Into His Image: God's Plan for Transforming Your Life.* Greenville, SC: Bob Jones University Press, 1999.

Berkhof, Louis. *Systematic Theology.* Grand Rapids: Eerdmans, 1941.

Berkouwer, G. C. *Faith and Sanctification.* Translated by John Vriend. Studies in Dogmatics. Grand Rapids: Eerdmans, 1952.

————. *Man: The Image of God.* Translated by Dirk W. Jellema. Studies in Dogmatics. Grand Rapids: Eerdmans, 1962.

Berquist, Jon L. *Controlling Corporeality. The Body and the Household in Ancient Israel.* New Brunswick, NJ: Rutgers University Press, 2002.

Best, Ernest. *A Critical and Exegetical Commentary on Ephesians.* ICC, ed. J. A. Emerton, C. E. B. Cranfield, and G. N. Stanton. Edinburgh: T&T Clark, 1998.

————. *One Body in Christ: A Study in the Relationship of the Church to Christ in the Epistles of the Apostle Paul.* London: SPCK, 1955.

Best, John Ernest. "Paul's Theology of the Corporate Life of the Local Church." Th.D. diss., Dallas Theological Seminary, 1983.

Betz, Hans Dieter. *Galatians.* Hermeneia, ed. Helmut Koester. Philadelphia: Fortress, 1979.

Bishop, Richard W. "Walking in the Spirit of Sanctification." *Paraclete* 24 (summer 1990): 25–30.

Black, David Alan. "The Pauline Love Command: Structure, Style, and Ethics in Romans 12:9–21." *Filologia Neotestamentaria* 1 (May 1989): 3–21.

Blass, F., A. Debrunner, and R. W. Funk. *A Greek Grammar of the New Testament and Other Early Christian Literature.* Chicago, 1961.

Bornkamm, Günther. *Paul.* Translated by D. M. G. Stalker. New York: Harper & Row, 1971.

Börschel, Regina. *Die Konstruktion einer christlichen identität: Paulus und die Gemeinde von Thessalonich in ihrer hellenistisch-römischen Umwelt.* Berlin: Philo, 2001.

Braaten, Carl F. *Principles of Lutheran Theology.* Philadelphia: Fortress, 1983.

Branick, Vincent. *The House Church in the Writings of Paul.* Wilmington, DE: Michael Glazier, 1989.

Breed, James L. "The Church as the 'Body of Christ': A Pauline Analogy." *Theological Reviews* 6, no. 2 (1985): 9–32.

Brondos, Joel A. "Sanctification and Moral Development: A Brief Investigation into the Principles and Methodologies of Lawrence Kohlberg in Light of Scripture and the Lutheran Confessions." *Concordia Journal* 17 (October 1991): 419–39.

Brown, Colin, ed. NIDNTT. 4 vols. Grand Rapids: Zondervan, 1975–1985.

Brown, Raymond E. *The Gospel According to John (I–XII): Introduction, Translation, and Notes.* AB, ed. William Foxwell Albright and David Noel Freedman, vol. 29. New York: Doubleday, 1970.

———. *The Gospel According to John (XIII–XXI): Introduction, Translation, and Notes.* AB, ed. William Foxwell Albright and David Noel Freedman, vol. 29A. New York: Doubleday, 1970.

Brown, William P., ed. *Character & Scripture: Moral Formation, Community, and Biblical Interpretation.* Grand Rapids: Eerdmans, 2002.

Bruce, F. F. *1 & 2 Thessalonians.* WBC, ed. David A. Hubbard, Glenn W. Barker, and Ralph P. Martin, vol. 45. Waco, TX: Word, 1982.

———. *The Epistle to the Galatians: A Commentary on the Greek Text.* NIGTC, ed. I. Howard Marshall and W. Ward Gasque. Grand Rapids: Eerdmans, 1982.

———. *The Epistles to the Colossians, to Philemon, and to the Ephesians.* NICNT, ed. F. F. Bruce. Grand Rapids: Eerdmans, 1984.

———. *The Epistle to the Hebrews.* Rev. ed. NICNT, ed. F. F. Bruce. Grand Rapids: Eerdmans, 1990.

———. *Paul: Apostle of the Heart Set Free.* Grand Rapids: Eerdmans, 1977.

———. *Romans.* Rev. ed. TNTC, ed. Leon Morris, vol. 6. Leicester: InterVarsity, 1985.

Brunner, Emil. *The Christian Doctrine of the Church, Faith and the Consummation.* Translated by David Cairns, vol. 3. Philadelphia: Westminster, 1962.

Buchanan, George Wesley. *To the Hebrews.* AB, ed. William Foxwell Albright and David Noel Freedman, vol. 36. New York: Doubleday, 1972.

Burge, Gary M. "Glory." In *DJG*, ed. Joel B. Green, Scot McKnight, and I. Howard Marshall, 268–70. Downers Grove, IL: InterVarsity, 1992.

Burrows, Millar. *More Light on the Dead Sea Scrolls: New Scrolls and Their Interpretations.* New York: Viking, 1958.

Butler, Phillip. *Well Connected: Releasing Power, Restoring Hope Through Kingdom Partnerships.* Waynesboro, GA: Authentic, 2005.

Calvert-Koyzis, Nancy. *Paul, Monotheism and the People of God: The Significance of Abraham Traditions for Early Judaism and Christianity.* JSNT, ed. Mark Goodacre, vol. 273. London: T&T Clark, 2004.

Carrez, Maurice. *La deuxième épître de saint Paul aux Corinthiens.* CNT, vol. 8. Geneva: Labor et Fides, 1986.

Carson, D. A. *The Gospel According to John.* Leicester, England: InterVarsity Press and Grand Rapids: Eerdmans, 1991.

———. "When Is Spirituality Spiritual? Reflections on Some Problems of Definition." *JETS* 37 (September 1994): 381–94.

Chamblin, J. Knox. *Paul & the Self: Apostolic Teaching for Personal Wholeness.* Grand Rapids: Baker, 1993.

———. "Psychology." In *DPL*, ed. Gerald F. Hawthorne and Ralph P. Martin, 765–75. Downers Grove, IL: InterVarsity, 1993.

Chester, Andrew, and Ralph P. Martin. *The Theology of the Letters of James, Peter, and Jude.* New Testament Theology, ed. James D. G. Dunn. Cambridge: Cambridge University Press, 1994.

Chung, Daniel. "Sanctify Them Through Thy Truth." *The Reformation Review* 25 (July 1980): 162–70.

Clines, David J. A. "Image of God." In *DPL*, ed. Gerald F. Hawthorne and Ralph P. Martin, 426–28. Downers Grove, IL: InterVarsity, 1993.

———. "The Image of God in Man." *TynBul* 19 (1968): 53–103.

Cloud, Henry, and John Townsend. *How People Grow: What the Bible Reveals about Personal Growth.* Grand Rapids: Zondervan, 2001.

Clowney, Edmund P. *The Church.* Contours of Christian Theology, ed. Gerald Bray. Downers Grove, IL: InterVarsity, 1995.

Collins, R. F. "Spirituality According to St. Paul." *Living Light* 38, no. 2 (2001): 44–56.

Conzelmann, Hans. *1 Corinthians: A Commentary on the First Epistle to the Corinthians.* Translated by James W. Leitch. Hermeneia, ed. George W. MacRae. Philadelphia: Fortress, 1975.

Crabb, Larry. *Connecting: Healing for Ourselves and Our Relationships a Radical New Vision.* Nashville, TN: Word, 1997.

———. *Finding God.* Grand Rapids: Zondervan, 1993.

———. *Inside Out.* Colorado Springs, CO: NavPress, 1988.

———. *Men & Women: Enjoying the Difference.* Grand Rapids: Zondervan, 1991.

———. *The Safest Place on Earth: Where People Connect and Are Forever Changed.* Nashville, TN: Word, 1999.

———. *Understanding People: Deep Longings for Relationship.* Grand Rapids: Zondervan, 1987.

Crabb, Larry, and Dan Allender. *Hope When You're Hurting: Answers to Four Questions Hurting People Ask.* Grand Rapids: Zondervan, 1996.

Crabb, Lawrence J., Jr. *Effective Biblical Counseling.* Grand Rapids: Zondervan, 1977.

———, and Dan Allender. *Encouragement: The Key to Caring.* Grand Rapids: Zondervan, 1984.

Cranfield, C. E. B. *The Epistle to the Romans.* 2 vols. ICC, ed. J. A. Emerton and C. E. B. Cranfield. Edinburgh: T&T Clark, 1975–79.

———. "Paul's Teaching on Sanctification." *RefR* 48 (spring 1995): 217–29.

Crowley, Michael. "The Way of Sanctification." *Epiph* 14, no. 4 (1994): 3–65, 74–86.

Culp, John E. "Supernatural and Sanctification: Comparison of Roman Catholic and Wesleyan Views." *Wesleyan Theological Journal* 31 (fall 1996): 147–66.

Davids, Peter H. *The Epistle of James.* NIGTC, ed. I. Howard Marshall and Gasque W. Ward. Grand Rapids: Eerdmans, 1982.

———. *The First Epistle of Peter.* NICNT, ed. Gordon D. Fee. Grand Rapids: Eerdmans, 1990.

Dayton, Wilber T. "Entire Sanctification As Taught in the Book of Romans." *Wesleyan Theological Journal* 1 (spring 1966): 1–10.

———. "Entire Sanctification: The Divine Purification and Perfection of Man." In *A Contemporary Wesleyan Theology: Biblical, Systematic, and Practical,* ed., Charles W. Carter, R. Duane Thompson, and Charles R. Wilson, vol. 1, 517–69. Grand Rapids: Francis Asbury, 1983.

Decker, Rodney J. "The Church's Relationship to the New Covenant." *BSac* 152 (July-September 1995): 290–305.

Deidun, T. J. *New Covenant Morality in Paul.* AnBib. Rome: Biblical Institute Press, 1981.

Dicker, Gordon S. "Sanctification: Three Models in Scripture and Theology." *St. Mark's Review* 112 (December 1982): 11–19.

Dieter, Marvin E. "The Wesleyan Perspective." In *Five Views on Sanctification,* 11–46. Grand Rapids: Zondervan, 1987.

Dockery, David S. "Fruit of the Spirit." In *DPL,* ed. Gerald F. Hawthorne and Ralph P. Martin, 316–19. Downers Grove, IL: InterVarsity, 1993.

———. "New Nature and Old Nature." In *DPL,* ed. Gerald F. Hawthorne and Ralph P. Martin, 628–29. Downers Grove, IL: InterVarsity, 1993.

Domché, étienne. "La croix et le sacrifice de sanctification." *ETR* 61, no. 2 (1986): 251–55.

Donfried, Karl Paul. *Paul, Thessalonica, and Early Christianity.* Grand Rapids: Eerdmans, 2002.

Doohan, Helen. *Paul's Vision of Church.* GNS, vol. 32. Wilmington, DE: Michael Glazier, 1989.

Duffield, Guy P., and Nathaniel M. Van Cleave. *Foundations of Pentecostal Theology.* Los Angeles: LIFE Bible College, 1983.

Dunn, James D. G. *Baptism in the Holy Spirit: A Reexamination of the New Testament Teaching on the Gift of the Spirit in Relation to Pentecostalism Today.* SBT, ed. C. F. D. Moule et al, 2d ser., vol. 15. Naperville, IL: Alec R. Allenson, 1970.

————. *The Epistles to the Colossians and to Philemon.* NIGTC, ed. I. Howard Marshall and Donald A. Hagner. Grand Rapids: Eerdmans and Paternoster Press, 1996.

————., ed. Paul and the Mosaic Law. Grand Rapids: Eerdmans, 2001.

————. *Romans 1–8.* WBC, ed. David A. Hubbard, Glenn W. Barker, and Ralph P. Martin, vol. 38A. Dallas, TX: Word, 1988.

————. *The Theology of Paul the Apostle.* Grand Rapids: Eerdmans, 1998.

————. *Unity and Diversity in the New Testament: An Inquiry into the Character of Earliest Christianity.* 2d ed. Harrisburg, PA: Trinity, 1990.

Edwards, Dwight. *Revolution Within: A Fresh Look at Supernatural Living.* Colorado Springs, CO: WaterBrook, 2001.

Edwards, J. R. "Unity Not of Our Making." *Christianity Today* 45 (October 2001): 48–50.

Elbert, Paul, ed. *Faces of Renewal: Studies in Honor of Stanley M. Horton.* Peabody, MA: Hendrickson, 1988.

Elgvin, Torleif. "'To Master His Own Vessel': 1 Thess 4:4 in Light of New Qumran Evidence." *NTS* 43 (October 1997): 604–19.

Elliott, John H. *1 Peter: A New Translation with Introduction and Commentary.* AB, ed. William Foxwell Albright and David Noel Freedman, vol. 37B. New York: Doubleday, 2000.

Emmons, Robert A., and Cheryl A. Crumpler. "Religion and Spirituality? The Roles of Sanctification and the Concept of God." *International Journal for the Psychology of Religion* 9, no. 1 (1999): 17–24.

Engberg-Pedersen, Troels, ed. *Paul in His Hellenistic Context.* Minneapolis, MN: Fortress, 1995.

Erickson, Millard J. *Christian Theology.* 2d ed. Grand Rapids: Baker, 1998.

Esler, Philip F., ed. *Modeling Early Christianity: Social-Scientific Studies of the New Testament in Its Context.* New York: Routledge, 1995.

————. *The First Christians in Their Social Worlds: Social-Scientific Approaches to New Testament Interpretation.* New York: Routledge, 1994.

Fanning, Buist M. *Verbal Aspect in New Testament Greek.* Oxford Theological Monographs, ed. J. Barton et al. Oxford: Clarendon, 1990.

Fee, Gordon D. *1 and 2 Timothy, Titus.* New International Biblical Commentary, ed. W. Ward Gasque, vol. 13. Peabody, MA: Hendrickson, 1988.

————. *The First Epistle to the Corinthians.* NICNT, ed. F. F. Bruce. Grand Rapids: Eerdmans, 1987.

————. *Paul, the Spirit, and the People of God.* Peabody, MA: Hendrickson, 1996.

————. *Paul's Letter to the Philippians.* NICNT, ed. Gordon D. Fee. Grand Rapids: Eerdmans, 1995.

Ferguson, David. *The Never Alone Church.* Wheaton, IL: Tyndale House, 1998.

Ferguson, Sinclair B. *Know Your Christian Life: A Theological Introduction.* Downers Grove, IL: Inter-Varsity, 1981.

————. "The Reformed View." In *Christian Spirituality.* Edited by Donald L. Alexander, 47–76. Downers Grove, IL: InterVarsity, 1988.

Fergusson, David. *Community, Liberalism and Christian Ethics.* New Studies in Christian Ethics, ed. Robin Gill et al. Cambridge: Cambridge University Press, 1998.

———. "Reclaiming the Doctrine of Sanctification." *Int* 53 (October 1999): 380–90.

Figgis, J. B. *Keswick from Within.* Edited by Donald W. Dayton. London: Marshall Brothers, 1914. Reprint, New York: Garland, 1985.

Fitzmyer, Joseph A. *Paul and His Theology: A Brief Sketch.* 2d ed. 1967. Reprint, Englewood Cliffs, NJ: Prentice Hall, 1989.

Ford, David C. "Saint Makarios of Egypt and John Wesley: Variations on the Theme of Sanctification." *GOTR* 33 (fall 1988): 285–312.

Forde, Gerhard O. "The Lutheran View." In *Christian Spirituality.* Edited by Donald L Alexander, 14–32. Downers Grove, IL: InterVarsity, 1988.

Fung, Ronald Y. K. "Body of Christ." In *DPL,* ed. Gerald F. Hawthorne and Ralph P. Martin, 76–82. Downers Grove, IL: InterVarsity, 1993.

Furnish, Victor Paul. *The Moral Teaching of Paul.* Nashville, TN: Abingdon, 1983.

———. *Theology and Ethics in Paul.* Nashville, TN: Abingdon, 1968.

Gaede, S. D. *Belonging: Our Need for Community in Church and Family.* Grand Rapids: Zondervan, 1985.

Gaffin, Richard B. "Glory, Glorification." In *DPL,* ed. Gerald F. Hawthorne and Ralph P. Martin, 348–50. Downers Grove, IL: InterVarsity, 1993.

García Martínez, Florentino, ed. *The Dead Sea Scrolls Translated: The Qumran Texts in English.* Translated by G. E. Wilfred Watson. 2d ed. Leiden: Brill, 1996.

Gatta, Julia. "Justification and Sanctification: Classical Concerns and Contemporary Context." *JES* 23 (summer 1986): 513–17.

Geertz, Clifford. *The Interpretation of Cultures.* New York: Basic Books, 1973.

Giles, Kevin. *What on Earth Is the Church? An Exploration in New Testament Theology.* Downers Grove, IL: InterVarsity, 1995.

Gottwald, Norman K. *The Hebrew Bible—A Socio-Literary Introduction.* Philadelphia: Fortress, 1985.

———. *The Hebrew Bible in Its Social World and in Ours.* Society of Biblical Literature Semeia Series, ed. Edward L. Greenstein. Atlanta, GA: Scholars Press, 1993.

———. "Sociological Method in the Study of Ancient Israel." In *Encounter with the Text: Form and History in the Hebrew Bible*, ed. Martin J. Buss, 69–81. Missoula, MT: Scholars Press and Fortress, 1979.

———. *The Tribes of Yahweh: A Sociology of Liberated Israel, 1250–1050 B.C.E.* Maryknoll, NY: Orbis, 1979.

Green, Michael. *2 Peter and Jude.* Rev. ed. TNTC, ed. Leon Morris. 1968. Reprint, Grand Rapids: Eerdmans, 1987.

Grenz, Stanley J. *Created for Community: Connecting Christian Belief with Christian Living.* Wheaton, IL: Victor /SP Publications, 1996.

———. *Renewing the Center: Evangelical Theology in a Post-Theological Era.* Grand Rapids: Baker, 2000.

———. *The Social God and the Relational Self: A Trinitarian Theology of the Imago Dei.* The Matrix of Christian Theology. Louisville, KY: Westminster John Knox, 2001.

———. *Theology for the Community of God.* Grand Rapids: Eerdmans, 1994.

Gritsch, Eric W., and Robert W. Jenson. *Lutheranism: The Theological Movement and Its Confessional Writings.* Philadelphia: Fortress, 1976.

Grogan, G. W. "The Old Testament Concept of Solidarity in Hebrews." *TynBul* 49 (May 1998): 159–73.

Grosheide, F. W. *Commentary on the First Epistle to the Corinthians: The English Text with Introduction, Exposition and Notes.* NICNT, ed. Ned B. Stonehouse. Grand Rapids: Eerdmans, 1953.

Grudem, Wayne. *1 Peter*. TNTC, ed. Leon Morris. Grand Rapids: Eerdmans, 1988.

Gundry, Robert H. *Sōma in Biblical Theology: With Emphasis on Pauline Anthropology*. SNTSMS, ed. Matthew Black and R. McL. Wilson, vol. 29. Cambridge: Cambridge University Press, 1976.

Guthrie, Donald. *The Epistle to the Hebrews: An Introduction and Commentary*. TNTC, ed. Leon Morris. Grand Rapids: Eerdmans, 1983.

Guthrie, George H. *Hebrews*. NIV Application Commentary, ed. Terry Muck. Grand Rapids: Zondervan, 1998.

Hafemann, Scott. "Paul's Use of the Old Testament in 2 Corinthians." *Int* 52 (July 1988): 246–57.

Hainz, Josef. *»Kirche« als Gemeinschaft bei Paulus*. Regensburg: Verlag Friedrich Pustet, 1982.

Haldane, John J. "The School of Sanctification." *First Things* 80 (February 1998): 31–35.

Hall, Roy W. "Ministry as Sanctification." *Memphis Theological Seminary Journal* 31 (spring-summer (1993)): 38–42.

Hanson, Paul D. *The People Called: The Growth of Community in the Bible: With a New Introduction*. Louisville, KY: Westminster John Knox, 2001.

Hanson, Stig. *The Unity of the Church in the New Testament: Colossians and Ephesians*. ASNU, ed. A. Fridrichsen, vol. 14. Uppsala: Almquist & Wiksells Boktryckeri, 1946. Reprint, Lexington, KY: American Theological Library Association, 1963.

Harris, Laird R., Gleason L. Archer Jr., and Bruce K. Waltke, eds. *TWOT*. 2 vols. Chicago: Moody, 1980.

Harris, Murray J. *The Second Epistle to the Corinthians*. NIGTC, ed. I. Howard Marshall and Donald A. Hagner. Grand Rapids: Eerdmans and Paternoster, 2005.

Hauerwas, Stanley. *Sanctify Them in the Truth: Holiness Exemplified*. Nashville, TN: Abingdon, 1998.

Hays, J. Daniel. *From every People and Nation: A Biblical Theology of Race*. NSBT, ed. D. A. Carson. Downers Grove, IL: InterVarsity and Apollos, 2003.

Hein, Steven A. "Sanctification: The Powerful Pardon." *Logia* 6 (1997): 19–23.

Helminiak, Daniel A. "Human Solidarity and Collective Union in Christ." *AThR* 70 (January 1988): 34–59.

Hendriksen, William. *Thessalonians, Timothy and Titus*. New Testament Commentary. Grand Rapids: Baker, 1957.

Herzog, William R. "Temple Cleansing." In *DJG*, ed. Joel B. Green, Scot McKnight, and I. Howard Marshall, 817–21. Downers Grove, IL: InterVarsity, 1992.

Hiebert, D. Edmond. *The Thessalonian Epistles: A Call to Readiness*. Chicago, IL: Moody, 1971.

Hoch, Carl B., Jr. *All Things New: The Significance of Newness for Biblical Theology*. Grand Rapids: Baker, 1995.

Hodge, Charles. *Systematic Theology*. Vol. 3. London: Scribner and Sons, 1872. Reprint, Grand Rapids: Eerdmans, 1940.

Hoehner, Harold W. *Ephesians: An Exegetical Commentary*. Grand Rapids: Baker, 2002.

Hoekema, Anthony A. *Created in God's Image*. Grand Rapids: Eerdmans, 1988.

———. "The Reformed Perspective." In *Five Views on Sanctification*, 59–90. Grand Rapids: Zondervan, 1987.

Holloman, Henry. *The Forgotten Blessing: Rediscovering the Transforming Power of Sanctification*. Swindoll Leadership Series, ed. Charles R. Swindoll. Nashville, TN: Word, 1999.

Holmes, Michael W. *1 and 2 Thessalonians*. NIV Application Commentary, ed. Terry Muck et al. Grand Rapids: Zondervan, 1998

Hooker, Morna D. "'Heirs of Abraham': The Gentiles' Role in Israel's Story." In *Narrative Dynamics in Paul: A Critical Assessment*, ed. Bruce W. Longenecker, 85–96. Louisville, KY: Westminster John Knox, 2002.

Horrell, D. G. "From ἀδελφοί to οἶκος θεοῦ· Social Transformation in Pauline Christianity." *JBL* 120 (February 2001): 293–311.

Horrell, D. G., and C. M. Tuckett, eds. *Christology, Controversy and Community: New Testament Essays in Honour of David R. Catchpole*. NovTSup, vol. 99. Leiden: Brill, 2.

Horton, Stanley M. "The Pentecostal Perspective." In *Five Views on Sanctification*, 105–35. Grand Rapids: Zondervan, 1987.

———. *What the Bible Says About the Holy Spirit*. Springfield, MO: Gospel Publishing House, 1976.

Hoy, Albert L. "Sanctification." *Paraclete* 15 (fall 1981): 1–7.

Hughes, Philip Edgcumbe. *The Second Epistle to the Corinthians*. NICNT, ed. F. F. Bruce. Grand Rapids: Eerdmans, 1962.

Hulme, William E. *Dynamics of Sanctification*. Minneapolis, MN: Augsburg, 1966.

Hurtado, Larry W. "God." In *DJG*, ed. Joel B. Green, Scot McKnight, and I. Howard Marshall, 270–76. Downers Grove, IL: InterVarsity, 1992.

Hutton, Rodney R. "Innocent or Holy? Justification and Sanctification in Old Testament Theology." *WW* 17 (summer 1997): 312–21.

Inwood, Charles. "The Fullness of the Spirit." In *Life More Abundant: Spirit-Filled Messages from the Keswick Convention*, ed. Herbert F. Stevenson. Grand Rapids: Francis Asbury, 1987.

Isaak, Jon M. "The Christian Community and Political Responsibility: Romans 13:1–7." *Direction* 32 (spring 2003): 32–46.

Jenney, Timothy P. "The Holy Spirit and Sanctification." In *Systematic Theology: A Pentecostal Perspective*, ed. Stanley M. Horton, 397–421. Springfield, MO: Logion, 1994.

Johnson, Aubrey R. *The One and the Many in the Israelite Conception of God*. 2d ed. Cardiff: University of Wales Press, 1961.

———. *The Vitality of the Individual in the Thought of Ancient Israel*. Cardiff: University of Wales Press, 1949.

Johnson, Luke Timothy. "The Church as God's Household." *TBT* 40, no. 4 (2002): 224–28.

———. *Letters to Paul's Delegates: 1 Timothy, 2 Timothy, Titus*. New Testament in Context, ed. Howard Clark Kee and J. Andrew Overman. Valley Forge, PA: Trinity, 1996.

Jonker, L. "The Influence of Social Transformation on the Interpretation of the Bible: A Methodological Reflection." *Scriptura* 72 (2000): 1–14.

———. "Social Transformation and Biblical Interpretation: A Comparative Study." *Scriptura* 77 (2001): 259–70.

Joyner, Russell E. "The One True God." In *Systematic Theology: A Pentecostal Perspective*, ed. Stanley M. Horton, 117–44. Springfield, MO: Logion, 1994.

Jung, Patricia B. "Sanctification: An Interpretation in Light of Embodiment." *JRE* 11 (spring 1983): 75–95.

Kaylor, R. David. *Paul's Covenant Community: Jew and Gentile in Romans*. Atlanta, GA: John Knox, 1988.

Katoppo, Pericles G. "Translating Hagiasmos 'Sanctification' in Paul's Letters." *BT* 38 (October 1987): 429–32.

Keener, Craig S. *1–2 Corinthians*. New Cambridge Bible Commentary, ed. Ben Witherington, III. Cambridge: Cambridge University Press, 2005.

Kille, D. A. "Psychology and the Bible: Three Worlds of the Text." *Pastoral Psychology* 51, no. 2 (2002): 125–34.

Kilmartin, Edward J. "The Active Role of Christ and the Holy Spirit in the Sanctification of the Eucharistic Elements." *TS* 45 (June 1984): 225–53.

Kirkpatrick, Frank G. *The Ethics of Community*. New Dimensions to Religious Ethics, ed. Frank G. Kirkpatrick and Susan F. Parsons. Oxford: Blackwell, 2001.

————. *Together Bound: God, History, and the Religious Community.* New York: Oxford University Press, 1994.

Kittel, Gerhard, and Gerhard Friedrich, eds. *TDNT.* 10 vols. Translated and edited by Geoffrey W. Bromiley. Grand Rapids: Eerdmans, 1964–74.

Knight, George W. *The Pastoral Epistles: A Commentary on the Greek Text.* NIGTC, ed. I. Howard Marshall and W. Ward Gasque. Grand Rapids: Eerdmans, 1992.

Knight, Henry H. III. "Worship and Sanctification." *Wesleyan Theological Journal* 32 (fall 1997): 5–14.

Koehler, Edward W. A. *A Summary of Christian Doctrine: A Popular Presentation of the Teachings of the Bible.* 2d ed. St. Louis, MO: Concordia, 1971.

Kolb, Robert. *The Christian Faith: A Lutheran Exposition.* St. Louis, MO: Concordia, 1993.

Köstenberger, Andreas J., and Peter T. O'Brien. *Salvation to the Ends of the Earth: A Biblical Theology of Mission.* NSBT, ed. D. A. Carson. Downers Grove, IL: InterVarsity and Apollos, 2001.

Kreitzer, Larry J. "Adam and Christ." In *DPL,* ed. Gerald F. Hawthorne and Ralph P. Martin, 9–15. Downers Grove, IL: InterVarsity, 1993.

Kruse, Colin G. *Paul, the Law, and Justification.* Peabody, MA: Hendrickson, 1996.

Lamb, Richard. *The Pursuit of God in the Company of Friends.* Downers Grove, IL: InterVarsity, 2003.

Land, Steven J. *Pentecostal Spirituality: A Passion for the Kingdom.* Journal of Pentecostal Theology Supplement Series, ed. John Christopher Thomas, Rick D. Moore, and Steven J. Land, vol. 1. Sheffield: Sheffield Academic Press, 1993.

Lane, William L. *Hebrews 1–8.* WBC, ed. David A. Hubbard and Glenn W. Barker, vol. 47A. Dallas, TX: Word, 1991.

Lattey, C. "Vicarious Solidarity in the Old Testament." *VT* 1 (October 1951): 267–74.

Leclerc, Thomas L. *Yahweh Is Exalted in Justice: Solidarity and Conflict in Isaiah.* Minneapolis, MN: Fortress, 2001.

Lemche, Niels Peter. *Prelude to Israel's Past: Background and Beginnings of Israelite History and Identity.* Translated by E. F. Maniscalco. Peabody, MA: Hendrickson, 1998.

Lenski, Richard C. H. *The Interpretation of St. Luke's Gospel.* Minneapolis, MN: Augsburg, 1946.

Letch, Ralph A. "Sanctification in the Old Testament." *London Quarterly and Holborn Review* 180 (April 1955): 129–31.

Lightfoot, J. B. *Saint Paul's Epistle to the Philippians.* Classic Commentary Library. London: Macmillan & Co., 1868. Reprint, Grand Rapids: Zondervan, 1953.

Lim, D. S. "Transformational Spirituality: Pauline Spirituality in Asian Context." *ATA Journal* 7, no. 1 (1999): 68–109.

Lincoln, Andrew T. *Ephesians.* WBC, ed. David A. Hubbard and Glenn W. Barker, vol. 42. Dallas, TX: Word, 1990.

————. *Paradise Now and Not Yet: Studies in the Role of the Heavenly Dimension in Paul's Thought with Special Reference to His Eschatology.* SNTSMS, ed. R. McL. Wilson and M. E. Thrall, vol. 43. Cambridge: Cambridge University Press, 1981.

Lindbeck, George. "Confession and Community: An Israel-Like View of the Church." *ChrCent* 107 (9 May 1990): 492–96.

Lindström, Harald. *Wesley and Sanctification: A Study in the Doctrine of Salvation.* Grand Rapids: Zondervan, 1980.

Lohse, Eduard. *Colossians and Philemon.* Translated by William R. Poehlmann and Robert J. Karris. Hermeneia, ed. Helmut Koester. Philadelphia: Fortress, 1971.

Longenecker, Bruce W. "Defining the Faithful Character of the Covenant Community: Galatians 2.15–21 and Beyond." In *Paul and the Mosaic Law,* ed. James D. G. Dunn, 75–97. Grand Rapids: Eerdmans, 2001.

————., ed. Narrative Dynamics in Paul: A Critical Assessment. Louisville, KY: Westminster John Knox, 2002.

Longenecker, Richard N. Galatians. WBC, ed. David A. Hubbard, Glenn W. Barker, and Ralph P. Martin, vol. 41. Dallas, TX: Word, 1990.

Louw, J. P., and Eugene A. Nida. Greek-English Lexicon of the New Testament: Based on Semantic Domains. 2d ed. New York: United Bible Societies, 1989.

Lowe, Chuck. "'There Is No Condemnation' (Romans 8:1): But Why Not?" JETS 42 (December 1999): 152–58.

Lloyd-Jones, D. Martyn. Christian Unity: An Exposition of Ephesians 4:1–16. Grand Rapids: Baker, 1980.

MacLeod, Donald. "The Doctrine of Sanctification." Banner of Truth 109 (October 1972): 16–25.

Mahlangu, E. "The Ancient Mediterranean Values of Honour and Shame as a Hermeneutical Procedure: A Social-Scientific Criticism in an African Perspective." Verbum et Ecclesia [Pretoria] 22 (2001): 85–101.

Malina, Bruce J. The New Testament World: Insights from Cultural Anthropology. 3d ed., rev. and exp. ed. Louisville, KY: Westminster John Knox, 2001.

————. The Social World of Jesus and the Gospels. New York: Routledge, 1996.

————. Christian Origins and Cultural Anthropology: Practical Models for Biblical Interpretation. Atlanta, GA: John Knox, 1986.

Marquardt, Manfred. John Wesley's Social Ethics: Praxis and Principles. Translated by John E. Steely and W. Stephen Gunter. Nashville, TN: Abingdon, 1992.

Marshall, I. Howard. A Critical and Exegetical Commentary on the Pastoral Epistles. ICC, ed. J. A. Emerton, C. E. B. Cranfield, and G. N. Stanton. Edinburgh: T&T Clark, 1999.

————. The Gospel of Luke. NIGTC, ed. I. Howard Marshall and W. Ward Gasque. Grand Rapids: Eerdmans, 1978.

Martens, Elmer A. God's Design: A Focus on Old Testament Theology. 2d ed. Leicester: InterVarsity Press, 1981. Reprint, Grand Rapids: Baker, 1994.

Martin, Ralph P. 2 Corinthians. WBC, ed. David A. Hubbard and Ralph P. Martin, vol. 40. Waco, TX: Word, 1986.

————. "Center of Paul's Theology." In DPL, ed. Gerald F. Hawthorne and Ralph P. Martin, 92–95. Downers Grove, IL: InterVarsity, 1993.

————. James. WBC, ed. David A. Hubbard, D. W. Watts, and Ralph P. Martin, vol. 48. Waco, TX: Word, 1988.

Matera, F. J. "Imitating Paul in Order to Follow Christ." Living Light 38, no. 2 (2001): 35–43.

Matthews, Victor H. and Don C. Benjamin. Social World of Ancient Israel, 1250–587 BCE. Peabody, MA: Hendrickson, 1993.

McCown, Wayne. "God's Will for You: Sanctification in the Thessalonian Epistles." Wesleyan Theological Journal 12 (spring 1977): 26–33.

McFadyen, Alistair I. The Call to Personhood: A Christian Theology of the Individual in Social Relationships. Cambridge: Cambridge University Press, 1990.

McGrath, Alister E. Christian Spirituality: An Introduction. Oxford: Blackwell, 1999.

Mcknight, Scot. "Gentiles." In DJG, ed. Joel B. Green, Scot McKnight, and I. Howard Marshall, 259–65. Downers Grove, IL: InterVarsity, 1992.

McQuilkin, J. Robertson. "The Keswick Perspective." In Five Views on Sanctification, 149–83. Grand Rapids: Zondervan, 1987.

McShea, Robert J. Morality and Human Nature: A New Route to Ethical Theory. Philadelphia: Temple University Press, 1990.

McVay, J. K. "The Human Body as Social and Political Metaphor in Stoic Literature and Early Christian Writers." *BASP* 37 (January-April 2000): 135–47.

Meeks, Wayne A. *The Moral World of the First Christians*. LEC, ed. Wayne A. Meeks, vol. 6. Philadelphia: Westminster, 1986.

———. *The Origins of Christian Morality: The First Two Centuries*. New Haven, CT: Yale University Press, 1993.

Meier, John P. "Structure and Theology in Heb 1,1–14." *Bib* 66, no. 2 (1985): 168–89.

Mendenhall, G. E. "The Relation of the Individual to Political Society in Ancient Israel." In *Biblical Studies in Memory of H. C. Alleman*, ed. J. M. Myers, 89–108. Locust Valley, NY: J.J Augustin, 1960.

Menzies, William W., and Stanley M. Horton. *Bible Doctrines: A Pentecostal Perspective*, ed. Stanley M. Horton. Springfield, MO: Logion, 1993.

Merrill, Eugene H. *Kingdom of Priests: A History of Old Testament Israel*. Grand Rapids: Baker, 1996.

Metzger, Bruce M. "Paul's Vision of the Church." *ThTo* 6 (April 1949): 49–63.

Meye, Robert P. "Spirituality." In *DPL*, ed. Gerald F. Hawthorne and Ralph P. Martin, 906–16. Downers Grove, IL: InterVarsity, 1993.

Michaels, J. Ramsey. *1 Peter*. WBC, ed. Glenn W. Barker, David A. Hubbard, and Ralph P. Martin, vol. 49. Waco, TX: Word, 1988.

Míguez Bonino, José. "Sanctification and Liberation." *AsTJ* 50–51 (fall-spring 1995–1996): 141–50.

———. "Wesley's Doctrine of Sanctification From a Liberationist Perspective." In *Sanctification and Liberation: Liberation Theologies in Light of the Wesleyan Tradition*, ed. Theodore Runyon, 49–63. Nashville, TN: Abingdon, 1981.

Miller, Ernest C. "Πολιτεύεσθε in Philippians 1:27: Some Philological and Thematic Observations." *JSNT* 15 (1982): 86–96.

Moltmann, Jürgen. *Man: Christian Anthropology in the Conflicts of the Present*. Translated by John Sturdy. Philadelphia: Fortress, 1974.

Montagu, Ashley. *Man in Progress*. New York: Mentor Books, 1961.

Moo, Douglas J. *The Epistle to the Romans*. NICNT, ed. Gordon D. Fee. Grand Rapids: Eerdmans, 1996.

———. "Law." In *Dictionary of New Testament Background*, ed. Craig A. Evans and Stanley E. Porter, 450–61. Downers Grove, IL: InterVarsity, 2000.

———. *The Letter of James: An Introduction and Commentary*. TNTC, ed. Leon Morris. Leicester, England: InterVarsity, 1985.

Morris, Leon. *The Epistle to the Romans*. Grand Rapids: Eerdmans, 1988.

———. *The First and Second Epistles to the Thessalonians: The English Text with Introduction, Exposition and Notes*. NICNT, ed. F. F. Bruce. Grand Rapids: Eerdmans, 1959.

———. *The Gospel According to John*. Rev. ed. NICNT, ed. Gordon D. Fee. Grand Rapids: Eerdmans, 1995.

Moule, H. C. G. *Colossian and Philemon Studies*. London: Pickering and Inglis, 1898. Reprint, Ft. Washington, PA: Christian Literature Crusade, 1975.

Moule, C. F. D. *An Idiom Book of New Testament Greek*. 2d ed. Cambridge: Cambridge University Press, 1959.

Mounce, William D. *Pastoral Epistles*. WBC, ed. Bruce M. Metzger and Ralph P. Martin, vol. 46. Nashville, TN: Thomas Nelson, 2000.

Mouton, Elna. *Reading a New Testament Document Ethically*. SBL: Academia Biblica, ed. Mark Allan Powell, vol. 1. Leiden: Brill, 2002.

Mueller, C. D. "People of God, Hear God Who Calls." *TBT* 40, no. 4 (2002): 211–17.

Murray, John. "Definitive Sanctification." *CTJ* 2 (April 1967): 5–21.

———. *The Epistle to the Romans*. 2 vols. NICNT, ed. F. F. Bruce. Grand Rapids: Eerdmans, 1959–65.

Nafziger, Samuel H. "Growing in Christ: The Proper Relationship between Justification and Sanctification." *Concordia Journal* 8 (November 1982): 206–13.

Nee, Watchman. *The Spiritual Man*. New York: Christian Fellowship Publishers, 1968.

Nettles, Tom J. "Sanctification and the New Perfectionism." *The Wicket Gate* 2 (spring 1983): 7–12.

New English Translation: NET Bible. Dallas, TX: Biblical Studies Press, 2001.

Newton, John A. "Spirituality and Sanctification." *OiC* 24, no. 3 (1988): 218–22.

Ngundu, Onesimus Annos. "Toward a Pauline Model of Progressive Sanctification." Th.D. diss., Dallas Theological Seminary, 1988.

Oakland, James A. "Self-Actualization and Sanctification." *Journal of Psychology and Theology* 2 (summer 1974): 202–09.

O'Brien, Peter T. *Colossians, Philemon*. WBC, ed. David A. Hubbard, Glenn W. Barker, and Ralph P. Martin, vol. 44. Waco, TX: Word, 1982.

———. *The Epistle to the Philippians: A Commentary on the Greek Text*. NIGTC, ed. I. Howard Marshall and W. Ward Gasque. Grand Rapids: Eerdmans, 1991.

———. *The Letter to the Ephesians*. Pillar New Testament Commentary, ed. D. A. Carson. Grand Rapids: Eerdmans and Apollos, 1999.

O'Neill, J. C. "'The Work of the Ministry' in Ephesians 4:12 and the New Testament." *ExpTim* 112 (October 2001): 336–40.

Overholt, Thomas. *Cultural Anthropology and the Old Testament*. GBS: Old Testament, ed. Gene M. Tucker. Minneapolis, MN: Fortress, 1996.

Packer, James I. *Keep in Step with the Spirit*. Old Tappan, NJ: Fleming H. Revell, 1984.

———. "'Keswick' and the Reformed Doctrine of Sanctification." *EvQ* 27 (July-September 1955): 153–67.

———. *Knowing God*. Downers Grove, IL: InterVarsity, 1973.

Pannenberg, Wolfhart. *What Is Man?* Translated by Duane A. Priebe. Philadelphia: Fortress, 1970.

Parsons, Michael. "Being Precedes Act: Indicative and Imperative in Paul's Writing." *EvQ* 60 (April 1988): 99–127.

Pauw, Amy Plantinga. "Theological Meditations on Ephesians 2:11–22." *ThTo* 62 (2005): 78–83

Pearlman, Myer. *Knowing the Doctrines of the Bible*. Springfield, MO: Gospel Publishing House, 1937.

Pecheur, David. "Cognitive Theory/Therapy and Sanctification: A Study in Integration." *Journal of Psychology and Theology* 6 (fall 1978): 239–53.

Perelewitz, Miriam Francis. "The Unity of the Body of Christ." *TBT* 18 (November 1980): 394–98.

Peterlin, Davorin. *Paul's Letter to the Philippians in the Light of the Disunity of the Church*. NovTSup, ed. A. J. Malherbe and D. P. Moessner, vol. 79. Leiden: Brill, 1995.

Peterson, David. *Possessed by God: A New Testament Theology of Sanctification and Holiness*. NSBT, ed. D. A. Carson. Grand Rapids: Eerdmans, 1995.

Pfammatter, Josef. *Die Kirche als Bau: eine Exegetisch-Theologische Studie zur Ekklesiologie Der Paulusbriefe*. Facultatis Theologicae, no. 110. Rome: Pontificiae Universitatis Gregorianae, 1960.

Pieper, Francis. *Christian Dogmatics*. Vol. 3. Saint Louis, MO: Concordia, 1953.

Pilch, John J., ed. *Social Scientific Models for Interpreting the Bible: Essays by the Context Group in Honor of Bruce J. Malina*. Leiden: Brill, 2001.

Pink, Arthur W. *The Doctrine of Sanctification*. Swengel, PA: Bible Truth Depot, 1953.

Plummer, Alfred. *A Critical and Exegetical Commentary on the Second Epistle of St Paul to the Corinthians.* ICC, ed. S. R. Driver, A. Plummer, and C. A. Briggs. Edinburgh: T&T Clark, 1915.

Pollock, J. C. *The Keswick Story: The Authorized History of the Keswick Convention.* Chicago: Moody, 1964.

Porter, J. R. "Legal Aspects of Corporate Personality." *VT* 15 (July 1965): 361–80.

Porter, Stanley E. *Idioms of the Greek New Testament.* 2d ed. Sheffield: Sheffield Academic and JSOT, 1996.

Porter, Steven L. "On the Renewal of Interest in the Doctrine of Sanctification: A Methodological Reminder." *JETS* 45 (September 2002): 415–26.

Powers, Daniel G. *Salvation through Participation: An Examination of the Notion of the Believers' Corporate Unity with Christ in Early Christian Soteriology.* Contributions to Biblical Exegesis & Theology, ed. Th. Baarda et al, vol. 29. Leuven: Peeters, 2001.

Prior, David. Creating Community: An Every-Member Approach to Ministry in the Local Church. Colorado Springs, CO: NavPress, 1992.

Raabe, Paul R. "The Law and Christian Sanctification: A Look at Romans." *Concordia Journal* 22 (April 1996): 178–85.

Rakestraw, Robert V. "Becoming Like God: An Evangelical Doctrine of Theosis." *JETS* 40 (June 1997): 257–69.

Rakover, Nahum. "The One Vs. The Many in Life and Death Situations." In *Proceedings of 1994 Conference in Jerusalem,* Jewish Law Association Studies, ed. E. A. Goldman, vol. 8, 129–54. Atlanta, GA: Scholars Press, 1996.

Rees, Paul S. "Adequacy for Life and Witness." In *Life More Abundant: Spirit-Filled Messages from the Keswick Convention.* Edited by Herbert F. Stevenson. Grand Rapids: Francis Asbury, 1987.

Reisinger, Ernest C. "The Biblical Doctrine of Sanctification." *The Wicket Gate* 2 (spring 1983): 13–19.

Richards, Lawrence O. *Becoming One in the Spirit.* Wheaton, IL: Victor, 1973.

Ridderbos, Herman N. *The Epistle of Paul to the Churches of Galatia: The English Text with Introduction, Exposition and Notes.* Translated by Henry Zylstra. NICNT, ed. N. B. Stonehouse. Grand Rapids: Eerdmans, 1953.

———. *Paul: An Outline of His Theology.* Translated by John Richard de Witt. Kampen, Netherlands: J. H. Kok, 1966. Reprint, Grand Rapids: Eerdmans, 1975.

Robinson, H. Wheeler. *Corporate Personality in Ancient Israel.* Rev. ed. Philadelphia: Fortress, 1980.

———. "Hebrew Psychology in Relation to Pauline Anthropology." In Mansfield College Essays Presented to the Reverend Andrew Martin Fairbairn, D.D. On the Occasion of His Seventieth Birthday, November 4, 1908, 265–86. London: Hodder & Stoughton, 1909.

Robinson, John A. T. *The Body: A Study in Pauline Theology.* Philadelphia: Westminster, 1952.

Rogers, William F. "Creation, Redemption, Sanctification, and Mental Health." *Pastoral Psychology* 12 (November 1961): 10–14.

Rogerson, J. W. *Anthropology and the Old Testament.* Atlanta, GA: John Knox, 1979.

———. "The Hebrew Conception of Corporate Personality: A Re-Examination." *Journal of Theological Studies* 21 (April 1970): 1–16.

Rosner, Brian S. Paul, Scripture and Ethics: A Study of 1 Corinthians 5–7. Leiden: Brill, 1994.

Rowland, A. N. "The Conception of Personality in Theology." In *Mansfield College Essays.* London: Hodder & Sloughton, 1909.

Russell, Walt. "The Apostle Paul's Redemptive-Historical Argumentation in Galatians 5:13–26." *Westminster Theological Journal* 57 (fall 1995): 333–57.

Rust, E. C. *Nature and Man in Biblical Thought.* London: Lutterworth, 1953.

Ryken, Leland, James C. Wilhoit, and Tremper Longman III, eds. *Dictionary of Biblical Imagery.* Downers Grove, IL: InterVarsity, 1998.

Sailhamer, John H. "Genesis." In *Expositor's Bible Commentary*, ed. by Frank E. Gaebelein, vol. 2, 1–284. Grand Rapids: Zondervan, 1990.

Sampley, J. Paul, ed. *Paul in the Greco-Roman World: A Handbook.* Harrisburg: Trinity, 2003.

————. *Pauline Partnership in Christ: Christian Community and Commitment in Light of Roman Law.* Philadelphia: Fortress, 1980.

Schlink, Edmund. *Theology of the Lutheran Confessions.* Translated by Paul F. Koehneke and Herbert J. A. Bouman. Philadelphia: Fortress, 1961.

Schmidt, F. *How the Temple Thinks. Identity and Social Cohesion in Ancient Judaism.* Translated by J. E. Crowley. Sheffield: Sheffield Academic Press, 2001.

Schnackenburg, Rudolf. *Ephesians: A Commentary.* Translated by Helen Heron. Edinburgh: T&T Clark, 1991.

Schroer, Silvia, and Thomas Staubli. *Body Symbolism in the Bible.* Translated by Linda M. Maloney. Collegeville, MN: Liturgical Press, 2001.

Scroggie, W. Graham. "Abounding Life." In *Life More Abundant: Spirit-Filled Messages from the Keswick Convention.* Edited by Herbert F. Stevenson. Grand Rapids: Francis Asbury, 1987.

Scroggs, R. *The Last Adam: A Study in Pauline Anthropology.* Philadelphia: Fortress, 1966.

Seifrid, Mark A. "In Christ." In *DPL*, ed. Gerald F. Hawthorne and Ralph P. Martin, 433–36. Downers Grove, IL: InterVarsity, 1993.

————. "Paul's Approach to the Old Testament in Rom 10:6–8." *TJ* 6 (spring 1985): 3–37.

Shackleford, J. M. *Biblical Body Language. The Figurative Face of Scripture.* Lanham, MD: University Press of America, 2000.

Shedd, Russell Phillip. *Man in Community: A Study of St. Paul's Application of Old Testament and Early Jewish Conceptions of Human Solidarity.* Grand Rapids: Eerdmans, 1964.

Shults, F. LeRon. *Reforming Theological Anthropology: After the Philosophical Turn to Relationality.* Grand Rapids: Eerdmans, 2003.

Silva, Moisés. *Interpreting Galatians: Explorations in Exegetical Method.* 2d ed. Grand Rapids: Baker, 2001.

————. *Philippians.* Wycliffe Exegetical Commentary, ed. Kenneth Barker. Chicago: Moody, 1988.

Sklba, R. J. "Body of Christ." *TBT* 40, no. 4 (2002): 219–23.

Smedes, Louis B. *Union with Christ: A Biblical View of the New Life in Jesus Christ.* Rev. ed. Grand Rapids: Eerdmans, 1983.

Smith, Jay E. "1 Thess 4:4–Breaking the Impasse." *BBR* 11, no. 1 (2001): 65–105.

Soards, Marion L. *1 Corinthians.* New International Biblical Commentary, ed. W. Ward Gasque. Peabody, MA: Hendrickson, 1999.

Son, Sang-Won. *Corporate Elements in Pauline Anthropology: A Study of Selected Terms, Idioms, and Concepts in the Light of Paul's Usage and Background.* AnBib. Rome: Editrice Pontificio Istituto Biblico, 2001.

Spittler, Russell P. "The Pentecostal View." In *Christian Spirituality*, ed. Donald L. Alexander, 133–54. Downers Grove, IL: InterVarsity, 1988.

Stacey, David W. *The Pauline View of Man in Relation to Its Judaic and Hellenistic Background.* London: Macmillan, 1956.

Stanger, Frank Bateman. "What Does It Mean to Be Sanctified?" *The Asbury Seminarian* 33 (April 1978): 5–12.

Staples, Rob L. "Sanctification and Selfhood: A Phenomenological Analysis of the Wesleyan Message." *Wesleyan Theological Journal* 7 (spring 1972): 3–16.

Stevenson, Herbert F., ed. *Keswick's Authentic Voice: Sixty-Five Dynamic Addresses Delivered at the Keswick Convention 1875–1957*. Grand Rapids: Zondervan, 1959.

————, ed. *Life More Abundant: Spirit-Filled Messages from the Keswick Convention*. Grand Rapids: Francis Asbury, 1987.

Stifler, James M. *The Epistle to the Romans: A Commentary Logical and Historical*. New York: Fleming H. Revell, 1897. Reprint, Chicago: Moody, 1960.

Stott, John R. W. *The Epistles of John*. TNTC, ed. R. V. G. Tasker, vol. 19. Grand Rapids: Eerdmans, 1960.

Strack, Wolfram. *Kultische Terminologie in ekklesiologischen Kontexten in den Briefen des Paulus*. BBB, ed. Frank-Lothar Hossfeld and Helmut Merklein, vol. 92. Weinheim, Germany: Beltz Athenäum Verlag, 1994.

Strom, Mark. *Reframing Paul: Conversations in Grace and Community*. Downers Grove, IL: InterVarsity, 2000.

Taylor, Charles. *Sources of the Self: The Making of the Modern Identity*. Cambridge, MA: Harvard University Press, 1989.

Theissen, Gerd. *Psychological Aspects of Pauline Theology*. Philadelphia: Fortress, 1986.

Thiselton, Anthony C. *The First Epistle to the Corinthians*. NIGTC, ed. I. Howard Marshall and Donald A. Hagner. Grand Rapids: Eerdmans, 2000.

Thomas, Robert L. *Revelation 1–7. An Exegetical Commentary,* ed. Kenneth Barker. Chicago: Moody, 1992.

Thompson, W. Ralph. "An Appraisal of the Keswick and Wesleyan Contemporary Positions on Sanctification." *Wesleyan Theological Journal* 1 (spring 1966): 11–20.

Thompson, William M. "The Saints, Justification, and Sanctification: An Ecumenical Thought Experiment." *ProEccl* 4 (winter 1995): 16–36.

Thrall, Margaret E. *2 Corinthians 1–7*. ICC, ed. J. A. Emerton, C. E. B. Cranfield, and G. N. Stanton. London and New York: T&T Clark, 1994.

————. *2 Corinthians 8–13*. ICC, ed. J. A. Emerton, C. E. B. Cranfield, and G. N. Stanton. London and New York: T&T Clark, 2000.

Tigay, Jeffrey H. "Sharing Weal and Woe: Expressions of Solidarity." In *Emanuel: Studies in Hebrew Bible, Septuagint, and Dead Sea Scrolls in Honor of Emanuel Tov*, ed. Shalom M. Paul et al., 811–26. Lieden: Brill, 2003.

Today's New International Version: TNIV Bible. Grand Rapids: Zondervan, 2001, 2005.

Tonlieu, L. L. "The Church as Family of God in the Pauline Corpus." *Hekima* 24 (2000): 16–27.

Toon, Peter. *Justification and Sanctification*. Westchester, IL: Crossway Books, 1983.

Trebilco, Paul R., and Craig A. Evans. "Diaspora Judaism." In *DNTB*, ed. Craig A. Evans and Stanley E. Porter, 281–96. Downers Grove, IL: InterVarsity, 2000.

Tresmontant, Claude. *A Study of Hebrew Thought*. Translated by Michael Francis Gibson. New York: Desclee Company, 1960.

Tyson, John R. *Charles Wesley on Sanctification: A Biographical and Theological Study*. Grand Rapids: Zondervan, 1986.

Van Rensburg, S. P. J. J. "Sanctification According to the New Testament." *Neot* 1 (1967): 73–87.

Vander Broek, Lyle D. *Breaking Barriers: The Possibilities of Christian Community in a Lonely World*. Grand Rapids: Brazos, 2002.

Vang, Preben. "Sanctification in Thessalonians." *SwJT* 42 (fall 1999): 50–65.

VanGemeren, Willem A., ed. *NIDOTTE*. 5 vols. Grand Rapids: Zondervan, 1997.

Vaux, Roland de. *Ancient Israel: Its Life and Institutions*. Translated by John McHugh. London: Darton, Longman & Todd, 1961.

Vincent, Marvin R. *A Critical and Exegetical Commentary on the Epistles to the Philippians and to Philemon.* ICC, ed. Charles Augustus Briggs, Samuel Rolles Driver, and Alfred Plummer. New York: Charles Scribner's Sons, 1906.

Vischer, Lucas. "Justification and Sanctification by Grace in a Time of Survival." *Reformed World* 49 (September 1999): 109–24.

Wadkins, Timothy. "Christian Holiness: Positional, Progressive and Practical: Martin Luther's View of Sanctification." *TJ* 7 (spring 1978): 57–66.

Wallace, Daniel B. *Greek Grammar beyond the Basics: An Exegetical Syntax of the New Testament.* Grand Rapids:, 1996.

Wanamaker, Charles A. *The Epistles to the Thessalonians: A Commentary on the Greek Text.* NIGTC, ed. I. Howard Marshall and W. Ward Gasque. Grand Rapids: Eerdmans, 1990.

Warrington, Keith, ed. *Pentecostal Perspectives.* Cumbria, England: Paternoster, 1998.

Webb, William J. *Slaves, Women & Homosexuals: Exploring the Hermeneutics of Cultural Analysis.* Downers Grove, IL: InterVarsity, 2001.

Wenham, David. *Paul: Follower of Jesus or Founder of Christianity?* Grand Rapids: Eerdmans, 1995.

Westcott, B. F. *The Epistles of St. John.* London: Macmillan Co., 1883. Reprint, Grand Rapids: Eerdmans, 1952.

Whitlock, Glenn E. "The Structure of Personality in Hebrew Psychology." *Int* 14 (January 1960): 3–13.

Williams, David J. *Paul's Metaphors: Their Context and Character.* Peabody, MA: Hendrickson, 1999.

Williams, Ernest Swing. *Systematic Theology,* Springfield, MO: Gospel Publishing House, 1953.

Witherington, Ben, III. "Christ." In *DPL*, ed. Gerald F. Hawthorne and Ralph P. Martin, 95–100. Downers Grove, IL: InterVarsity, 1993.

———. *Conflict and Community in Corinth: A Socio-Rhetorical Commentary on 1 and 2 Corinthians.* Grand Rapids: Eerdmans, 1995.

———. *Grace in Galatia: A Commentary on St Paul's Letter to the Galatians.* Grand Rapids: Eerdmans, 1998.

Wolff, Hans Walter. *Anthropology of the Old Testament.* Translated by Margaret Kohl. Philadelphia: Fortress, 1974.

Wong, E. K. C. "The De-Radicalization of Jesus' Ethical Sayings in Romans." *NovT* 43 (March 2001): 245–63.

Wood, Laurence W. "The Wesleyan View." In *Christian Spirituality: Five Views of Sanctification,* 95–118. Downers Grove, IL: InterVarsity, 1988.

The Works of John Wesley. Vol. 6. London: Wesleyan Methodist Book Room, 1872. Reprint, Grand Rapids: Baker, 1978.

Wortham, R. A. *Social-Scientific Approaches in Biblical Literature.* Texts and Studies in Religion, vol. 81. Lewiston, NY: Edwin Mellen, 1999.

Wright, Christopher J. H. *An Eye for an Eye: The Place of Old Testament Ethics Today.* Downers Grove, IL: InterVarsity, 1983.

———. *God's People in God's Land: Family, Land, and Property in the Old Testament.* Grand Rapids: Eerdmans, 1990.

———. *Walking in the Ways of the Lord: The Ethical Authority of the Old Testament.* Downers Grove, IL: InterVarsity, 1995.

Wright, N. T. *The Challenge of Jesus: Rediscovering Who Jesus Was and Is.* Downers Grove, IL: InterVarsity, 1999.

———. *Christian Origins and the Question of God.* Vol. 1, *The New Testament and the People of God.* Minneapolis, MN: Fortress, 1992.

————. *Christian Origins and the Question of God.* Vol. 2, *Jesus and the Victory of God.* Minneapolis, MN: Fortress, 1996.

————. *Christian Origins and the Question of God.* Vol. 3, *The Resurrection of the Son of God.* Minneapolis, MN: Fortress, 2003.

————. *The Climax of the Covenant: Christ and the Law in Pauline Theology.* Minneapolis, MN: Fortress, 1992.

————. *Paul for Everyone: The Prison Epistles Ephesians, Philippians, Colossians and Philemon.* London: SPCK, 2002.

————. *Paul: in Fresh Perspective.* Minneapolis, MN: Fortress, 2005.

————. *What Saint Paul Really Said: Was Paul of Tarsus the Real Founder of Christianity?* Grand Rapids: Eerdmans, 1997.

Wyckoff, John W. "The Baptism in the Holy Spirit." In *Systematic Theology: A Pentecostal Perspective,* ed. Stanley M. Horton, 423–55. Springfield, MO: Logion Press, 1994.

Yorke, Gosnell L. O. R. *The Church as the Body of Christ in the Pauline Corpus: A Re-Examination.* New York: University Press of America, 1991.

Zappone, Katherine E. "Sanctification of the Person and the Transformation of Society." *RelEd* 79 (fall 1984): 558–76.

AUTHOR INDEX

B

Banks, R., 172
Barabas, S., 21, 38
Barrett, C., 131, 132, 139
Barth, K., 4, 5, 8
Barth, M., 137, 173
Beale, G., 103, 123, 137
Beasley-Murray, G., 49, 57
Behm, J., 80
Berkhof, L., 4, 5, 8, 35
Berkouwer, G., 14, 35
Bertram, G., 180
Best, E., 100, 101, 139
Black, D., 153, 154, 155, 176, 177
Brown, R., 49, 50, 57, 77
Bruce, F., 78, 81, 82, 127, 137, 138, 139,
    147, 162, 171, 172, 173, 174, 177, 178,
    180, 181
Brunner, E., 4
Büchsel, F., 180
Burge, G., 77

C

Calvert-Koyzis, N., 135
Chamblin, J., 70, 81
Chester, A., 58
Clines, D., 76
Conzelmann, H., 131, 174, 180
Crabb, L., 25–28, 29, 30, 33, 39, 40
Cranfield, C., 78, 118, 135, 139, 175, 176

D

Davids, P., 58
Dayton, W., 34
Delling, G., 124, 138
Dieter, M., 34
Dockery, D., 69, 80, 81, 171
Donfried, K., 144, 172, 173
Duffield, G., 17, 36
Dunn, J., 76, 77, 79, 81, 105, 113, 130, 131,
    132, 133, 134, 135, 137, 139, 152, 156,
    171, 175, 176, 177

E

Elliott, J., 56
Erickson, M., 4, 5, 8, 75, 76, 82
Evans, C., 102

F

Fanning, B., 79, 133, 138
Fee, G., 66, 78, 79, 123, 132, 136, 137, 149,
    174, 175, 179, 182
Ferguson, S., 16, 35
Forde, G., 19, 37

G

Gaffin, R., 77, 79
Geertz, C., 84, 89, 99, 100, 101
Grenz, S., 4, 8, 28–30, 33, 40, 61, 62, 63,
    64, 65, 67, 68, 70, 72, 75, 76, 77, 78, 79,
    80, 81, 82, 130, 139
Grogan, G., 99, 100, 130

Grosheide, F., 131, 137, 150, 175

H

Hanson, S., 99, 100, 101, 102, 131, 174
Helminiak, D., 99
Hendriksen, W., 174
Herzog, W., 102
Hiebert, D., 172, 174
Hodge, C., 4, 8
Hoehner, H., 124, 126, 127, 130, 138, 139,
    163, 179, 180, 181, 182
Hoekema, A., 35, 139
Hooker, M., 171
Horton, S., 17, 36, 37
Hoy, A., 37
Hughes, P., 64, 68, 77, 79
Hurtado, L., 101

I

Inwood, C., 24, 39

J

Jenney, T., 8, 36
Joyner, R., 8

K

Kaylor, R., 177
Keener, C., 136, 175
Kittel, G., 63, 77, 80
Knight, G., 182
Koehler, E., 20, 37
Kolb, R., 38
Kreitzer, L., 132
Kruse, C., 118, 135, 136, 174

L

Land, S., 36, 37
Lattey, C., 99
Leclerc, T., 86, 101
Letch, R., 55
Lincoln, A., 131, 133, 138, 139, 179, 180,
    181
Lloyd-Jones, D., 130

Lohse, E., 180, 181
Longenecker, B., 171

M

Marshall, I., 169, 182
Martin, R., 58, 64, 67, 68, 77, 79, 80, 131
Maurer, C., 127, 138, 173, 175
McComiskey, T., 54, 55, 100
McKnight, S., 102
McQuilkin, J., 23, 24, 38, 39
Menzies, W., 17, 36
Meye, R., 107, 130
Michaels, J., 56, 58, 59
Miller, E., 179
Moo, D., 78, 80, 93, 102, 118, 132, 134,
    135, 136, 176, 177
Morris, L., 78, 135, 172, 174
Moule, C., 175, 176
Mounce, W., 182
Mouton, E., 177
Murray, J., 65, 78, 132, 134

N

Naudé, J., 54, 55, 56

O

O'Brien, P., 70, 80, 81, 114, 124, 125, 127,
    130, 132, 133, 134, 137, 138, 159, 162,
    165, 166, 178, 179, 180, 181
Oepke, A., 182
Overholt, T., 90, 101

P

Parsons, M., 171
Pearlman, M., 17, 36
Perelewitz, M., 174
Peterlin, D., 178, 179
Peterson, D., 30–32, 33, 40, 51, 55, 56, 57,
    62, 76, 146, 174
Pieper, F., 37
Pollock, J., 38
Porter, J., 100
Porter, S., 176
Procksch, O., 55, 56, 146, 173

R

Raabe, P., 37
Ridderbos, H., 132, 139, 171, 175, 177
Rogerson, J., 99
Roland, P., 82
Rosner, B., 136, 137
Russell, W., 171, 172

S

Sailhamer, J., 82
Schnackenburg, R., 180
Schneider, J., 139
Schreiner, T., 171
Scroggie, W., 38
Seebass, H., 54, 55, 56
Seifrid, M., 129, 135, 139
Shedd, R., 99
Shults, F., 76
Silva, M., 171, 172, 177, 179
Smedes, L., 35, 139
Soards, M., 131, 174
Spittler, R., 36
Stauffer, E., 107, 130
Strathmann, H., 133

T

Thiselton, A., 131, 137, 174, 175
Thompson, W., 39
Thrall, M., 80
Tigay, J., 100
Trebilco, P., 102

V

Van Cleave, N., 17, 36
Vang, P., 172, 174
Vincent, M., 132

W

Wallace, D., 134, 135, 165, 174, 179, 181
Wanamaker, C., 145, 172, 173, 174
Webb, W., 8
Weiss, K., 79
Williams, E., 18, 36
Witherington, B., 131
Wood, L., 34
Wright, N., 68, 80, 84, 90, 91, 95, 99, 101,
    102, 112, 113, 132, 133, 134, 135, 176,
    178

SCRIPTURE INDEX

Genesis
1:26, 76
1:26–27, 65
1:28, 71
2:3, 56
2:7, 66
2:16–17, 71
3:8–10, 71
3:15–16, 71
3:21, 71
3:22–24, 71
12, 85, 89
12:1–3, 46
19:10, 46
19:14, 46
19:20, 76
19:22, 46
34:23, 76
45:5, 72

Exodus
3:5, 42
3:7, 72
13, 56
15:11, 41
15:17, 125
19, 52, 71
19:1, 53
19:4, 53
19:5–6, 46, 52, 53, 86
20:18, 71
20:19, 71
20:20, 44, 72
26:34, 43
28, 42

28:3, 47
28:38, 41
28:41, 47
29:1, 47
29:21, 47
29:27, 47
29:29, 41
29:33, 41
29:37, 42
30:26–30, 47
30:35, 41
31:13, 56
31:14–15, 41, 42
32, 109
32:11–32, 109
33:2–3, 44
37:28, 56

Leviticus
10:10, 41
11:44, 42
19:2, 44, 49
19:8, 42
19:18, 93
20:3, 41
20:8, 51, 56
20:26, 45, 55, 86
21:6, 41
21:8, 56
21:15, 51
22:14–16, 55
22:32, 56
23, 42

Numbers
  4:20, 42
  15:30, 100
  16, 109
  16:20–35, 109
  21:9, 109
  25, 109
  25:6–8, 109
  35:25, 41

Deuteronomy
  7:2–4, 46
  7:5–6, 46
  7:6, 45, 55, 86
  9:4, 116
  12, 88, 102, 152
  12:10–11, 88
  14:2, 86
  17:7, 119
  19:19, 119
  22:21, 119
  22:24, 119
  24:7, 119
  26:15, 41, 43
  26:16–18, 45
  26:18–19, 47
  26:19, 45, 86
  30:11–14, 116, 119

Joshua
  7:1, 100
  7:11, 100

1 Samuel
  2:2, 42
  6:19–20, 44

2 Samuel
  3:21, 76

1 Kings
  8:4, 41
  8:10, 43
  8:39, 125

2 Chronicles
  6:30, 125
  23:6, 41

30:27, 125

Ezra
  9, 55

Psalms
  2:6, 43
  3:4[5], 43
  11:4, 43
  15:1, 43
  20:6[7], 43
  24:4, 45
  24:5–6, 45
  30:4[5], 42
  32:13–14, 125
  33:21, 43
  42, 101
  43:3, 43
  46:1–7, 88
  74:12–14, 88
  77:13[14], 41
  79:9–12, 85
  86:8–10, 89
  89:6–15, 88
  93:2–5, 88
  95, 73
  95:3, 48
  96, 48
  96:1, 48
  96:1–3, 89
  96:3, 48
  96:10, 48
  97, 48
  97:1, 48
  97:1–2, 89
  97:6, 48
  97:12, 42
  110, 125
  119:14, 44
  119:40, 45

Proverbs
  29:14, 86

Isaiah
  1:10–14, 87
  1:10–17, 87
  1:15, 87

1:16–17, 87
1:17, 87
8:14, 117, 134
28:16, 117
33:15–16, 87
46:3–4, 72
48:2, 41
52:10, 41
56:1, 95
56:3, 95
56:7, 95, 96
63:10, 41

Jeremiah
7:5, 96
7:6, 96
7:11, 95
7:14–15, 96
31:31–34, 92
31:33, 52

Lamentations
4:1, 41

Ezekiel
36:23, 52
36:25–27, 52
36:26, 122
36:27, 87
37:27–28, 88

Hosea
1, 52
2, 52
13:4–5, 72

Joel
2:32, 117

Zechariah
1:14–15, 86

Matthew
1:20–23, 73
7:2, 90
9:2, 90
9:3, 90
17:2, 69

18:21–22, 90
19:28, 63
23:19, 56
24:15, 56
24:30, 63
25:31, 63
26:64, 125
27:53, 56

Mark
3:34–35, 92
8:38, 48
9:2, 69
12:29–31, 93
12:36, 125
12:40, 94
12:41–44, 94
13:26, 63
14:24, 50

Luke
1:30–33, 73
1:49, 48
1:70, 48
1:72, 48
2:23, 56
2:9, 63
4:18, 94
4:21, 94
5:13, 94
7:13, 94
9:26, 48
9:31, 63
20:41–44, 125
20:45–47, 94
21:27, 63
22:19, 50

John
1:14, 63, 92, 94
1:29, 92
4:20, 102
4:21–24, 103
6:51, 50
7:18, 63
10:35, 57
10:36, 49, 57
11:40, 63

12:28, 63
13:31–32, 63
14:9, 63
14:13, 63
17, 50, 51
17:1, 50
17:4–5, 63
17:9, 50
17:11, 48, 50
17:14, 50
17:16, 50
17:17, 4, 50, 57
17:18, 50
17:19, 49, 50, 57
17:20–24, 51
17:21, 51
17:22, 51
17:23, 51

Acts
22:11, 63

Romans
1:2, 48
2:14–15, 115
3:2, 115
3:3, 116
4, 117, 120
4:13, 117
4:15, 115
5, 110, 114
5:12–21, 110
5:15, 111
5:17, 111
5:18–19, 111
6:6, 81
7:1–6, 135
7:12, 48
8, 65, 117, 118, 120
8:3–4, 118
8:18, 65
8:22, 65
8:23, 65
8:26, 65
8:28–29, 65
8:29, 65
9:1–29, 116
9:30–32, 116

9:32–33, 116
9:33, 117, 134
10, 115
10:3, 116
10:4, 116, 124
10:5, 116
10:5–8, 116
10:6, 116
10:6–8, 119
10:9, 117
10:9–10, 117
10:11, 117
10:13, 117
12, 152
12:1, 69, 81, 152
12:1–2, 152, 153
12:2, 15, 26, 69
12:9, 153, 154, 156
12:9–13, 176
12:9–16, 156
12:9–21, 153
12:10, 154
12:10–13, 153, 154
12:11, 154, 155
12:12, 154
12:13, 154
12:14, 153
12:14–16, 155, 176
12:17–21, 155, 156, 176
12:19, 153
12:21, 153
13, 117, 118, 120
13:1–5, 156
13:1–10, 156
13:6, 156
13:8, 156
13:8–10, 118
13:9–10, 156
13:10, 156
14:17, 173
16:17, 157
16:17–18, 157
16:18, 157

1 Corinthians
1, 148
1:8, 133
1:9, 149

1:10, 148, 149
1:12–13, 148
1:13, 149
3, 120, 128
3:3, 121
3:7, 121
3:8, 122
3:9, 121
3:10–15, 121
3:12–15, 121
3:16, 120, 122, 125
3:17, 121, 123
4:14, 148
4:20, 173
5, 118, 120, 136
5:1, 119
5:2–3, 119
5:4–5, 119
5:6, 148
5:6–8, 136
5:6–13, 119
5:13, 119
5:8, 119
6, 120, 128
6:1, 148
6:15, 122
6:16–17, 122
6:18, 122
6:19, 122, 123, 125
6:19–20, 137
6:20, 123
10, 109, 114
10:4, 109
10:5, 109
10:5–10, 109
10:7–8, 137
10:11, 110
10:12, 110
10:13, 110
10:14–22, 109
10:17, 109
11:18, 110
11:21–22, 148
11:23–26, 110
11:24, 50
11:30, 131
12:7, 150
12:12, 150

12:21–22, 150
12:25, 150
12–13, 150
13, 150
13:4–8, 151
13:8–13, 151
14, 151
14:1–5, 151
14:3, 151
14:4–5, 151
14:26, 151
15, 111
15:20–22, 110
15:20–28, 66
15:42, 66
15:42–43, 66
15:42–49, 78
15:44, 66
15:45, 66, 113
15:45–47, 66
15:46–48, 66
15:47–48, 79
15:49, 65, 66, 79

2 Corinthians
1:21, 174
2:1–4, 148
3:7, 64, 67
3:7–8, 67
3:7–11, 79
3:9, 67
3:11, 67
3:13–14, 67
3:14–15, 67, 68
3:16, 68
3:18, 64, 67, 68, 80, 173
4:1, 69
4:2, 69
4:3–4, 64
4:4, 64
4:4–6, 64
4:6, 64, 69, 81
7:2–3, 148
7:8, 148
10:9–11, 148
11:16, 148

Galatians
1:6, 141
3, 117
3:8, 117
3:19–22, 72
3:23, 135
3:23–24, 117
3:23–25, 117
5, 142
5:1, 142
5:6, 143
5:13–14, 143
5:13–26, 142
5:14, 142
5:15, 142, 143
5:16, 143
5:19–21, 147
5:22–23, 143
5:26, 142, 143
6, 143
6:1, 143
6:2–5, 143
6:6–10, 143
6:10, 143

Ephesians
1:3, 125
1:6, 16
1:12, 16
1:20, 125
2, 94, 123, 125, 128
2:1, 127
2:2, 163, 178
2:6, 126
2:7, 163
2:10, 178
2:11, 124
2:11–13, 124
2:11–19, 124
2:14–15, 124
2:15, 70, 124
2:15–16, 124, 165
2:20–22, 124, 168
2:21, 125, 126, 127
2:21–22, 127
2:22, 126
3:6, 126, 158, 165
3:10, 126, 158

3:11, 158
3:16, 158
3:17, 158
3:18–19, 158
3:21, 138, 159
4, 159
4–6, 178
4:1, 107, 159, 166, 178
4:1–16, 159
4:1–3, 166
4:2, 160
4:3, 107, 160, 168, 178
4:4–6, 107
4:7–16, 108
4:11–16, 160
4:13, 127, 160
4:15, 15, 160
4:16, 108, 127, 160
4:17, 166, 178
4:22, 81
4:28–29, 108
5:2, 166, 178
5:6, 163
5:6–14, 180
5:8, 162, 163, 166, 178
5:9, 163
5:10, 163
5:11, 163
5:15, 164, 166, 178
5:15–16, 164
5:15–6:9, 178
5:17, 164
5:18, 164
5:19, 164
5:19–21, 164
5:20, 164, 165
5:22–6:9, 165
5:25–27, 166
6:10, 178
6:10–11, 168
6:10–20, 168
6:11, 168
6:12, 126, 168
6:16, 168

Philippians
1:1, 159
1:4, 159

1:6, 159
1:7, 159
1:8, 159
1:9–10, 159
1:11, 16, 159
1:27, 112, 161
2, 111, 114
2:1–4, 111
2:2, 161
2:5–11, 111
2:9–11, 112
3:20, 112
3:21, 78
4:18, 159
4:19–20, 159

Colossians
1, 112
1:3–8, 161
1:5, 161
1:6–7, 161
1:9–14, 161
1:10, 161
1:11, 161
1:11–12, 161
1:15, 63, 70
1:15–17, 113
1:15–20, 112
1:18–20, 113
1:20, 113
1:22–23, 113
1:24, 167
1:28, 134, 167
2, 114
2:2–3, 167
2:11, 70
2:15, 70
3:8, 70
3:9, 70
3:9–10, 69, 70
3:10, 81
3:12–13, 70
3:16, 167
3:18–4:1, 181

1 Thessalonians
1–2, 144
1:4–5, 145

1:6, 145, 173
1:6–10, 146
1:6–7, 146
1:7, 144, 145
1:9, 146
1:12, 145
2:2, 145
2:6, 173
2:7, 145
2:9, 145
2:11, 145
2:11–12, 145, 146
2:13, 145
2:14, 146, 173
4–5, 146
4:1–8, 147
4:3, 146
4:3–5, 146
4:4, 147
4:6, 147
4:8, 147
4:9, 148
4:9–12, 148

2 Thessalonians
1:3, 144
2:13, 58

1 Timothy
1:5, 13
2:1–7, 35
3:1–12, 169
3:4–5, 169
3:7, 169
5:17–25, 182
5:22, 182
5:24–25, 182

2 Timothy
2:1–7, 169
2:2, 170

Titus
1:5–9, 169
1:6, 169

Philemon
9, 162

14, 162
16, 162
18, 162

Hebrews
1:1–2, 73
1:3, 73
2:17, 73
3:12–13, 74
3:7–8, 74
4:14–10:18, 6
4:16, 31
10:10, 51
10:11–18, 51
10:14, 51
10:19–13:19, 6
10:19–20, 74
10:19–22, 6
10:23, 6
10:24–25, 74

1 Peter
1:2, 51, 58
1:14–16, 49
1:15, 48, 56
2:4–10, 51
2:4–5, 121
2:5, 52
2:6, 52
2:9, 51, 52, 53, 56
2:21, 56, 57
3:9, 56, 57
5:10, 56

2 Peter
1:17, 63

Revelation
4:8, 48
6:10, 48
18:2, 138

Studies in Biblical Literature

This series invites manuscripts from scholars in any area of biblical literature. Both established and innovative methodologies, covering general and particular areas in biblical study, are welcome. The series seeks to make available studies that will make a significant contribution to the ongoing biblical discourse. Scholars who have interests in gender and sociocultural hermeneutics are particularly encouraged to consider this series.

For further information about the series and for the submission of manuscripts, contact:

Dr. Hemchand Gossai
Georgia Southern University
Department of Literature and Philosophy
P.O. Box Office 8023
Statesboro, GA 30460-8023

To order other books in this series, please contact our Customer Service Department:

(800) 770-LANG (within the U.S.)
(212) 647-7706 (outside the U.S.)
(212) 647-7707 FAX

or browse online by series at:

WWW.PETERLANG.COM